Freedom Narratives
of African American Women

Freedom Narratives of African American Women

A Study of 19th Century Writings

JANAKA BOWMAN LEWIS

McFarland & Company, Inc., Publishers
Jefferson, North Carolina

LIBRARY OF CONGRESS CATALOGUING-IN-PUBLICATION DATA

Names: Lewis, Janaka Bowman, 1981– author.
Title: Freedom narratives of African American women : a study of 19th century writings | Janaka Bowman Lewis.
Description: Jefferson, North Carolina : McFarland & Company, Inc., Publishers, 2017. | Includes bibliographical references and index.
Identifiers: LCCN 2017038911 | ISBN 9781476667782 (softcover : acid free paper) ∞
Subjects: LCSH: American literature—African American women authors—History and criticism. | American literature—19th century—History and criticism. | Slave narratives—United States—History and criticism. | African American women in literature. | Liberty in literature.
Classification: LCC PS153.N5 L457 2017 | DDC 810.9/928708996073—dc23
LC record available at https://lccn.loc.gov/2017038911

BRITISH LIBRARY CATALOGUING DATA ARE AVAILABLE

ISBN (print) 978-1-4766-6778-2
ISBN (ebook) 978-1-4766-3036-6

© 2017 Janaka Bowman Lewis. All rights reserved

No part of this book may be reproduced or transmitted in any form or by any means, electronic or mechanical, including photocopying or recording, or by any information storage and retrieval system, without permission in writing from the publisher.

On the cover: Frances Ellen Watkins Harper (Atlanta, Georgia, J.L. Nichols & Co., New York Public Library Digital Collections).

Printed in the United States of America

McFarland & Company, Inc., Publishers
  Box 611, Jefferson, North Carolina 28640
    www.mcfarlandpub.com

Table of Contents

Preface   1

Introduction: Black Women and the Materiality of Freedom   3

One. Women Writing Black: Literary Glimpses into African American History   21

Two. Moving Free: Black Women's Bodies and Freedom   35

Three. Elizabeth Keckley and Freedom's Labor   65

Four. "Fiction"ing Freedom: Frances Ellen Watkins Harper's Novelistic Tradition   105

Five. Reflections on Freedom, or Freedom Retold   119

Epilogue: Freedom's Promise: Coming of Age Narratives in African America   141

Chapter Notes   159

Bibliography   168

Index   173

Preface

> "This nation cannot nourish your soul."
> —The Rev. Otis B. Moss, III, Trinity United
> Church of Christ, January 8, 2017

This project, in its entirety, has endured three presidential campaigns, as I began my research in the age of George W. Bush when I was a graduate student and continued in the age of Barack H. Obama as I accepted my first academic position as a full-time instructor at Spelman College and then began as an assistant professor at the University of North Carolina at Charlotte. I conclude these notes at another moment of transition, at the end of the Obama era and, literally, at the dawn of the Trump era, which we don't know yet as a country what will bring. Yet, I find it appropriate to turn to the notion of civil discourse at this very moment because the African American women writers in this study were also in states of uncertainty as they declared their freedom even when society did not.

I had been trying to write a true prologue to this book, which now extends over a decade in its thought and structure, for several months. In July 2016, as I put together final thoughts from a hotel room in Philadelphia, Pennsylvania, I turned on the news to hear of the deaths by murder of first Alton Sterling in Baton Rouge, Louisiana, and then Philando Castile in St. Paul, Minnesota, within the same week.[1]

These murders added to a long list of names of gone-too-soon men and women both before since I worked on the book in March 2012 at a conference in Chicago, after the shooting of Trayvon Martin in Sanford, Florida, and between the births of my first child, a son, in 2010 and my second, a daughter (as I gave birth, with the television on, while the trial of George Zimmerman—accused but not convicted of killing Martin—was televised in July 2013).

Add to this that I have been living in Charlotte for seven years and endured changes in political climate, widely televised and covered (at least

1

in local media) killings of black men (Jonathan Ferrell and Keith Lamont Scott) by police on at least two occasions, both without initial indictments and one where protests in the streets are still very fresh, and yet the stories in this book about black women's lives still demand to be told. In an era where we are reminded and encouraged to remind others that "#BlackLivesMatter," it is certainly appropriate, in my opinion, to go back to the nineteenth-century stories of women who made their lives and the lives of others under and emerging from the institution of slavery matter.

That being said, civil discourse is not the language that society dictates or validates. It is the very choice to write or to speak the words that certify one's existence to oneself or to those in the communities that matter. Civil discourse, from the beginning of what we know as African American literature, in various moments in the nineteenth and twentieth century, and continuing into our present day, is how one is able to define and negotiate uncertain circumstances through language and through literature. It is the selection and definition of terms that tell one's story. It is my hope that these stories remain timeless but also that they help readers gain a greater understanding of what these women endured and overcame to assert freedom on their own terms.

So while this project was not envisioned in this current climate or even largely shaped in its ideas throughout this climate, the times in which we live certainly make it more relevant. In the spirit of the work being done by the African American Policy Forum to include black women's narratives in those who are taken away in some instances with little to no clear explanation, work that demands us to "#SayHerName," I add and repeat these names: Harriet Ann Jacobs, Charlotte Forten (Grimke), Ellen Craft, Elizabeth Keckley, Frances Ellen Watkins Harper, Lucy Craft Laney, Anna Julia Cooper, Zora Neale Hurston, Nikki Giovanni, Toni Morrison, and the stories continue.

Introduction
Black Women and the Materiality of Freedom

> "The cause of freedom is not the cause of a race or a sect, a party or a class—it is the cause of humankind, the very birthright of humanity."
> —Anna Julia Cooper

In this quote from Anna Julia Cooper's 1892 book of essays *A Voice from the South*, which has also been featured in the United States of America passport since 2007, Cooper argues that freedom belongs not to just one group or even to one race, but to all of humankind by *birthright*. Cooper, a formerly enslaved woman from Raleigh, North Carolina, who went on to have a distinguished teaching and educational administration career in Washington, D.C., and to earn a doctorate of philosophy from the University of Paris–Sorbonne in 1924, could certainly speak to what she thought was her right to freedom from her own perspective. However, this narrative on behalf of all of humanity also illustrates the idea of freedom as demanding social recognition while rejecting exclusion from social constructs including marriage, family, and prescribed spaces of labor and education.

In *Sister Citizen*, Melissa Harris Perry asks the very important question, "What does it mean to be a black woman and an American citizen?"[1] She argues of Zora Neale Hurston's *Their Eyes Were Watching God* and other texts authored by black women that "to understand black women's politics, we must explore their often unspoken experiences of hurt, rejection, faith, and search for identity."[2] This exploration takes place by examining those lived experiences which are documented in writing. As Harris Perry uses these experiences to understand "the social construction of black women's citizenship and identity around the theme of self-sacrificial strength [as] a recurrent motif in black women's lives and politics,"³ I am interested in how they construct this conception of citizenship and identity through discourse surrounding freedom (both lived and imagined).

As African American men and women came to understand themselves as citizens of the United States, they also described ways in which they used traditional narratives to write or rewrite their own. Thus, concerns about marriage, family, and mobility that culminate (or perhaps pause) in Harlem Renaissance and migratory narratives are not just about aspirations, but about investment in a version of freedom that is more permanent than fleeting. For many women, their desire was not just to "re-claim" their physical bodies from the institution of slavery, but in some cases to conceal their individual bodies in favor of creating a sense of a national identity for themselves and their families. Many of these women also contributed to the idea of "one nation under God" in lieu of dedicating their attention to themselves.

In seeking to illustrate versions of freedom that are both specific and universal, this book discusses narratives of freedom authored by nineteenth-century African American women (described in their time as black or Colored American women). Some of these women were recently or even still legally enslaved at the time of writing, but others were born free or into free or emancipated families; regardless of legal or social position, they all specifically create or engage narratives of freedom in print. I argue that these women define and negotiate their social positions and ways that they enter a "free" society through narrative representation. Therefore, the term "civil discourse" represents how they engage with their own and larger communities while adapting language of existing social structures to meet their own needs.

Theoretically, assessing the discursive nature of narratives of freedom is already relevant in other disciplinary frameworks. In *On Making Sense*, Ernesto J. Martinez argues that "queer race narratives offer us access to subjugated ways of seeing and feeling, to complex processes of resistance and agency."⁴ He advocates for "more familiarity with these knowledges and subjectivities, not on the grounds that they explain everything about the social world, or that they explain the social world well in every instance, but on the grounds that they are attempts at epistemic decolonization, and that as such, they represent possibilities for new knowledge and social critique."⁵ Along these lines, narratives of women of color who imagine themselves as free subjects of their own making offer readers ways to make sense of society and social transitions at critical points in American history. During their transitions into freedom as they, not as society, define it, these women's narratives are the means by which they take responsibility for representing America on their own terms. They offer a new framework for understanding black American women's citizenship even before it is viewed as a real legal possibility.

A New Framework for Freedom

Robert Reid-Pharr's representation of Black American identity as "not only socially constructed but also historically contingent," in addition to being chosen "both for and by us," offers an accurate framework of how these women view themselves.[6] Along with men, black American women also came to understand themselves as citizens of the United States, a process that began before and continued after President Abraham Lincoln's Emancipation Proclamation of 1863. They likewise wrote or rewrote their own versions of what it means to be part of the nation, whether it claimed them as human beings or not. Coming out of a period filled with challenges that harnessed their physical and intellectual power, black women writers of the mid- to late nineteenth century used literature to reflect upon and even to define what freedom looked like through their own experiences. Their efforts included attempts to reconstruct and negotiate romantic and familial relationships and the desire to literally construct or reconstruct their own identities. Concerns about marriage, family, and mobility that are highlighted in black women's narratives from this period are not just about aspirations, but also about investment in versions of freedom that are more permanent than fleeting. For many enslaved women, their desire was not just to "re-claim" their physical bodies from the institution of slavery, but in some cases to conceal their individual bodies in favor of creating a sense of a national identity for themselves and their families. Even women who were not born into the institution of slavery but were aware of its existence contributed through writing to the idea of "one nation under God" in lieu of dedicating their attention solely to themselves.

While narratives of enslavement have become a defined genre within the canon of African American literature, freedom narratives are much more loosely constructed. They include writing of women who were

Introduction

born free, those manumitted by their masters, those who escaped from slavery, and those who reflect on a period of legal emancipation. These women are married, unmarried, and widowed, but their reflections extend beyond even these categories. Looking at their narratives in their own rights makes it clear that freedom is not a concept that was simply issued or proclaimed.

Texts such as *Narrative of the Life of Frederick Douglass* (1845) and Harriet Jacobs' *Incidents in the Life of a Slave Girl* (1861), for example, end with freedom, and subsequent texts pick up the mantle of individual engagement during freedom, but a thematic subtext seems to beg the question of what freedom means not just individually, but collectively as well. Critical readings of these and other narratives have also bemoaned the loss of what enslaved subjects could not have or could not do—marry legally and have legal claim to their children, for example. Although much scholarship has explored the genre of slave narratives, or narratives of enslaved peoples and populations, critical analysis is beginning to include their narratives of freedom as well.

This book argues that the definitions of freedom and citizenship that these women articulate in nineteenth-century narratives are shaped both by understanding connections to a larger national identity and by personal desires to achieve a greater sense of mobility on their own terms. In addition to the marriage trope, which has been examined by Candice Jenkins, Tess Chakkalakal, and Ann du Cille as both a public and private means of visibility and legal recognition for women after emancipation, there are other legal discursive practices in which men and women sought to ensure their civil rights, both before and after the period of legal emancipation. These practices largely depended on community engagement, as black women writers represented a transition from focus on enslavement to focus on self-liberation to formation of a cultural identity. "Rights" they pursued in addition to marital contracts included a right to become educated and to educate others, the right to travel for work or for pleasure, and the right to represent themselves as community leaders.

From silences, in many cases, about their own sexuality, we can read instead a desire of black women authors to both produce and reproduce a sense of a national identity through travel, labor, education, and authorship. To this end, I discuss what the idea of "nation" meant to these women through these tropes and also how they both define an individual identity but also include a sense of collective identity.

Literature across genres is also instrumental, especially for women, in efforts toward what they believed were "respectable" representations of black female subjectivity.[7] From diary to autobiography to novel, each of these authors emphasizes black women's labor and community participation. This book first discusses the genre of narratives of freedom and then examines women's relationships to the community as they seek to illustrate a collective free identity. Finally, it presents ways in which these texts represent a sense of civil rights that emerges prior even to the ideas of racial uplift that reached a height for women in the late nineteenth century.

I read nineteenth-century black women's narratives of education, individual progress, marriage and family, labor, and intellectual commitments to see how they both reflected and produced national and community rebuilding projects. I argue that these black women defined freedom through all of the means listed above, but what is most significant for the purposes of this project was the freedom to choose their paths and to tell their own stories, in their own words and on their own terms. While these texts are not representative of a comprehensive body of work that discusses freedom, they represent examples in which women are literally inscribing their notions of freedom within more systematic legal discourse (that did not always address or initiate their means of emancipation).

My version of "freedom narratives" lies in between the narratives of enslavement and "liberatory narratives," as defined by Angelyn Mitchell in *The Freedom to Remember*. These narratives often end with freedom, but the terms on which freedom is achieved, I argue, are as significant as the efforts and experiences leading toward it. With attention to both literary and historical aspects of these women's lives, I trace changes in subjectivity from slave to free, from persons objectified by the oppressive institution of slavery to reconstructing subjects in their own rights.

Initializing Freedom

In *Incidents in the Life of a Slave Girl*, Harriet Jacobs (writing as Linda Brent) asserts: "Reader, my story ends with freedom; not in the usual way, with marriage. I and my children are now free! We are as free from the power of slaveholders as are the white people of the north; and though that, according to my ideas, is not saying a great deal, it is a vast improvement in *my* condition. The dream of my life is not yet realized."⁸ Beginning with Jacobs, whose well known narrative serves as a story both of slavery and of freedom, allows me to consider possibilities of freedom beyond its legal implications. There is something else, she suggests, beyond legal attachment to a male figure through marriage as the conclusion to her tale. Jacobs' utterance of having earned freedom not in the traditional sense, "with marriage," suggests a recognition of the legal contracts to which black women were not necessarily privy. However, writing her story by her own hand gives Jacobs the privilege to determine by which means her freedom will come.

Jacobs disputes marriage as the only means of freedom, claims herself and her children from the power of slavery, and offers hope for her future as a free woman. In her narrative, discussions of her body and even her sexuality are bound to white men. Each of these declarations, however, reflects layers of the quest for *self*-actualization after emancipation. Although Jacobs was manumitted in 1852, the publication of this text in 1861 parallels national conversations about the emancipation of slaves that marginally address relationships between the soldiers and their wives but neglect to detail women's freedom on individual terms. Jacobs' declaration of freedom "from the power of slaveholders" is an example of the relationship that becomes evident between black women and legal constructs/contracts through Emancipation and Reconstruction legislation, through labor, and through external regulation of marital and family status.

In *Black Women as Custodians of History*, Paula Sanmartin argues that texts such as Jacobs' played a foundational role in national literary discourse. At points, these texts have been dismissed as inauthentic "given that the slave narratives dealt simultaneously with the personal issues of a slave's life and with the public issues of the antislavery crusade," but Sanmartin argues that black women were also held to the standards of women authors in general.⁹ She states that "the existence of gender-specific conventions intensifies the problem of authorial control for female slave authors. Harriet Jacobs's struggle to write and publish her autobiography offers a 'representative' example of the constraints female slave authors faced to establish their authorship."¹⁰ This argument suggests that even ideas of self-authorship and a framework of the dialogic character of black women's writing are relevant, as the "discourse of abolitionism is enhanced by the civil-tongued discourse of black women writers as they represent themselves within the domestic values of genre and of society."¹¹

Representation is key for black women writing in the years during and after the institution of slavery was responsible for shaping many of their public identities. In *Mastering Slavery*, Jennifer Fleischner argues that "Jacobs's image of black women as other is integrated into her self-perception."[12] However, I add that as these women narrate their lives, they also shape the perception of themselves and of the society in which they live.

African American women writers are also responding to social circumstances. Eighteen sixty-one, when Jacobs' text was published, also marks a historical transition, as initial efforts were made to free slaves of rebelling Southern owners.[13] Although rejected by President Abraham Lincoln in favor of plans of gradual emancipation, these initiatives began a series of attempts to free enslaved Americans throughout the country in the ensuing years.[14] I trace this political history both to show the proliferation of emancipation rhetoric around and shortly after the time of Jacobs' publication and to illustrate the disconnection between legal and discursive representations of freedom. For Jacobs, freedom is more than a concept or even a contract. It is a lived experience that is accompanied by liberty both to produce and to circulate her reflections. She foresees problems with black women's integration into national citizenship and concerns of freedom in the "nontraditional" sense.

From Jacobs' connection of "mother-love" and freedom in 1861 (also the beginning of the formal emancipation process, as General John Frémont drafted legislation to free slaves in Missouri) through the writing of the "Women's Era" of the 1890s, when many black women's civic organizations, including the National Association of Colored Women (1896) also became official, I ask by which means African American women authors attend to a free black female subjectivity through their work. I discuss the complex nature of freedom for black women in narratives of women who gained freedom prior to Emancipation, those who were freed by national legislation, and those were are born legally free. At the time these works were circulating, women were only vaguely implicated in much of the legal rhetoric of Emancipation and Reconstruction. Some legislation, including a resolution issued by Congress in 1865, even made their freedom contingent on their status as wives.[15] Furthermore, this "freedom" as issued by national leaders came with no practical strategies, no pre-issued roles or outlined changes in responsibilities. Yet, black women, I argue, were as concerned with their status as American citizens as were their male counterparts.[16]

Introduction

Black women's narratives of the mid- to late nineteenth century represent increased visibility of black women as reading and writing subjects themselves as well as of the ways in which they create characters or versions of themselves through which political and historical crises are brought to light. African American women writers of this era also created or related stories of freedom to a readership that was attentive to a changing society of which they were also a part. Within and through these narratives, dreams are created, initiated, illustrated, and, to return to Jacobs' statement, even realized.

Collectively, these "freedom narratives" document transitions into a new phase in American history, but they also detail literal engagement with freedom as it is lived, constructed, and imagined. Additionally, this body of texts serves as a prehistory to later black women's literary efforts by developing themes of racial pride, relationships, and opportunity. *Freedom Narratives of African American Women* interprets the work of memory, history, and critique in black women's cultural productions around the meanings of *and* at the sites of emancipation, as I read the ways in which early black feminist writing responds to what Linda Grasso catalogues as "exclusion, absence, misrepresentation, [and] disinheritance."[17] I argue that these texts are in themselves literary, political, and historical documents that illustrate lived experiences of freedom.

I focus on the mid- to late nineteenth century first because many people associate Abraham Lincoln's Emancipation Proclamation of 1863 with "freedom" for black Americans; however, as it is now more widely known, the proclamation neither "freed" all black Americans, as it focused predominantly on rebelling states, nor did it specifically address the plight of black women who were already unprotected by the institution of slavery. Additionally, narratives and historical research have circulated about the vulnerability of women who were subject to constant surveillance by and physical, psychological, and emotional intrusion from their masters. These narratives, including *Incidents in the Life of a Slave Girl*, also show a sense of protection and resistance on behalf of their authors and women in their communities. For Jacobs, a transition into a "freedom consciousness" meant an ability to know and connect with her family, especially her grandmother, "Aunt Martha," in whose small attic space she hid for seven years until she could escape to freedom. In this example, it also meant access to protection that was not immediately available in slavery. Identification of family had a direct connection to protection of family even when the "state" (and literally, the state of society) was not concerned with the safety of black women's bodies.

By drawing her reading audience's attention to the physical state of her body (including pregnancies by a man with whom she birthed two children in attempts to escape oppression by her master and the institution of slavery), Jacobs also draws attention through print culture to the presence of African American women who gained mobility and agency during enslavement. This interpretation does not assume that a consciousness of freedom led directly to a perception of freedom by society. Instead, it focuses on the articulations and rhetoric of individual and collective freedom in texts that seemed to be concerned with telling personal stories of and about enslavement.

In her study of whiteness and American imagination in *Playing in the Dark*, Toni Morrison argues, "The contemplation of this black presence is central to any understanding of our national literature and should not be permitted to hover at the margins of the literary imagination."[18] In this book, the personae—black women authors—reflect and are based upon the ways they see themselves and project their own future and the future of their race. Their individual, and, at times, collective consciousness, is critical to an understanding of political history after the Civil War. Attempts to resolve the conflicted nature of black bodies are manifested in narratives of freedom and liberation, which I use interchangeably only because the means of emancipation these women pursued were so diverse.[19]

After emancipation, African Americans were instrumental in founding and maintaining schools in order to promote literacy among male and female children and adults, and women were essential to these efforts. The desire for the freedom of expression is the principle upon which much of black women's writing is based and is also essential after enslaved men and women are formally emancipated. After they are proclaimed to be "free," they must define for themselves what that freedom means against the rules prescribed by and for white and black men and white women. They must base their concept of freedom on their own lives: what they can do as "free" people, where they can go, and how they can circulate ideas of what it means to be liberated.

Black women had their own feelings, passions, plans, goals, and anxieties that only taking up their own pens could allow them to reveal. They wrote against misrepresentation by laws and writing that deemed them inferior. For example, the American Tract Society of the American Missionary Association, which, published most of the materials used in schools, issued texts such as *The Freedmen's Primer* that "portrayed blacks in subservient roles and frequently assumed that blacks were morally and mentally inferior."[20] These were ideas that black men and women had to counter in their own writing, but black women who served as domestic leaders also had to help their children counter misrepresentations of themselves that pervaded both educational material and published literature. Motherhood was certainly not the only rationale for women's efforts to represent themselves. Authorship literally allowed authority in the ways their views were circulated.

After Emancipation, print media are common texts that all are literally *free* to read. African American national identity was established, then preserved, by the ability of African American men and women both to read and to tell their own stories as African American women assumed and continued the responsibility of telling their own truths. This was done through newspapers, as Frances Ellen Watkins Harper published her earliest work in the African Methodist Episcopal Church's *Christian Recorder*, but also through published journals, autobiographies, and novels (a genre which Harper also executes with success).[21] Genre becomes less significant than content, as printed literature is often intertextual as well. Novels could contain autobiographical information, just as fiction could be published in newspapers. What is most important during this period is the information that is able to be circulated in writing.

In *Iola Leroy* (1892), Frances Ellen Watkins Harper's use of newspapers connects the value of literacy to the pursuit of freedom for African Americans. The novel opens with a conversation between two enslaved characters about the success of the Union army: Robert, a young man, is literate and Linda, and older woman, is not, but the story in the paper of Union victory becomes a common ground for anticipating freedom: "'Splendid news in the papers. Secesh routed. Yankees whipped 'em out of their boots. Papers full of it,'" Robert says, to which Linda responds: "'Oh, sho, chile.... I can't read de newspapers, but ole Missus' face is newspaper nuff for me...'"[22] Robert's and Linda's abilities to read two texts that tell the same story connect them in the potential for communal liberation. They are part of the same plight, hopeful that the war will bring freedom for all enslaved Americans. Both responses also express the value of literacy; reading, whether literal or metaphorical, is directly connected to freedom. Robert continues to "read" to his community, telling a group at a secret meeting that runaway slaves will no longer be returned to their masters. When asked, "'how did you yere it?'" by his compatriots, Robert responds simply, "'I read it in the paper.'"[23]

This book considers what is "in the papers" of African American women, who are writing in the shadows of African American men even as African American literature is coming into existence. I discuss ways in which black women authors attend to black female subjectivity through their work, how they represent increased visibility as reading and writing subjects themselves, and the types of subjects they create to speak to and about African American women's experiences in the nineteenth century. Finally I argue that black women writers create or relate stories of freedom to a discursive readership through which political and historical crises are brought to light.

Drawing from the dubious status of African American freedom as represented through the lens of Bill Lawson's and Howard McGary's *Between Slavery and Freedom* (in which they examine the rhetoric of emancipation and its moral failures), I address literal and discursive representations of freedom for black women after legal emancipation. Attempts to inscribe their own discourses of freedom against abstract ideas prompt such women as Harriet Jacobs, Elizabeth Keckley, Charlotte Forten, Frances E.W. Harper, and Anna Julia Cooper to produce texts about the various implications of freedom. The circulation and reception of their work is evidence that legal emancipation is connected to the freedom of black women to write and to have their experiences represented in writing.[24]

Democracy has come to represent the American dream; in its ideal sense, every person has a voice and the ability to be heard. The concept became so strong as America came to be formed that the government felt the need to stipulate who would and who would not be included.[25] In 1787, before emancipation-at-large was even under consideration, African Americans were a significant part of the debate about who could be represented in America. Existing antislavery discourse was suppressed in the final decision to divide bodies in the "three-fifths" accounting of slaves for voting purposes.

By determining how to account for the slaves that year, among other conversations that have taken place throughout American history, the debate about the meaning of freedom was taking root. Scientists, historians, and politicians had already tried to account for the difference between blacks and those of other ethnic backgrounds in America in various ways that included color, physiognomy (including size of brain and body parts), and assumptions about mental versus physical abilities. When it ultimately became beneficial for sixteenth president Abraham Lincoln to fit African Americans into his plan for a unified America, stereotypes and misrepresentations abounded, if not increased due to fear about what their "inclusion" in the category of those represented would mean even after the Fifteenth Amendment granted black males the vote. Black women were not able to cast their own votes until women were granted suffrage in 1920. Thus, even the sense of national inclusion that seemed to represent freedom was neither promised nor guaranteed for blacks. Because of the unsubstantiated fear and racial typecasting that accompanied legal emancipation in addition to the denial of legal rights, black men and women had to make their own stories of freedom in order to actually be included in rhetoric of emancipation.

Democracy offered a way for the country to begin anew, and visions of freedom and being part of a democratic ideal were also written by black women, arguably the last to even be thought of as deserving of the rights granted other Americans. From diary to autobiography to novel, these texts all emphasize black women's labor and community participation. These pervasive themes suggest common goals for integration into the national sphere. Each text speaks to the challenges of representing history, creating an audience, and adapting texts to the people and time period among which they circulate. While recognizing distinct differences in the formal elements of these texts, I look for the common ways in which writers in this study make abstract notions of freedom more accessible through literary representations.[26]

Through their narratives, the women in this book renegotiate both absence from national discourse about citizenship and dependence upon men for legal rights by describing their lived experiences. They offer notions of freedom that are not, as Jacobs suggests, explicitly dependent legal contracts such as marriage; instead, they offer alternative means of mobility.[27] Historian Darlene Clark Hine argues that economic resources for black women were still severely limited after the war but they pioneered in art, education, and literacy. She states: "while white America debated about what to do with them, black women and men went about trying to construct lives, to construct freedom."[28] Hine describes efforts of black women to reimagine themselves and their families when the South is placed under military rule from 1865 to 1877; they immediately seek employment, begin to engage in the political sphere (even actively contesting their denial of the right to vote in 1870), and educate in classrooms, churches, and in their communities.

I read black women's narratives of education, individual progress, marriage and family, labor, and intellectual commitments to see how they both reflect and produce national and community rebuilding projects. I argue that black women define freedom through all of the means listed above, but what is most significant for the purposes of this project is freedom to choose their paths and to tell their own stories, in their own words and on their own terms. While these texts are not representative of a comprehensive body of work that discusses freedom, they represent examples in which women are literally inscribing their notions of freedom within more systematic legal discourse (that did not always address or initiate their means of emancipation).

As Saidiya Hartman reads the ways in which contracts and rules restore systems of black subordination—as she determines that blacks are problems, projects, and aliens to national constructs—I seek to describe how black women write themselves into national history as free persons with active roles to play in society. They work both within and against contracts of marriage, prescribed labor, and most of all, freedom as legislated by the national government.[29] With both attention to literary and historical aspects of these women's lives, I trace changes in subjectivity from slave to free, from persons objectified by the oppressive institution of slavery to reconstructing subjects in their own rights.

Chapter One, "Women Writing Black: Literary Glimpses into African American History," provides an overview into the ways that black women authors have engaged themes of life, including their own freedom, in centuries of writing. Chapter Two, "Moving Free: Black Women's Bodies and Freedom," analyzes Charlotte Forten's journal of her travel and assistance in reconstructing lives in the South by educating freedmen and women, published as *Life in the Sea Islands* in 1864. Reading this diary as a documentary for how freed people's efforts and experiences are represented, but also as a class based analysis of a scene of cultural contact, reveals the ways in which the text is both a missionary allegory and a revised domestic scene amongst black people in a single community. Forten, part of the free northern black elite, encounters a very different world of free black

Introduction

southerners when she becomes their teacher.[30] She both embodies and creates conflicting versions of freedom for African Americans as she maintains the central position of her narrative and describes the newly emancipated people as "other."

The chapter also discusses Ellen Craft, wife of William Craft (author of *Running a Thousand Miles for Freedom: The Escape of William and Ellen Craft from Slavery*), as a subject of freedom in her own right. She and her husband staged an escape from Georgia by way of New York, and then to England, yet the Crafts returned to the Southern state to build a school on their own land. Ellen Craft's narrative of travel is markedly different from Forten's, yet they end up in similar geographical locations to realize their own freedom and the freedom of those they teach. Read together, these narratives demonstrate the freedom of physical mobility and relocation from two very different sets of circumstances.

Chapter Three, "Elizabeth Keckley and Freedom's Labor," studies Elizabeth Keckley's *Behind the Scenes, or Thirty Years a Slave, and Four Years in the White House* (1868), as a model for African American Reconstruction writing. In this text, Keckley uses her experience as a seamstress for Mary Todd Lincoln as an example of new opportunities for former slaves. Keckley deftly weaves her own experiences as a former slave and those of freedpersons who migrate to Washington, D.C., into descriptions of her association with the Lincolns. Keckley writes in the margins of the story of this first family, using stories of popular figures as background for her agenda to articulate the plight of emancipated black Americans. She furthermore shows the inextricable nature of freedpersons and members of the black middle class, some formerly enslaved themselves. Keckley's narrative serves multiple purposes on its own terms and in this project. As a formerly enslaved woman (free woman at the time of writing) who becomes proprietor of her own labor, Keckley inscribes a newly developing black middle class and a revised model of black free womanhood. Her narrative reveals the ways in which freedom allows expanded employment and activist roles for women, and Keckley's analysis of her labor shows that her personal testimony, political commentary, and cultural work are intertwined. Her freedom is the freedom to contract her own labor, to have free children, to consent to marry and divorce, and to help improve the freedmen's and freedwomen's plight. As a result, the reader sees a narrative of independent labor that dictates freedom on one's own terms in addition to the ability to contract work for even the most well-known clients.

Chapter Four, "'Fiction'ing Freedom: Frances Ellen Watkins Harper's Novelistic Tradition," reads the way Frances Ellen Watkins Harper represents the freed woman's role in reconstructing her community through fiction. As her character Iola Leroy in the book of the same name states, "My life-work is planned. I intend on spending my future among the colored people of the South ... they need me."[31] Sacrifice and education are the means articulated in Harper's fiction for women to take up the responsibility of racial leadership. Both her shorter novel *Minnie's Sacrifice*, which appeared in the African Methodist Episcopal-sponsored *Christian Recorder* in 1869, and her longer and most-well known novel, *Iola Leroy* (published in 1892), feature mixed-race female characters who are raised as white women and have to decide how to live their lives once they discover they are black.

Both Minnie and Iola choose to educate fellow members of their race as their contribution to African American freedom. *Iola Leroy* is historical fiction; it addresses post–Emancipation issues such as the reconnecting of families, but more generally, what black people should do "on the threshold of a new era."[32] In Iola's decision to "teach in the Sunday-school, help in the church, [and] hold mothers' meetings to help these boys and girls to grow up to be good men and women,'" Harper's text is fiction about the virtues of education (similar to the doctrine of Republican motherhood, as Linda K. Kerber coins it about a population a century earlier in *Women of the Republic: Intellect and Ideology in Revolutionary America* and also proof of how black women can be instrumental race leaders.[33]

This reading determines that the novel is simultaneously the culmination of these different generic efforts and a way to imagine or idealize the effects of emancipation; additionally, subjectivities represented in it and other genres are cyclical and intertwined. This chapter also connects the relationship of African American novels during the nineteenth century to the content of journalistic writing, speeches, and essays that preceded them.[34]

Chapter Five, "Reflections on Freedom, or Freedom Retold," draws from Anna Julia Cooper's statement "We look back, not to become inflated with conceit because of the depths from which we have arisen, but that we may learn wisdom from experience."[35] I use Anna Julia Cooper's *A Voice from the South* to discuss where black women positioned themselves in national discourse toward the turn of the century.[36] Cooper specifically refers to progress that has been made since Emancipation but suggests

Introduction

that change is needed in the ideologies of black people to include women on the intellectual stage.

Frances Smith Foster argues that Cooper begins a new era of writing in 1892, and I use her work as a way to reflect upon the efforts that these women have used to project their voices into national dialogue.[37] As a prelude to several organized efforts of women's activism, including the Women's Conference of 1893, National Association of Colored Women in 1893, and National Conference of Colored Women in 1895, Cooper uses her singular voice to argue that black women are the foundation of the race, and therefore regeneration begins with them: "Only the BLACK WOMAN can say when and where I enter, in the quiet, undisputed dignity of my womanhood, without violence and without suing or special patronage, then and there the whole Negro race enters with me."[38] Cooper faults men for not encouraging the development of black women's roles after Emancipation and expounds upon the stakes of black women's involvement in efforts of racial progress.

Arguing that "we can give ourselves," Cooper writes black women into conversations of racial uplift.[39] Although Cooper is usually discussed as an originator of black women's activism of the twentieth century, I argue that Cooper is as concerned with past efforts of racial progress as with future opportunities for black women. Also integral to this chapter is a discussion of educator Lucy Craft Laney, a woman who began her life enslaved in Macon, Georgia who, after gaining her freedom went on to start the first black kindergarten and the first nursing school for black women in Augusta, Georgia, in addition to a very reputable school called Haines Industrial and Normal Institute in 1886 that was recognized by such figures as W.E.B. Du Bois and Booker T. Washington. Through speeches and essays, Laney also reflected on the distance from which blacks had come in just a short period of freedom and instructed mothers on how to build their children up at home to be successful and productive as the first generation of free adults. By setting up both narratives and ideals of social progress, Cooper and Laney argue for education and institutional opportunities as means for women (and in effect, men as well) to achieve real social progress.

The epilogue, "Freedom's Promise: Coming of Age Narratives in African America," argues that women's writing in the late nineteenth century develops themes of racial pride, relationships, and opportunity while documenting transitions into a new phase in American history at the turn of through the mid-twentieth century. Through engagement with "civil discourses" about rights, education, travel, and even means of publication into the twentieth century (including codas about liberation writing from Hurston, Gwendolyn Brooks, and Nikki Giovanni), these texts illustrate literal engagement with freedom as it is lived, constructed, and imagined. As a result, these narratives both argue for and demonstrate examples of economic freedom, social progress, physical mobility, and community narratives.

At the time these women were writing, women in America had not even secured the vote and wouldn't for several decades. Women did not, however, undervalue their influence on husbands, brothers, fathers, and even other women through their domestic activism and their writing. For this reason, these texts can be looked at as literature of African American women's citizenship. African American women would have to continue to agitate for decades later for their constitutional rights, but their writing served as an effective foundation for articulating their needs from society.

Like those who wrote before her, including Harriet Jacobs in her plea for Northern white women to recognize the ways she was unable to write herself into respectable femininity, Elizabeth Keckley knew that her own freedom depended on recognition from women that she was also one of them. Key to Keckley's version of freedom, however, was her domestic work for these women. She desired to earn social credit so that they were unable to write her out of even their own versions of femininity; in the end, her efforts not only earned her freedom with money owed to her for her work, but also allowed her to transcend the status of formerly enslaved woman to a woman who worked on by her own hands (and on her own terms) for not only one, but three of the most notable political families of her time.

Likewise, *Iola Leroy* shows the journey of a young black woman from slavery to public leadership through community work, shifting the focus on the black community from subjugation to the way in which they labor and progress. The unity Iola achieves within her own domestic setting once her family is reunited is not an individual triumph, but a triumph of the community through dedication and education. A success story is written, therefore, on Iola's body that speaks to the success of a black woman, a black family, and a black community. Similar cases can be argued with male protagonists such as Martin Delany's *Blake; or, the Huts of America* (1859–1861) and Frederick Douglass's Madison Washington in *The Heroic Slave* (1853). As women are included in the conversation, their journeys are affixed to the journeys of their communities, creating an alternate national discourse that is situated within dominant narratives.

We can argue, then, that the struggle for rights of citizenship continued from the time of enslavement well into the twentieth century, and the fight for social recognition even until today. The women represented in this sample of nineteenth-century texts specifically narrated the transition from freedom to citizenship in a way that allowed others to see not only their struggles, but their triumphs as well. They wrote about rights as individual women, as mothers, as travelers, as educators, and as speakers and writers. They wrote about their character and defended their rights to not only their bodies, but to their entire physical and psychological beings.

"Civil discourse" refers to the ways these authors used words to establish their civil presence in society during their transitions from either legal, social, or mental enslavement to the ways that they defined freedom on their own terms. I look at the terms in which they wrote about freedom, the definitions they offered through their own lived experiences, and finally, how they outline versions of freedom for others through their writing. To be free, these texts suggest, one must assume one's own version of femininity and demand that she be recognized as such.

CHAPTER ONE

Women Writing Black
Literary Glimpses into African American History

In 1851 at the Woman's Rights Convention in Akron, Ohio, formerly enslaved woman Sojourner Truth stood before white women and asked what came to be known as the now famous question, as documented by journalist Frances Gage and Truth's biographer, Olive Gilbert, "'Ar'n't I a Woman?'" The question has since been repeated in various forms and served as the title of black woman historian Deborah Gray White's first book, published in 1985 and revised in 1999. But it is still worth looking at the language of these four words that demanded that white women look at Truth's black body and offer, or at least consider, an affirmative answer to her question. The expanded version of Truth's contraction, Are not, suggests that she has been defined outside of the rhetoric of womanhood but needs to be written in. She does not ask her audience whether she is a woman (and therefore give them license to define her); instead, she dares them to prove that she is not.

Truth's address demonstrates oratory empowerment in its most explicit form. Standing in front of an audience who already has some interest or investment in women's rights gives her the space to physically convince others that she, like they, deserves justice. But what happens when language has to substitute for physical presence? What are the strategies of formulating the relationship of speaker and audience between a woman writer and her designated or anonymous audience? Before we end where we began, I invoke Truth's speech first as an entry into a discussion of nineteenth-century print feminist text, specifically beginning with Harriet Jacobs' *Incidents*. I argue that a national feminist discourse can be read from aspects of staging and address in the writing of an enslaved black woman. But several texts that come later in the African American women's literary tradition continued to contend with dominant discourses to demand reconsideration of the status of black American womanhood.

"Reader, be assured this narrative is no fiction" is the of-quoted opening line used to discuss Jacobs' assertion of authenticity. Implicit in this and other direct addresses throughout the book is the staging of a confidential relationship between Jacobs and each individual Northern white woman who may peruse her book. She writes, "I trust my readers will excuse deficiencies in consideration of circumstances" (xiii). This is not an outright demand or apology, but a gentle assurance of pardon from someone familiar. So familiar, in fact, that she claims the book is not for her at all, but for them:

> I have not written my experiences in order to attract attention to myself; on the contrary, it would have been more pleasant to me to have been silent about my own history. Neither do I care to excite sympathy for my own sufferings. But I do earnestly desire to arouse the women of the North to a realizing sense of the condition of two millions of women at the South, still in bondage, suffering what I suffered, and most of them far worse [xiv].

It is critical for Jacobs to assert herself as a woman from the very beginning of her text. How else can she converse with her targeted audience if not, even by her own determination, on equal ground? Because they have failed to create conditions that are conducive to her freedom and equality, Jacobs assumes the work of convincing them, and strategy is essential in such a significant task. Jacobs denies that her efforts are for her own benefit, but her mission is much bigger: she is a representative for two million women, by her own count, whose liberty depends on her literary success.

Jacobs' narrative and other pre and antebellum African American narratives mentioned above have been read widely for their characteristics as narratives of enslavement, but to focus only on genre obscures the effects of style and address. Jacobs does not ask or request that people pay attention; instead, she writes as if she knows they are already doing so. Each subsequent address, therefore, is an attempt to convey a specific piece of information that is crucial to the plight for freedom. Jacobs is the voice of knowledge and reason that calls upon readers to observe her life in slavery, then adjust their own attitudes about the brutal and oppressive institution.

As in the preface, Jacobs allows that her audience may or may not know specific details of slavery. Her incidents are shaped by this effort to reveal while never accusing them of ignorance. Thus, she marks several incidents with commentary to the reader, to make clear the implications of the stories she shares. This happens as early as the fourth page of the text, when Jacobs relates the theft of "Linda's" grandmother's money by her mistress. Under the pseudonym Linda Brent, she writes, "The reader probably knows that no promise or writing given to a slave is legally binding; for, according to Southern laws, a slave, *being* property, can *hold* no property" (4). In this statement, Brent directs information on Southern laws and slaves' (lack of) rights to the reader—if they did not know beforehand that slaves could not hold property, there is no excuse for ignorance after the first few pages of the text.

This is the most objective address that Jacobs employs. She does not speak directly to the reader in this instance, but places herself in a position to comment to them indirectly instead. This indirect discourse also permits other readers, those who Brent does not address in the preface, to be part of the conversation. If the reader already knows property laws, he or she can now see specifically how they affect the lives of enslaved men and women.

After the point of introduction, Jacobs uses the knowledge she has of free women to make them see her condition. She moves from conversational mode to enlightenment through contrast. After she draws the reader in, she shows them that all women do not share the same comforts and privileges. She affirms her gender through references to womanhood but also reveals inconsistency in what enslaved women can do as mothers:

> O, you happy free women, contrast your New Year's day with that of the poor bondwoman! With you it is a pleasant season, and the light of the day is blessed.... But to the slave mother New Year's day comes laden with peculiar sorrows. She sits on her cold cabin floor, watching the children who may all be torn from her the next morning; and often does she wish that she and they might die before the day dawns. She may be an ignorant creature, degraded by the system that has brutalized her from childhood; but she has a mother's instincts, and is capable of feeling a mother's agonies [14].

Jacobs places the reader in a specific moment in time, one that brings joy to those not laden with the pain of slave motherhood. Jacobs appeals to the free mother by reminding her that the enslaved mother can never share her happiest times. "You *happy* free women," she suggests, should look at the unhappy slave mother and see the irony in the very next phrase. Motherhood is not a permanent condition for the enslaved mother because of the pervasiveness of her condition in slavery.

Jacobs has already written Linda into womanhood through the text but cannot yet truly writer her as mother until the end of the text. She also reveals the paradox of motherhood by taking the reader into other slave cabins and domiciles and into the perspectives of the women who may soon be separated from their children. Here, Jacobs begins to unfold the horror of slavery from the lens of the mother; fatalism becomes real in this scene, and it is an effect of the system's brutality. Jacobs also challenges free women to look beyond their own perspective of the enslaved mother as an "ignorant creature"; despite the degradation caused by this system, the enslaved mother is still mother by instinct, and despite the inflictions of brutality, she can still feel the agonies of any other mother.

Over the course of the text, Jacobs' identification with the reader progresses. She challenges her audience to question the information they have already been provided through the Fugitive Slave Law of 1850. Jacobs gives her reader the reasons to refuse participation—her text gives them the truth to keep them from assisting in "cruel bondage." "Surely" if they know good from evil, they will not help keep women in this condition. If Jacobs can show a Northern white audience that "slavery is a curse to the whites as well as to the blacks," there is a possibility that they will move to action against this institution.

Through the study of Jacobs' staged discourse with an assumed civil society, I am interested in the way that she and other authors position themselves as mediators of experiences their readers may never have. Jacobs directs her descriptions directly to them so that ignorance can no longer be an excuse, but she also sacrifices her own rights to privacy in the process.

Jacobs's ambivalent witnessing is evident in her discussion of her pregnancy by Mr. Sands, which she expresses that she only reveals for the sake of her audience: "And now, reader, I come to a period in my unhappy life, which I would gladly forget if I could. The remembrance fills me with sorrow and shame. It pains me to tell you of it; but I have promised to tell you the truth, and will do it honestly, let it cost me what it may" (54). Yet, Jacobs does not end by simply discussing what may be perceived as a sexual indiscretion in their eyes. Jacobs uses the position she has established within a national circle of women to demand reevaluation of determining factors of womanhood.

Reflecting on an instance of what some may call "fallen" womanhood, Jacobs asserts that readers must look at the experiences of enslaved women

One. Women Writing Black

in order to determine how they fit into national dialogue. She demands that another system is needed that takes the paradox of enslaved womanhood and motherhood into account. Jacobs demonstrates through the "incidents" she shares that narratives of enslavement are not so much about offering information of to the nation as about bringing the masses "down" to sites where men and woman are suffering.

Each of the aforementioned moments of address, culminating with the use of confession to demand a revision of the standards of womanhood, demonstrates the way in which Jacobs literally writes herself into a national feminist discourse. Jacobs addresses the reader as peer from the very beginning, which establishes a dynamic of camaraderie that she can then use to assert their implication in the continuation of American slavery. Therefore, Jacobs simultaneously writes and holds up a mirror that requires the reader to look at herself and see that she, by denying the humanity of other women, is also hindering women's rights.

This mirror is continued in the twentieth century with the desire to represent, in the terms of Alain Locke, the "new Negro" as the impetus of the Harlem Renaissance of the 1920s and 1930s. Locke wrote in his book of that name, "He now becomes a conscious contributor and lays aside the status of beneficiary and ward for that of a collaborator and participant in American civilization" (15). Houston Baker and other scholars have emphasized the gendered component of this quest, as Baker asked, "What then is the Negro, this new man?" (Baker, *Modernism and the Harlem Renaissance*). In a conflict that would play out repeatedly during the twentieth century, rhetoric of manhood motivates this black nationalist project. Zora Neale Hurston wrote herself into the cultural movement by employing this rhetoric. Although she would later be recognized for the feminist implications of *Their Eyes Were Watching God*, Hurston's first published short story features a male protagonist—John Redding. Published in May 1921 in the *Stylus* literary society magazine at Howard University, "John Redding Goes to Sea" is Hurston's negotiation of the new Negro and the modern man within the setting of a rural Florida town.

Hurston, who spent much of her childhood in an all-black town of Eatonville, Florida, uses a similar locale as the crux of her narrative. Both Locke, who sponsored the Stylus society, and co-sponsor Montgomery Gregory, were "excited about expressing the folklife of rural black people through plays, stories, and poems" (Hemenway 19). The excitement and the potential Locke saw in Hurston's writing motivated him to send her work to Charles Johnson, editor of *Opportunity* magazine (the second major magazine, after *Crisis*, of the Harlem Renaissance). Johnson then featured several of Hurston's stories in the magazine, including "John Redding" in January 1926 (Cheryl Wall, *Women of the Harlem Renaissance*, 146).

Even at the beginning of her career, Hurston had the makings of success as a writer, as she could contribute information about non-urban black Americans to a primarily urban cultural project. This story, however, does not portray "folklife" in this Florida town romantically. Instead, the location is the site of contestation between folk culture and an expanding consciousness of the world tied to rhetoric of gender. Hurston uses civil discourse to address issues of black masculinity even as she prepares to continue stories of black women.

The premise of the story is that ten-year-old John Redding, a black boy, wants to follow the twigs he casts into the St. John River "down stream to Jacksonville, the sea, and the wide world." Many residents of the town perceive this wish to travel as "queer" behavior. His mother, Matty Redding, thinks that John has a spell on him that makes him want to leave her. John's father, however, seems to understand John's fantasies to travel to the horizon. He repeatedly tells his wife Matty to "stop dat talk 'bout conjure" and encourages his son to continue to dream.

Traveling in this story is a desire of manhood, which is why John's mother seemingly does not understand. Hurston narrates an interaction between young John and his father Alfred in which John cries because the weeds sweep away his "ships" (the twigs), preventing them from going off to "sea." John's father is concerned, however, not that John invests so much time in this activity, but that his son is weeping. "Well, well, doan cry. Ah thought youse uh grown up man. Men doan cry lak babies," he says (2). When John reiterates his wish to go "farther than them ships," his father replies: "'Well, son, when Ah wuz a boy Ah said Ah wuz goin' too, but heah Ah am. Ah hopes you have bettah luck than me'" (2). While Matty Redding (who is described as a small, wiry, weepy woman) is at home setting the table for supper, the "men" discuss fantasies that only they can understand. John's father has failed in his own venture for nautical freedom but supports the possibility that his son, who he wishfully refers to as a "grown up man," will fulfill this masculine quest. In this pair of characters, Hurston illustrates a gender construct that is defined by inherent potential to imagine and to achieve even as the woman is still bound to the home.

One. Women Writing Black

As the story progresses, John does not give up his dreams to "go roving about the world for a spell." In attempts to "fix" John's "queer" notions, his mother insists that he get married. After a brief courtship, John fulfills his mother's wishes but still wants to join the Navy. The family is at odds over the idea of John's departure when he goes off to help build a bridge near the town. After an uneasy night, his wife and parents go looking for John at the construction site, where no one has seen him. His father Alfred finally sees something floating in the river. Hurston writes:

> Sure enough there was a man floating on a piece of timber. He lay prone upon his back. His arms were outstretched, and the water washed over his brogans but his feet were lifted out of the water whenever the timber was buoyed up by the stream. His blue overalls were nearly torn from his body. A heavy piece of steel or timber had struck him in falling for his left side was laid open by the thrust. A great jagged hole wherein the double fists of a man might be thrust, could plainly be seen from the shore. The man was John Redding [16].

John's tragic end, in which his father makes the decision to let his body float off to sea, is brought about by an initial and final masculine desire to escape. Sadly and ironically, the narrative does not proclaim John to be a man until his death.

There are a number of ways to read Hurston's ending, including the relationship between the sea to the slave trade as the military and modern technology also connect Europe, Africa, and the Americas. The story can also be read as an allegory—John can perceive the world beyond his Florida town; he is aware of the role of the Navy (which may also be a reference to world War I) and a quest for universal manhood. Yet, he ultimately cannot participate in this quest because of racial constraints. When "John Redding Goes to Sea" is examined as a site of multiple contestations, the following tensions are most evident: that between male potential and female limitations and that between a folk culture/location and progress of the modern world.

Hurston's evident preoccupations in the context of this story are her social position and the hometown setting she desires to portray. She is writing as a black woman in a dominant literary tradition. She initially navigates gender constraints by writing a story about men in order to discuss concerns that are unweighted by feminine oppression. Furthermore, she is motivated by a desire to portray a rural Florida experience that looks beyond a single town; in other words, to write this locale into the modern world. From the banks of the St. John River, John can imagine

Jacksonville, the sea, and the wide world by means of water. Through John Redding, Hurston constructs her own literary tradition within developing artistic constructs (the Harlem Renaissance and American modernist period). In doing so, she enters larger conversations of black mobility (in both its possibilities and its limitations) and universal modernity.

In one of my favorite twentieth-century novels, Zora Neale Hurston's *Their Eyes Were Watching God* (1934), sixteen-year-old protagonist Janie Crawford's grandmother catches her kissing a young boy by the gate and decides she needs to marry for "protection." "Nanny" sits Janie in her lap "lak yo' use tuh" and tells her about the plight of the black woman in the world. "Honey, de white man is de ruler of everything as fur as Ah been able tuh find out.... De nigger woman is de mule uh de world so fur as Ah can see. Ah been prayin' fuh it tuh be different wid you."[1] As Nanny "half sung, half sobbed a running chantprayer" over her granddaughter, who she has raised since Janie's mother went awry, Janie continues to protest an early marriage. "'Lemme wait, Nanny, please, jus' a lil bit mo'" Janie pleads, to which Nanny responds, "You ain't got no papa, you might jus' as well say no mama, for de good she do yuh. You ain't got nobody but me.[2] And mah head is ole and tilted towards de grave. Neither can you stand alone by yo'self. De thought uh you bein' kicked around from pillar tuh post is uh hurtin' thing.... Ah got tuh try and do for you befo' mah head is cold.'"[3] This scene, which is the first flashback to Janie telling her best friend Pheoby Watson about her life when she returns to the small town her second husband (of three marriages) helped to incorporate, helps the reader understand why Janie searched so hard for the perfect marriage and why Nanny was so concerned for her wellbeing.

As much as we read this text in a contemporary context about Janie's independence, we see initially Nanny's second attempt, after Janie's mother, at single motherhood and fear that she might fail Janie, too. Thus, she tries to protect Janie's womanhood by entrusting it to a much older man who will provide a home for her although it may not be the marriage of beauty and nature that Janie seeks.

From Nanny's description of her life in slavery, where she witnesses her master riding off after the announcement that General Sherman had taken Atlanta, one week after her own daughter was born and after he ran into her cabin and made her let down her hair for "de last time," after her mistress demands to see the baby "wid gray eyes and yaller hair" and asks several times why the baby "look white," we see why she wants Janie to be protected.⁴ Nanny's mistress plans to have her whipped and the baby sold away, so she ran through snakes and trees with her baby and hid until the announcement of the men in blue (Union soldiers) that all of the slaves were free. This is Nanny's freedom story, although she offers the disclaimer that it was a long time "befo' de Big Surrender at Richmond ... and all de men in gray uniforms had to go to Moultrie, and bury their swords in de ground to show they was never to fight about slavery no mo,'" but she chooses not to marry because she worries about her child Leafy.⁵ "Ah wouldn't marry nobody, though ah could have uh heap uh times, cause Ah didn't want nobody mistreating mah baby."⁶

Nanny's version of freedom then becomes making sure Leafy is provided for—she moves to West Florida "to work and make de sun shine on both sides of de street for Leafy."⁷ Additionally, she puts her in school to help her become a school teacher, until Leafy is raped by the school teacher at age seventeen and takes to "drinkin' likker and stayin' out nights."⁸ After Leafy's innocence is taken, Nanny argues that she "couldn't git her to stay here and nowhere else."⁹ Before Janie's story truly begins, her mother's narrative becomes one of wandering in search of satisfaction that she was not allowed to initiate for herself.

Over the course of the novel, the reader learns about Janie's successive marriages to Logan Killicks, Joe (Jody) Starks, and Vergible "Tea Cake" Woods. After a connection to natural freedom is established, Janie goes in pursuit, not of a greater knowledge of her history, but of a fulfilling relationship with a suitable mate. Freedom for Janie is not then about "marriage" per se, but about seeking fulfillment for her "natural desires." When she leaves Logan for Joe, deciding that even if he was waiting for her, "the change was bound to do her good" (33), she decides that "from now on until death she was going to have flower dust and springtime sprinkled over everything. A bee for her bloom."¹⁰ Janie decided that marriage to her second husband Joe Starts was "not a marriage," and we can argue that her third marriage to Tea Cake was only "marriage" for a time. So we end both removed from and continuing where we began, with freedom "other than marriage." Janie returns to her community (the last community she knew), where she helps her friend Pheoby realize the possibilities of life with her husband Sam. "'Lawd!' Pheoby breathed out heavily, 'Ah done growed ten feet higher from jus' listenin' tuh you, Janie. Ah ain't satisfied wid mahself no mo.' Ah means tuh make Sam take me fishin' wid him after this.'"¹¹ After Janie realizes that her own freedom is not tied up in marriage to any of these men, but in a true marriage to herself and to her friendships, at least in this next phase, she is able to help them realize the joys of their own lives with themselves and with their mates.

For Harriet Jacobs, freedom meant being reunited with her family. For the fictional Janie, it meant a return to and a reunion with her community. Throughout these stories, black women's desires for freedom from the institution of slavery were strongly connected to the legacy that they wanted to leave for future generations. As Jacobs was motivated to seek freedom for her children, so was Harper's Iola Leroy determined to remain in the south, to commit herself to educating freedpeople and their children, and to create a new awareness of self and possibility. When Ellen Craft finally decided to have children after she and her husband William escaped to free land, she came back to Georgia to educate as well. Finally, Lucy Craft Laney was referred to for her efforts as "Mother of the Children of the People" after slavery had formally ended.[12] Education (both formal and self-teaching) is a consistent link through these narratives because each author's motivation to write is based on the desire to document and to communicate their experiences. Through these narratives, readers can see themes of motherhood, independent labor, education, and democratic ideals as means of achieving freedom.

Perhaps the literary references to mothers and children in freedom are connected to the notion that the status of slavery was passed through the mother, yet even the maternal lineage was ambiguous. In "Mama's Baby, Papa's Maybe," Hortense J. Spillers discusses the impossibility of finding the "female" in "Middle Passage" although the "*internal* African slave trade ... according to Africanists, remained a predominantly *female* market."[13] She writes: "We get very little notion in the written record on the life of women, children, and infants in 'Middle Passage,' and no idea of the fate of the pregnant female captive and the unborn."[14] Spillers demonstrates the irony of tracing the history of black women when in many cases, their lives were undocumented.

This ambiguity continues through the institution of slavery on American soil; biological connections, specifically maternal bloodlines, were used in order to separate children "of color" from slave owners, but blood gets "mixed" through sex and conception. In cases of rape, a slaveholder could both distance himself from a child with an enslaved woman and ensure the continued growth of his labor force by attaching the child to its mother's bloodline. The literal bloodline became a metaphorical one as women raised other children on plantations in addition to their own (and the master's).[15] From this institution into emancipation, "mothering" came to assume a meaning beyond simply raising the child from one's womb. It meant, for many women, ensuring that their children had opportunities that they could only imagine.

In order to guarantee that these opportunities were realized, a number of black women writers in addition to Lucy Laney took the responsibility to educate black mothers in print as to how they could fulfill this role.

In *The Colored Girl Beautiful* (1916), Emma Azalia Hackley writes: "What a privilege to carve the destiny of a race!... A colored mother lives not only for herself and for her own children, but she must live for the race.... The colored mother beautiful must ... study more about the laws of heredity and child culture to prepare the child for its race battle, unhampered by inherited mental or physical tendencies."[16] The duties of motherhood are thus intertwined in the duties that Cooper, Laney, and others dictated for women to uplift the race. Hackley suggests that it is imperative for black women (specifically mothers) to actively study to prepare their children for racial obstacles ahead. This, in effect, is part of the mission of freedom. The idea of passing "blood" through generations is extended to the transfer of consciousness of a free status. The transfer then becomes one of "freedom-knowledge"; what to do and how to behave, that depends less on "blood"/biological connections than on by whom and how one is raised. In freedom, connections through biological blood lines expanded into connections through lines of history and literature; anyone who had experienced the plight of slavery or been affected by it could participate in dialogue that print and circulation facilitated.

This metaphor of "extended bloodlines" represented the intellectual community as well. Black women knew each other in literary and academic communities and also came into contact with each other through social networks and intellectual circles. Lucy Craft Laney established a legacy for Mary McLeod Bethune, who she taught and also taught with, in addition to Nannie Helen Burroughs, Charlotte Hawkins Brown, and others. Once reunited after separate journeys to New York, Harriet Jacobs and her daughter went on to start The Jacobs School in Alexandria, Virginia (1865) and, like Keckley, "worked to clothe, feed, and counsel refugees from the Civil War, open several boarding houses for both whites and black public officials, and travel between the north and south trying to help establish rights for free black folks and women."[17]

By the 1890s, these methods of perpetuating freedom were organized through women's clubs such as the National Association of Colored Women in 1896, and what came to be known as the "Women's Era" (a proliferation of writing by black women in the 1890s) began. Black women finally had ways to address the needs of their communities and could create their own contracts and agendas to serve this purpose.[18] In *Too Heavy a Load*, Deborah Gray White discusses speeches such as one by NACW first president and educator Mary Church Terrell that "'those of us fortunate enough to have education must share it with the less fortunate of our race. We must go into our communities and improve them; we must go out into the nation and change it.'"[19] "Changing the nation" was, in effect, the mission of the women who wrote their experiences from slavery to freedom. They never remained isolated in their social ascension but always extended assistance to those around them to secure opportunities for their freedom as well.

Narratives of freedom as authored by black women became the precursors for both these organizations and for more recognized literary "movements" of the late nineteenth and early twentieth centuries. "Freedom narratives" articulated black women's demands to be recognized as human beings and as citizens of the United States. Clubs provided collective and collaborative ways for these desires to be brought to fruition. They also created an environment which widened the audience, and therefore often increased the circulation of later publications by black women. Freedom narratives also established the ground and the audience for prescriptive literature, which instructed men and women on proper behavior: "From at least the early 1890s, conduct literature disseminated purposeful narratives about race women, men, and children, narratives that simultaneously produced and reproduced guidelines to be consumed, circulated, and perpetuated."[20] Those who aspired to achieve success could look to models in narratives and in more directly instructional texts such as manuals, pamphlets, tracts, and sermons.[21]

Audience reception of this literature was evidence of the need for texts written by black women. Michele Mitchell writes: "bound texts at once disseminated and codified values: publication and mass production made it easier for authors to reach wider audiences; both phenomena preserved information so that a daughter could receive the same wisdom as her mother."[22] This "wisdom" included, for both adult and younger women, information on "moral" sexual practices so that they would be viewed as "respectable."[23] Guidelines served as forms of reproduction in themselves, as authors reached mothers and fathers to establish a behavioral legacy.

Mitchell states: "Afro-American conduct literature thus attempted to perpetuate moral ideals as it strove to develop and reproduce a new people."[24] These earlier efforts to document women's experiences through literature and to "reproduce" acceptable versions of womanhood were enhanced in the Harlem Renaissance of the 1920s and 1930s by poets such as Angelina Weld Grimke and fiction writers such as Zora Neale Hurston. Grimke, notably, was Charlotte Forten (Grimke's) niece, her husband's brother's daughter who moved in with her in her later years.[25] Desires for various forms of "freedom" would persist throughout twentieth-century literature, as women gained visibility through literature in the "Black Arts Movement" of the 1960s and 1970s.[26]

Ideas of circulating and recirculating similar ideas through various points in history is made evident in such events as the 1980s reclamation by Alice Walker of Zora Neale Hurston and similar efforts of black feminist writers to discuss, republish, and rearticulate the claims of women who came before them. In addition to creating a sense of "motherhood" for those who came after them, black women writers of "freedom narratives" also created a sense of *sisterhood* in their efforts to rhetorically address various concerns of women. As in the examples of Keckley helping the refugees, freedmen and freedwomen in Washington, freedom for one was never independent of freedom for others.

Michele Mitchell writes: "It was with emancipation that freed people faced formidable pressures to make a way for themselves, and it was with emancipation that race activists devised an array of strategies built around and upon notions of collective destiny."[27] Some of these women may not have been thought of as traditional "race women," but their efforts represented and proclaimed progress for the newly free. For this reason, the end of the nineteenth century is actually a beginning, as earlier work of black women who documented experiences of freedom also gained wider circulation.[28]

This story ends where it began; our stories all begin with "freedom," and the desire to achieve it both initiated and has continued throughout the African American women's literary tradition. In her introduction to the *Cambridge Companion to the African American Novel*, Maryemma

Freedom Narratives of African American Women

Graham traces the history of the novel from the numerous versions of William Wells Brown's *Clotel* to the more than 25 African American novels, many written by black women, which appeared in 1970 alone. (This list includes, Graham notes, the first novel by Toni Morrison.)[29] As Graham argues about novels written by African Americans, the wealth of writing by black women about black women also needs to be investigated. She asserts: "The African American novel was capable of representing the broadest human concerns, it could absorb multiple forms of expressive culture, and it could engage readers across economic and racial lines."[30] This assessment is an effect of *and* represents the effects of what black women's writing in the nineteenth century was able to do. The value of writing oneself free or writing one's self freely, of being able to express feelings, passions, plans, family and career goals, and anxieties, is continuously revealed through analysis of black women's narratives of freedom. To both borrow and invert a phrase from Toni Morrison's now classic representation of Margaret Garner's story in *Beloved* (1988), freedom is indeed a story "to be *passed* on."

CHAPTER TWO

Moving Free
Black Women's Bodies and Freedom

Read together, the stories of Ellen Craft and Charlotte Forten articulate two "voices" from the South and illustrate two ways of writing and creating freedom and history. One woman literally writes a story and another woman inspires one, but both narratives represent ways of living *and* leaving legacies, of creating new possibilities, and of passing on knowledge. This chapter traces the circumstances that led Charlotte Forten, a free woman from Philadelphia's middle class in the mid-nineteenth century, and Ellen Craft, a formerly enslaved woman from Macon, Georgia, during the same period, to establish educational institutions in the South as a means of freedom.

Charlotte Forten (later Charlotte Forten Grimke) was formally educated and went to the Sea Islands of South Carolina to teach contraband black families; she shared her experiences with a broader audience through published journals and autobiographical articles before and after the Civil War. Ellen Craft did not write her own narrative but had her very significant story of freedom told by her husband, William Craft, in *Running a Thousand Miles for Freedom*. Craft played an integral part in her husband's narrative because she helped him design their plan of escape from Macon, Georgia. She later supported and embodied the efforts of northern abolitionists toward securing freedom; Craft created a life for her family in England and returned to the South to continue the legacy of freedom through education.

Both women *authorize* narratives that illuminate obstacles and successful efforts toward freedom. They also share an awareness of the value of literacy to racial progress, both by having their own lives represented and by sharing knowledge with others. Concerned both with preserving her image as a free woman and with documenting the experiences of those trying to achieve a permanent state of freedom, Forten discusses her attempts to help African Americans reconstruct their lives in *Life in the Sea Islands* (published as such in selections in 1864 in *Atlantic Monthly*).

William Craft's *Running a Thousand Miles for Freedom: The Escape of William and Ellen Craft from Slavery* (1860) is seldom discussed as biography of Ellen Craft, but Ellen is as much a primary character from the book's initial phrase, "My wife and myself." Having been enslaved in Georgia until 1848, then escaping to the north and traveling abroad to establish her family in England, Craft offers a narrative of freedom that culminates in her founding the Woodville Plantation School in 1870.

I explore the relationship between perceptions of freedom for African American women and the ways that they enable and engage this freedom with physical mobility and physical labor. These women transform the south into a place where liberation is adopted by some, enacted by others, and still enabled for others. For these women, the American south becomes a space where new narratives are created at the very sites of previous oppression. In these cases, they become places where identities of free American citizens are created

In the mid- to late nineteenth century, "newly emancipated" women were creating a role in society and on paper that they were also working to fulfill—that of self-determined intellectuals who cared for the minds in their charge. In considering the ideas that "the identity of the emancipated as rights bearer, free laborer, and calculable [wo]man must be considered in regard to processes of domination, exploitation, and subjection..." I argue that Charlotte Forten and Ellen Craft then manipulate these exploitative and subjective processes through mobility and visibility of their respective selves.[1] Their subjectivity is reconstituted by their respective journeys as they integrate themselves into new economies of bodies (both in numbers and in accounts of collective experiences).

I define freedom both by these women's abilities to move and by the access to opportunities in specific locations.[2] The body (in both its material state and its location) tells much in these narratives—where one goes, where one has been, and the journey in between.[3] Forten executes her ability to move as a free woman and notably uses that mobility to assist at a site of oppression far from her home (South Carolina's Sea Islands). Craft adopts the disguise of a white man (with her husband as her slave) to escape to Philadelphia, New York, and finally to England; she moves from a partially free status in America, where the threat of being returned is still present, to being permanently free abroad. She then returns to her original site of enslavement in the southern United States in order to create a new narrative for those emerging from slavery. These women "position" themselves literally and figuratively both to tell their stories and to have their stories told.

Even as a woman who was never legally enslaved, Charlotte Forten describes moments of feeling oppressed as she strives to be an intellectual, conflicted about how to help "the race." Her inability to resolve this feeling in the north compels her to travel to South Carolina, where she illustrates scenes of life on the Sea Islands and also struggles to find her place. Feeling marginalized as a woman and potential scholar as she grows up may have created her desire to make herself central to her narratives of educating southern blacks. Her movement from the outside of society (where she feels she is placed) to the center of the texts she writes is partly metaphorical but is also an effect of her physical movement from one actual location to another. As her body moves, she undergoes a transformation from feeling helpless to writing her own narrative of agency. She comes to "embody" the role of a missionary as she claims her social privilege as educated woman and even assumes the "privileges" of whiteness both by traveling with "white" people and by pronouncing the "blackness" of those she meets.

Ellen Craft's narrative is also written on her body as her husband chronicles how her disguise as a white man aids them toward freedom, the physical locations through which she travels, and, significantly, the ability of her body to bear children as a free woman (a point to which I return). Craft's life story is "written" by her body—how it was legally owned, escapes through physical transformation, then returns to assume a different role in a familiar location.

Charlotte Forten, Scenarios of Freedom

Forten lived the life of a scholar from a young age. She began her first published journal on May 24, 1854, at the age of sixteen while in Salem, Massachusetts to complete her studies after years of private instruction.[4] The daughter of middle class Philadelphians, Charlotte Forten was educated, familiar with the best social circles, and had social and educational liberties that many women of color did not. Forten's father refused to send her to the segregated schools of Philadelphia, and Stevenson writes that Forten "preferred" the life of a scholar and writer and lived with father's friends, abolitionist Charles Lenox Remond and wife Amy. While in the Remond's company, Forten met noted abolitionists William Lloyd Garrison, John Greenleaf Whittier, Lydia Maria Child, and former slave William Wells Brown.[5] She lived with Remond's sister after his wife's death and prospered in Salem—graduating, continuing a self-imposed study of Latin, French, and German, and publishing poetry in Garrison's *Liberator*.[6]

Brenda Stevenson writes in the introduction to a collection of Forten's journals that the Fortens were "among the most prestigious and wealthy of the Philadelphia free black community. Moreover, they used their financial and social standing to support local and regional reform movements, most particularly the efforts to abolish slavery and to establish legal equality for free blacks."[7] Although she was viewed as exceptional by abolitionists, Stevenson suggests that Forten felt a sense of negative self-perception from racism and rejection by whites that led to great unhappiness.[8] Her challenge seemed to be exactly how to translate her individual efforts into collective "improvement." Coupled with family issues—physical and emotional distance from her father and personal health concerns—Forten had to end her teaching career at Epes Grammar School in Salem early in order to return to Philadelphia.[9] There, she sought an opportunity to inspire change in the lives of others.

After Forten published articles in the *Christian Recorder* and the *National Anti-Slavery Standard*, Whittier suggested that she teach the contraband slave populations in Union camps in the Confederate south. Stevenson writes: "Under the auspices of the Port Royal Relief Association, Charlotte secured the position of teacher among the contraband slaves of the South Carolina Sea Islands. She was among hundreds of teachers from the Northeast who had come South for various reasons, but primarily to prepare the recently released slaves for their new role as free citizens of the United States."[10] Although Forten was legally free, she felt oppressed in another sense. She had the freedom to earn an education (in some places) and to teach, but still did not feel that she was able to use her efforts to the fullest.

Forten determined that traveling to Port Royal would allow her satisfaction that did not come from her daily studies and observations. She writes: "The accomplishments, the society, the delights of travel which I have dreamed of and longed for all my life, I am now convinced can never be mine. If I can go to Port Royal, I will try to forget all these desires. I will pray that God in his goodness will make me noble enough to find my highest happiness in doing my duty."[11] She hoped that her actions could do what her words were not previously to—allow her to feel free.

Forten thought that fulfillment would come through physical movement. Relocation would allow her to situate herself in a different environment and to therefore create a new narrative for her life. She felt the need to leave home, where she was legally "free," to achieve some greater social impact than that in her own community. Forten left for Port Royal, South Carolina, on October 22, 1862, where she lived for eighteen months.[12] Her efforts were not purely from a desire to exert missionary influence; her writings in her journal suggest that they were also inspired by her search for a greater sense of self-fulfillment.

Like women who wrote and published before her, Forten is also trying to "write" a place for herself—to make herself visible before an audience and to convince others of the value of her work. She is, however, less sure of her convictions and less confident in her position. Brenda Stevenson writes that Forten experienced unhappiness and negative self-perception from racism and rejection by whites although she was viewed as exceptional by abolitionists.[13] She was also conflicted about how African Americans could achieve equal status to that of their white counterparts. It is possible that Forten undertook a journey South in order to gain further understanding of the circumstances of the newly free "members of her race" in addition so seeing how she could help. Yet, her self-consciousness seems to come through in her writing even as she discusses the plights of others.

Perhaps in response to the restrictions she felt as a black woman, Forten sets up a clear contrast between herself and the people she goes to the Sea Islands to help. She becomes visible by locating herself at the center and distinguishing herself from other blacks. Ironically, Forten has to leave her domestic sphere to see herself. She has to put herself in the company of blacks with fewer social and educational privileges than she possesses in order to appreciate her own privilege. She also, however, displays an anxiety about her visibility by creating an "us"/"them" dichotomy between herself and the newly freed blacks. For example, she never describes her own appearance but is very attentive to such details as skin color and other physical attributes amongst members of the Sea Islands community. She also discusses their freedom extensively but never reflects on her own status as a free woman.

Through the lens (and pen) of a schoolteacher, Forten focuses on her own agency in addition to what she sees and recognizes amongst her pupils and their families. Her theories of freedom are attached to the bodies that now move fluidly where they were once restricted. Forten's own feelings of oppression give her insight on how others negotiate their freedom; observing the physical manifestations of the liberation of others helps Forten to define herself.

The version of her narrative journals published as *Life on the Sea Islands* begins symbolically, as Forten describes sailing to Hilton Head on a steamer called the "United States." Upon arrival, she writes, "A motley assemblage had collected on the wharf,—officers, soldiers, and 'contrabands' of every size and hue: black was, however, the prevailing color."[14] Forten literally represents the "nation" coming to the black people in South Carolina, but whether or not she likens herself to the black "contrabands" is not evident here. Forten's initial descriptions actually seem more like the notes of an outsider than of one who plans to situate herself in the community. She describes the "desolate" first view of the island, "a long, low, sandy point ... with no visible dwellings [except] the rows of small white-roofed houses which have lately been built for the freed people" but just as soon begins to describe military General Saxton as "handsome, courteous, and affable."[15] As she described scenes of nature in her earlier journals, Forten seemingly desires to paint a picture of her overall journey rather than a specific investment in the plight of her charges. Although this is not an explicit personal critique, it shows the ways in which she, a free woman of the north, is able to transfer her attentions among multiple worlds of soldiers, freedmen, and those with whom she traveled.

Forten is also, however, invested in maintaining the boundaries between these worlds. She describes freedpeople and Southerners as "they" and "them" and clings to her northern background by using the pronoun "we." She writes: "We saw no one in the streets but soldiers and freed people. There were indications that already Northern improvements had reached this Southern town. Among them was a wharf, a convenience that one wonders how the Southerners could so long have existed without. The more we know of their mode of life, the more are we inclined to marvel at its utter shiftlessness."[16] Observations such as these confirm the dichotomy between Forten, who is clearly representative of both a certain region and class, and those she comes to help. She critiques the conveniences they lack but shows more amazement than explicit concern. To "marvel" at the "shiftlessness" of other's lives is the perspective of a spectator, an onlooker to crisis rather than an initiator of change. Forten's initial perspective is important, yet it shows her superficial understanding of her very serious task.

Other examples of the manner in which Forten separates herself from the black people she goes to help are her descriptions of the "little colored children of every hue ... playing about the streets, looking as merry and happy as children ought to look,—now that the evil shadow of Slavery no longer hangs over them."[17] As she observes, Forten seems particularly concerned—in an anthropological sense—with literally painting a picture of the "Negroes." She is interested in their skin color, but also in their actions and the ways they are treated. On one hand, she describes how the officers talked "sneeringly of the negroes, whom they found we had come down to teach."[18] On another, her descriptions of "negroes" extend to the "rich tones of the negro boatmen" who sing as they row her party to Ladies Island. Forten's observations are generally complimentary as to the abilities of those she describes, but she draws no likeness to these Southern blacks. Furthermore, she NEVER defines the "we" of which she is part. She even feels "a sense of unreality about everything": "I felt that nothing less than a vigorous 'shaking-up' ... would arouse me thoroughly to the fact that I was in South Carolina."[19] Such phrases suggest that the differences between her own background and her southern environment are too great for Forten to overcome.

Forten's notable effort to come to the South to teach the freedmen is not, however, to be diminished. In fact, the most significant parts of her narrative are descriptions of them. She watches the women from the window of her new abode and is warmed by their happiness: "On every face there was a look of serenity and cheerfulness. My heart gave a great throb of happiness as I looked at them, and thought, 'They are free! So long down-trodden, so long crushed to the earth, but now in their old homes, forever free!' And I thanked God that I had lived to see this day."[20] For Forten, seeing the freedom of others reminds her of the privileges for which she can be thankful. Being able to *witness* this scene (in both the observational and testimonial senses of the word) gives her a sense of purpose and a feeling of joy. In this description, Forten looks at their faces and is able to tell a significant story—a story of freedom. She also writes herself into the scene because she is able to give thanks for being able to see this transformation take place. Scenes such as this also help Forten realize that the condition of these men and women is a result of the conditions under which they have been forced to live. She writes: "Were they, under such circumstances, intellectual and refined, they would certainly be vastly superior to any other race that ever existed."[21] Although Forten is concerned with the change in consciousness of the freed men and women, it is also evident that her own consciousness changes as she comes to understand the physical, mental, and psychological challenges that they have had to endure.

Prior to visiting the Sea Islands, Forten's writing was primarily based on materials that she read instead of events that she saw firsthand. Being part of the process to enable the freedom of former slaves, however, allows Forten to cross the line from consumer of stories written by others to producer of her own. She can both see and create firsthand knowledge of the inspiration that freedom brings to the people of the Sea Islands. Her testimony also allows her to define her own role in helping them realize their freedom. Forten writes: "The freed people on the place seemed glad to see us. After talking with them, and giving some directions for cleaning the house, we drove to the school, in which I was to teach."[22] In her interaction with the "freedpeople," Forten gains some sense of authority in her mission on the Sea Islands.

Forten's freedom, however, is also characterized by the liberty to observe rather than to participate in the everyday activities of those who she helps. Forten's sense of "us" and "them" is very apparent in this narrative; she, already free in name, is part of the mission to educate people that are in many ways different from her. A primary difference is their class status. Forten, well-educated and from a middle class northern background, does not share the cultural background of other black people on the Sea Islands. The practices that are most significant to them, namely their worship experiences, are as foreign to Forten as if she were visiting another country.

The school Forten describes is held in a Baptist church, and Forten describes the "rich, sweet tones" of the children as they sing.[23] In the same lines in which she describes the land and nature (without stating their particular significance to her), Forten describes the black church and the singing that takes place there.[24] It is almost as if her journey to the Sea Islands and to these people is equivalent to a return to a natural state that she never inhabited. The black people she encounters are simultaneously strange and fascinating to her, and discussing their ways becomes Forten's new intellectual enterprise.

After attending a black church on the Islands, she writes that the Baptist preacher's sermon is "quite unintelligible" to our unaccustomed ears" but, after attending the white Episcopal church, she states that the "old-fashioned New-England church-music, [was] pleasant to hear, but ... did not thrill us as the singing of the people had done."[25] Forten seems to be within two worlds as she situates herself in the Sea Islands. She is a stranger to the cultural traditions of the black people and thus describes and interprets them almost as an anthropological case study. Yet, she takes interest in them in a way that she does not with the whites in the same space. In her descriptions, Forten inhabits the "in-between" as a place of comfort, as she is still unfamiliar with some of their ways, but also to maintain the distance from which she observes.

As spectator, Forten has a curious investment in the details of the lives of the black people with whom she interacts. She describes "Cupid," her "right hand" man, as having a "face nearly black, very ugly, but with the shrewdest expression I ever saw, and the brightest, most humorous twinkle in the eyes."[26] Amaretta, the cook, is "a neat-looking black woman, adorned with the gayest of head-handkerchiefs."[27] Her descriptions are not necessarily derogatory, but more curious as to the things and people she observes. Forten's training as a scholar and influence of white abolitionists may be evident in her observations. She was influenced largely by noted abolitionists William Lloyd Garrison, Lydia Maria Child, and John Greenleaf Whittier (also a Quaker poet who initially suggested that she teach among contraband slaves in Union camps in the Confederate south).[28] Along this line, there may be distance from approaching across a northern-southern divide. As Whittier writes of Virginia and slavery, in his poem "Massachusetts to Virginia," "All that a sister State should do, all that a free State may/Heart, hand, and purse we proffer, as in our early day;/But that one dark loathsome burden ye must stagger with alone,/And reap the bitter harvest which ye yourselves have sown!"[29] The states may feel kinship but there is a sense in these lines, as in Forten's writing, that observations are made from a different position.

Because she comes from a background of free blacks, Forten is more aware of the restrictions of blackness through bodies on the Sea Islands and also more aware of the opportunities that freedom offers. Her observations are not just about her own mobility, but about what she sees as these former slaves move through domestic and community environments. Of her pupils, Forten writes, "I never before saw children so eager to learn, although I had had several years' experience in New-England schools."[30] Even the grown people want to read, Forten notes, stating that it is wonderful how people "who have been so long crushed to the earth ... can have so great a desire for knowledge."[31] "Were they, under such circumstances, intellectual and refined, they would certainly be vastly superior to any other race that ever existed," she states, developing an awareness of the privileges necessary to achieve success.[32] She even tries to promote such achievement by reminding the students of Toussaint L'Ouverture, leader of the Haitian Revolution. Forten told this story "thinking it well they should know what one of their own color had done for his race."[33] But the question as to why Forten speaks to "them" about "their" circumstances remains unanswered.

It is quite possible that for Forten, class status, geography, and cultural background spoke as much if not more than race in distinguishing some people from others. "These" people had not had the privileges of formal education, had no refined domestic spheres or socially elevated communities. "These" people, Forten writes, carry things on their heads and live in "miserable little huts."[34] She compliments their taste, "We noticed that the people had much better taste in selecting materials for dresses than we had supposed," and adds that they are fond of jewelry, polite in manner, and solemn in hand-shaking.[35] They also have faith in northerners to help them. Such descriptions make it seem as if Forten is trying to figure out for herself who they are through their manners and customs.

Southern blacks and former slaves seem to be from a completely different world for Forten, and she also associates them with Africa (which she never does for herself). Forten describes the "shouts" of the musicians, children, and adults as "rather solemn and impressive ... we cannot determine whether it has a religious character or not."[36] She decides that it is probably an expression of religion, "handed down to them from their African ancestors, and destined to pass away under the influence of Christian teachings."[37] Forten adds in a related conversation that "Prince, a large black boy from a neighboring plantation," performed "most amusing specimens of Ethiopian gymnastics" for the visitors.[38] Is the exoticism of their religion and ethnic traditions explicit separatism or merely acknowledged unfamiliarity with their ways? Furthermore, what does Forten achieve by separating herself from these Africanisms (or are they already separated *for* her)?

By describing the differences of the black people on the Sea Islands, Forten positions herself as narrator to a larger reading community. Not only does she educate the contrabanded black people of the Civil War, but she educates others *about* them. Although it is noticeable that Forten describes no initial connection with the freedmen as fellow blacks, it is clear that she is also coming under the influence of (and in the company of) white northerners who also approach their pupils from different class and educational backgrounds.

Throughout Forten's narrative, she is transformed by the actual impact that the realization of freedom has on the members of the community. She describes how people listened to General Saxton's proclamation at church on the Sunday before Thanksgiving with emotion: "The people listened with the deepest attention, and seemed to understand and appreciate it."[39] It is at this point that she begins to penetrate the legal implications of freedom for the community. She states: "General Saxton is truly worthy of the gratitude and admiration with which the people regard him. His unfailing kindness and consideration for them—so different from the treatment they have sometimes received at the hands of other officers—have caused them to have unbounded confidence in General 'Saxby,' as they call him."[40] When it comes to understanding how deeply the language of freedom affects black people on the Sea Islands, Forten adopts a more empathetic position that brings her closer to what "the people" are experiencing.

Perhaps Forten realizes at this point that many people take part in the freedom process, including General Saxton and missionaries and educators (including herself). The consciousness of self that Forten carries from her previous life experiences—feeling oppressed and isolated as a free black woman in the north—has to disappear in order for her to truly see others. Ironically, watching another journey toward liberation as it takes place helps Forten free herself from a restrictive perspective. Forten ceases to be as concerned with herself in her observations and can therefore issue commentary about broad implications of freedom through her narrative. The transformation in her position at this point makes important dialogues of freedom available to her audience.

In this shift in perspective from spectator to insider, Forten is able to represent more objectively the different forms that freedom takes for this community—education, reunion of families, and the ability to establish domestic life on their own terms. The significance of these opportunities is demonstrated by the initiative that couples take to make their unions official. Forten describes a marriage ceremony for six couples after the Proclamation service. She writes that the items utilized for the marriages were cast-off dresses with decayed decorations "but, comical as the costumes were, we were not disposed to laugh at them."[41] Although Forten is unmarried at this time, she shows a sincere appreciation for the legally recognized endeavour which these former slaves seek to undertake: "We were too glad to see the poor creatures trying to lead right and virtuous lives. The legal ceremony, which was formerly scarcely known among them, is now everywhere consecrated ... nearly every Sunday there are several couples married in church. Some of them are people who have grown old together."[42] Although she still sees through her own social lens—in this case, attempts of "poor creatures" to lead righteous lives modeled by those from more privileged circumstances—Forten does recognize the inability of her subjects to even participate in some forms of "virtuous" behavior such as marriage prior to this point.[43] She also acknowledges that the unions among them are genuine although previously unrecognized by the law. This is important, especially when read with the story of William and Ellen Craft as an example of the ways the marriage plot was directly connected to emancipation, because it shows that intimate relationships persisted under some of the most horrible circumstances and the challenges that couples endured.

However, the cultural gaps that Forten displays earlier in her narrative are also narrowed by her observations of events to which she can relate, such as marriage and celebration of holidays. Her ultimate realization of freedom for this community—a freedom consecrated by state law and civil rights—comes through such celebrations. The opportunity to observe nationally recognized holidays symbolizes inclusion if not yet full citizenship.[44] On Thanksgiving, they are "forever free," she writes—a crowd of "eager, happy black faces."[45] As men are urged to enlist in the armed forces to protect their freedom, Forten writes: "Over all shone gloriously the blessed light of Freedom, Freedom forevermore!"[46] The second section of Forten's narrative incorporates celebrations of Christmas and New Year's Day. She describes the soldiers, the *"first"* Black regiment "mustered into the service of U.S." and illustrates the body of people in their company singing "My Country 'tis of Thee." Forten responds: "It was a touching and beautiful incident, and sent a thrill through all our hearts."[47] Although her descriptions are still not entirely complimentary (she eventually refers to the people as "sweetest, wildest humans," it is clear that Forten's concern with representing the humanity of the Sea Islanders increases.[48]

Under a backdrop of military pomp and holiday celebrations, Forten incorporates bodies into a national narrative. As the boatmen sing, she writes: "We knew that Freedom was surely born in our land that day."[49] This is a turning point in the narrative, one of the few times that Forten speaks of a collective "we," a communal "land." Through her account, Forten begins to articulate that efforts to achieve freedom are larger than what she is doing. By this point, she is able to focus on her agency in relation to that of others. She gradually lends more attention to their life stories than to her own.

A perceptive narrator is characterized by awareness of one's subject and the ability to represent this subject with complexity. In Forten's case, her growth as a narrator comes from the ability to recognize the many levels of her subjects' experiences. While they were initially just external characters to her—numbers of people who needed help—her observations allow her to go beneath the exterior of this community and the issue on the surface (the need for education). By witnessing their desire for inclusion in the realm of freedom that education would allow, Forten also finds inclusion in their community by seeing that their goals were similar to hers—visibility, voice, mobility, and opportunity. Thus, her individual effort as part of the mission becomes linked to a collective effort toward freedom. She finds that freedom is not a singular effort; it depends on both individual and cooperative efforts and wider recognition of them.

The stories that Forten includes "are things too heart-sickening to dwell upon, God alone knows how many hundreds of plantations, all over the south, might furnish a similar record."[50] Yet, by telling them, the black freedmen/contraband slaves become more than bodies to her. They have names, such as Bess, a former house-servant who "bears on her limbs many marks of the whip, [some of the scars] three and four inches long."[51] Another girl whose story Forten chronicles threw herself in creek and drowned for refusing to degrade herself by giving in to her master's "licentiousness": "Outraged, despised, and black, she yet preferred death to dishonor."[52] Forten adds these women to the number of descriptions she offers throughout the text but represents their significance beyond their physical appearances. In documenting an economy of bodies—numbers that resisted in addition to numbers that were lost—Forten recognizes the value of black women's lives other than her own. Through her attention to these individuals, Forten's perspective literally grows wider and their subjectivity is enhanced through the tales of their activism in Forten's text.

Forten's journey to the Sea Islands is simultaneously a physical, spiritual, and psychologically transformative experience in that it allows her to see herself, and through that process, "see" others. Her vision is at first limited to their outward appearance and their differences from her, but as she situates herself more comfortably in her new space, she is then able to see her own freedom as connected to theirs. Ultimately, she can best tell the tale of free bodies when she literally becomes *one of them*. It is ironic that Forten had to journey to a place previously controlled by slave owners in order to see freedom realized. It is also symbolic that she reflects more on her greater role in the emancipation effort at a site where she sees liberation taking place. Forten's conclusions in her study of people in one location serves as a model for studies of freedom—one must actually see (by experiencing *or* gaining knowledge of) the plight of one's subjects in order to understand the implications of their liberation.

Forten also seems to be within two worlds as she situates herself in the Sea Islands. She is a stranger to the cultural traditions of the black people and thus describes and interprets them almost as an anthropological case study. Yet, she takes interest in them in a way that she does not with the whites in the same space. In her descriptions, Forten inhabits the "in-between" as a place of comfort, as she is still unfamiliar with some of their ways, but also to maintain the distance from which she observes.

Prior to visiting the Sea Islands, Forten's writing was primarily based on materials that she read instead of events that she saw first hand. Being part of the process to enable the freedom of former slaves, however, allows Forten to cross the line from consumer of stories written by others to producer of her own. She can both see and create firsthand knowledge of the inspiration that freedom brings to the people of the Sea Islands. Her testimony also allows her to define her own role in helping them realize their freedom.

For Forten, seeing the freedom of others in its "natural," or original state, reminds her of the privileges for which she can be thankful. Being able to *witness* this scene (in both the observational and testimonial senses of the word) gives her a sense of purpose and a feeling of joy. In this description, Forten looks at their faces and is able to tell a significant story—a story of freedom. She also writes herself into the scene because she is able to give thanks for being able to see this transformation take place. Scenes such as this also help Forten realize that the condition of these men and women is a result of the conditions under which they have been forced to live. She writes: "Were they, under such circumstances, intellectual and refined, they would certainly be vastly superior to any other race that ever existed."[53] Although Forten is concerned with the change in consciousness of the freed men and women, it is also evident that her own consciousness changes as she comes to understand the physical, mental, and psychological challenges that they have had to endure.

Forten's journey to the Sea Islands is simultaneously a physical, spiritual, and psychologically transformative experience in that it allows her to see herself, and through that process, "see" others. Her vision is at first limited to their outward appearance and their differences from her, but as she situates herself more comfortably in her new space, she is then able to see her own freedom as connected to theirs. Ultimately, she can best tell the tale of free bodies when she literally becomes *one of them*. It is ironic that Forten had to journey to a place previously controlled by slave owners in order to see freedom realized. It is also symbolic that she reflects more on her greater role in the emancipation effort at a site where she sees liberation taking place. Forten's conclusions in her study of people in one location serves as a model for studies of freedom—one must actually see (by experiencing *or* gaining knowledge of) the plight of one's subjects in order to understand the implications of their liberation.

Ellen Craft: A Body Transformed

As Charlotte Forten describes the bodies of others, Ellen Craft's husband is concerned with *her* body in *Running a Thousand Miles for Freedom: Or, the Escape of William and Ellen Craft from Slavery* (1848). The movement of Ellen Craft in this text occurs on multiple levels. First, she moves throughout the actual inscription, as she is present in name and as a featured character of the plot. Then, the story traces her physical movement as she escapes with her husband to freedom and returns to reestablish her life as a free woman in Georgia.

The opening paragraphs of *Running* offer a comprehensive synopsis of its plot, at length:

> My wife and myself were born in different towns in the State of Georgia, which is one of the principal slave States. It is true, our condition as slaves was not by any means the worst; but the mere idea that we were held as chattels, and de-prived of all legal rights ... the thought that we could not call the bones and sinews that God gave us our own: but above all, the fact that another man had the power to tear from our cradle the new-born babe and sell it in the shambles like a brute, and then scourge us if we dared to lift a finger to save it from such a fate, haunted us for years.
>
> But in December, 1848, a plan suggested itself that proved quite successful, and in eight days after it was first thought of we were free from the horrible trammels of slavery, rejoicing and praising God in the glorious sunshine of liberty.[54]

The story could conceivably end here. The reader is given the most salient points of the story in this brief summary—that the two were born slaves but were somehow able to marry, that besides having no rights they were opposed to the power that another man had over their bodies and any children they bore, and that they escaped by means of a successful plan. Yet, the subtext that is not explicit in this preview is the negotiation of bodies and physical space that allowed this escape. Craft goes into great detail about how they then reclaim control of the "bones and sinews" given by God but usurped by their masters.

Dorothy Sterling notes that Ellen traveled with her mistress's daughter to Macon, Georgia, where she met William (who hired his time as a cab-inetmaker there).[55] Ellen Craft's principles quickly become apparent. After the two meet in the company of "persons who held us as property" and develop a relationship, Ellen wishes to postpone marriage because of "mother laws"—"the father of the slave may be the President of the Repub-lic; but if the mother should be a slave at the infant's birth, the poor child is ever legally doomed to the same cruel fate."[56] To document this analysis, William Craft cites a case of a slave woman and her children who are seized although she had lived with her master as his wife; when the master died without a will, a man claiming to be his relative separated the family and took two of the children. Being nearly white, they escaped without attention, but the mother died before her children could find her.[57] Craft acknowledges the influence of this story on his own life, for the "mother" was "[his] wife's own dear aunt."[58] This ending is tragic for William as narrator but even more so because it is so close to his own situation. It is impetus for he and Ellen to create another story with a different ending than that of her aunt.

With the knowledge of this family history and numerous other stories, Ellen Craft refuses to let the laws that benefit slaveholders keep any children she might bear in the same condition of enslavement. Separated from her own parents, the thought of becoming a mother "filled [Ellen's] soul with horror," and William agreed to assist her in devising a plan "to escape from [their] unhappy condition, and then be married."[59] After the marriage, Ellen maintains her desire not to have children before they are free. Sterling suggests that she may have used "crude homemade devices"— sponges, citrus fruits, or stones in order—that some "desperate slave women used to prevent conception."[60] Betty DeRamus also suggests that Ellen may have used homemade contraceptives but asserts that there is no evidence of induced miscarriages in her case, as with "some slave women."[61] Whether or not Ellen Craft used contraceptives, this shows the critical decisions that slave women had to make to keep from having children taken into slavery. William and Ellen Craft have a strong desire to live together in freedom; unwilling to stay in this dubious condition for much longer, the two plan to escape during the Christmas holiday so that they can use passes available to slaves to leave their masters' homes without suspicion. Through the discussions of her moral dilemmas, more of Ellen's interiority is revealed to the reader. She is not just an enslaved woman or merely a subject of William's narrative, but also a principal character in how their lives evolve before and during their journey toward emancipation.

In planning to escape, the couple thought it impossible to travel immediately across slave states and first resolved to marry and continue to plan, prayerfully "[keeping] dim eyes steadily fixed upon the glimmering hope of liberty."[62] William and Ellen married in December 1848, at which time a plan came to William to escape: "Knowing that slaveholders have the privilege of taking their slaves to any part of the country they think proper, it occurred to me that, as my wife was nearly white, I might get her to disguise herself as an invalid gentlemen, and assume to be my master, while I could attend as his slave."[63] Although Ellen was at first fearful of the idea of escaping in disguise because of the potential to get caught, William Craft writes that "she also thought of her condition. She saw that the laws under which we lived did not recognize her to be a woman, but a mere chattel, to be bought and sold..."[64] These laws that kept her enslaved did not consider Ellen's humanity, thus she had to go against them to establish her own version of freedom. Going against the laws, in Ellen's case, means to transform herself—to physically alter the ability to recognize her as a woman.

Once she is resolved to make the escape, Ellen is instrumental in helping with the plan to disguise herself: "'If you will purchase the disguise,'" she tells her husband, "'I will try to carry out the plan.'"[65] William goes around town to collect items and takes them to his wife's house. Since Ellen was "a ladies' maid, and a favourite slave in the family,'" she had her own room and a chest of drawers that William made her in which to lock the items.[66] Ellen also made the trousers to wear in the escape.

William writes that the two obtain their holiday passes, which neither he nor his wife can read.[67] Their similar inability to write causes Ellen great distress when she recalls that travelers must register their names in hotel visitor books, but this moment of trepidation leads her to a breakthrough: "All at once my wife raised her head, and with a smile upon her face, which was a moment before bathed in tears, said 'I think I have it!' … 'I think I can make a poultice and bind up my right hand in a sling, and with propriety ask the officers to register my name for me.'"[68] Ellen's husband concurs, at which point her planning continues to add a poultice in a white handkerchief "to be worn under the chin, up the cheeks, and to tie over the head" to hide her facial expressions and beardless chin.[69] Finally, she suggests that they hide the final telltale feature, her eyes: "My wife, knowing that she would be thrown a good deal into the company of gentlemen, fancied that she could get on better if she had something to go over the eyes; so I went to a shop and bought a pair of green spectacles."[70] Thus, Ellen is disguised as a white man who is both ill and visually challenged. In these few paragraphs, William Craft shows not only the skill of their collaboration, but highlights his wife's insight. After cutting her hair and having her put on the disguise that they thought of within the hours of a day, William Craft writes: "I found that she made a most respectable looking gentleman."[71]

This was not, of course, the first use of disguise of which the Crafts were aware. In an earlier documented story of Ellen's aunt in the narrative, the older brother Frank comes for his younger siblings disguised as a white man after several failed attempts to buy them in his own "skin."[72] Craft writes that Frank "cultivated large whiskers and moustachios, cut off his hair, put on a wig and glasses, and went down as a white man" to buy his sister, a disguise so successful that she did not even know him after he purchased her and their brother. The young girl would not speak until "he showed their mother's likeness."[73] Together, these stories demonstrate the understanding that one literally had to "become" white in order to have the privilege to own other bodies (including, ironically, their own). In order to free themselves from the system of slavery, they had to obtain a position from which to buy themselves. They had to perform the role of whiteness—both physical and economic—in order to access the benefits associated with it. Pursuing the guise of whiteness was a strategy of physical transformation to achieve social transformation.[74]

When Ellen contemplates her own condition of enslavement, she realizes that nothing could be worse than remaining in it. She is then charged with altering her appearance so as to be completely unrecognizable. The background William offers is that even free blacks are banished from certain states, including Tennessee, Missouri, Kentucky, and Georgia, so even to escape in disguise would be dangerous.[75] She ironically assumes the identity of the farthest thing from her and the most dangerous thing to her—a white slave master. The final piece of the Craft's disguise is that William appears as Ellen's slave, which Ellen had "no ambition whatever" to incorporate. William writes: "[she] would not have done so had it been possible to have obtained our liberty by more simple means; but we knew it was not customary in the South for ladies to travel with male servants; and therefore, notwithstanding my wife's fair complexion, it would have been a very difficult task for her to have come off as a free white lady, with me as her slave."[76] Therefore, Ellen has to become a white man, and she has to appear in the position of power that a slave master holds. She has to become what she most despises to get what she most desires, freedom from enslavement.

Ellen Craft even refuses to let the laws that benefit slaveholders keep any children she might bear in the same condition of enslavement. Separated from her own parents, the thought of becoming a mother "filled [Ellen's] soul with horror," and William agreed to assist her in devising a plan "to escape from [their] unhappy condition, and then be married."[77] In planning to escape, the couple thought it impossible to travel immediately across slave states and first resolved to marry and continue to plan, prayerfully "[keeping] dim eyes steadily fixed upon the glimmering hope of liberty."[78] William and Ellen married in December 1848, at which time a plan came to William to escape: "Knowing that slaveholders have the privilege of taking their slaves to any part of the country they think proper, it occurred to me that, as my wife was nearly white, I might get her to disguise herself as an invalid gentlemen, and assume to be my master, while I could attend as his slave."[79] Although Ellen was at first fearful of the idea of escaping in disguise because of the potential to get caught, William Craft writes that "she also thought of her condition. She saw that the laws under which we lived did not recognize her to be a woman, but a mere chattel, to be bought and sold..."[80] These laws that kept her enslaved did not consider Ellen's humanity, thus she had to go against them to establish her own version of freedom. Going against the laws, in Ellen's case, means to transform herself—to physically alter the ability to recognize her as a woman.

In order to make their extraordinary story plausible to a reading audience, William Craft describes the lineage that contributed to his wife's light complexion early in the text: "My wife's first master was her father, and her mother his slave."[81] He goes on to clarify that slavery is not limited to any particular skin color: "slavery in America is not at all confined to persons of any particular complexion; there are a very large number of slaves as white as any one; but as the evidence of a slave is not admitted in court against a free white person, it is almost impossible for a white child, after having been kidnapped and sold into or reduced to slavery, in a part of the country where it is not known (as often is the case) ever to recover its freedom."[82] In this description, even whites who are sold as slaves are often unable to regain freedom, so the case is even more difficult for slaves of color. It is an illogical institution that depends on financial rather than moral sustenance to keep it alive. Throughout the narratives that William Craft relays, including a court case about a German emigrant taken for a slave in New Orleans, he articulates the arbitrary and often violent nature of slavery and is consoled only by belief in God's justice.[83]

Returning to his own history, William Craft focuses on the manner in which his master sold his two siblings and both parents. He was apprenticed to learn the trade of cabinet-maker, while his master sold his brother and mortgaged his sister to a bank for money to speculate in cotton.[84] When his master was unable to make his payments, the bank put them on auction, selling his sister first despite his requests to bid her farewell. Thus, he sees the effects of slavery firsthand as his siblings are sent away for his master's financial mismanagement. They receive no financial contributions, yet they must suffer for his greed in speculation.

Significantly, however, he includes a happier ending that involves his wife even in the early portion of the narrative—he recalls later finding his sister living with a family in Mississippi and being "nearly" able to purchase her freedom with profits from occasional lectures, the help of friends, and "through the sale of an engraving of my wife in the disguise in which she escaped."[85] In this section, William Craft literally inscribes the stories of black women into his own. His sister, and later his wife—women he loves dearly but also seeks to protect—contribute to his impression of the emotional distress that slavery could cause and the urgent need to escape.

As the Crafts execute their escape, Ellen is scared and both see difficulties in playing roles from which they are trying to escape.[86] As she is disguised as a white man, both Ellen's color *and* gender disappear in order for her and her husband to appear in their "proper roles" as prescribed by society. Although Ellen makes the greatest physical transformation, it is important to remember that William also gives up his sense of dignity as he must become more convincing as an enslaved man in order to achieve freedom. William must not only *be* but also "play" the role of the slave to make his relationship to a "white" person believable. He cannot display intellect or talent, he cannot speak, he must completely submit. Ironically, as they seek to live their full humanity as free people, they must temporarily erase and transform themselves through disguise.

After they leave the house to escape from Macon, William and Ellen Craft shake hands and say "farewell" as they start on different directions to the train. This is also a "farewell" to their former identities, at least for a time: "My *master* (as I will now call my wife) took a longer way round, and only arrived there with the bulk of the passengers. He obtained a ticket for himself and one for his slave to Savannah, the first port, which was about two hundred miles off. My master then had the luggage stowed away and stepped into one of the best carriages."[87] The challenge of impersonation falls on Ellen—she has to be convincing in physical appearance and voice, especially as she asks for tickets to various locations. In their process of obtaining freedom, Ellen Craft is continually referred to as "master" and "he" from this point in William's narrative.[88] This is evidence of what she becomes to him, of the way in which they must completely remove themselves from their former roles even as husband and wife. Even the process of writing about his wife in this role seems challenging in the text. When the Crafts see an old friend of Ellen's master on the train, William writes that "she" feigns deafness.[89] His slipping back into the feminine gender descriptive of Ellen is not just a textual lapse, but a way to show difficulty between describing who Ellen is and the role she enacts.

In "becoming" master, Ellen has to both mimic and adopt a slave master's ways. She must sit in the first-class carriage, knowing that her husband is in the "Jim Crow" car.[90] On this same train ride, she must endure her master's friend in silence as he discusses "the three great topics of discussion in first-class circles in Georgia, namely, Niggers, Cotton, and the Abolitionists."[91] "Feigning" deafness is perhaps the only way that she can keep herself from taking offense; she does, however, learn for the first time that abolitionists "were persons that were opposed to oppression" and comes to think of them as "not the lowest, but the very highest, of God's creatures."[92]

Ellen is challenged several times over on the way North. When they arrive in Savannah, "she" retires to bed so as not to have to talk with the other passengers. William covers for her by preparing warm flannels to aid her "rheumatism," then sleeping outside on the deck because there is no place "provided for coloured passengers."[93] He serves her faithfully, even carving her food because of the sling, to the point where a slave dealer offers to buy William "for any price."[94] Ellen responds, "'I cannot get on well without him,'" to which the dealer retorts that "he" will have to get on without him if he takes him North: "'It always makes me mad to hear a man talking about fidelity in niggers. There isn't a d——-d one on 'em who wouldn't cut sticks, if he had half a chance."[95] This is one of the best textual examples when Ellen *does* speak of the way those invested in the slave trade feel about slaves in general, to the point of discussing them with perfect strangers. All Ellen can do is thank the man for his advice, at which point he continues to deride blacks who pursue their own freedom. Ellen relies on her illness again to remove herself from a conversation in which she cannot safely defend herself.[96] On this same trip, she is scolded by an officer for telling William "thank you" and must silently witness the man swearing at his "poor dejected slave."[97] Ellen is treated gently by others, likely because of "her" illness, but the mistreatment that she sees of others in William's position is additional pain that she must endure.

In the next stage of the trip, a steamer to Wilmington, North Carolina, the officer nearly refuses to sell them the tickets because Ellen cannot write "his" name and the name of "[his] nigger."[98] Ellen pays the dollar duty and points to the poultice to no end, until the officer from the last trip steps in to "sign" for them as "Mr. William Johnson and slave."[99] Again, William and Ellen must not only benefit from the privilege of whiteness

Two. Moving Free

in order to be free, but also could delight in knowing that they tricked all of these people into helping them gain their freedom. Theirs is a game of negotiation and manipulation for Ellen; she has to determine when to speak and when to be silent, when to exert her role as a "white man" and when to adopt the weakness of her illness. She is in effect a master performer who, with the help of her husband, becomes a convincing alternate persona.

Ellen is treated well on the train from Wilmington to Richmond although she is almost stopped in Baltimore due to lack of proof as to her identity. William Craft describes his trepidation at their potential discovery as such:

We felt as though we had come into deep waters and were about being overwhelmed, and that the slightest mistake would clip asunder the last brittle thread of hope by which we were suspended, and let us down for ever into the dark and horrible pit of misery and degradation from which we were straining every nerve to escape.[100]

His metaphor of feeling as if their bodies were hanging to a last thread is appropriate, as being found out would in effect be to be disposed into a pit. Fortunately, however, the bell rings to board the train and the officer decides to tell the conductor to "'let this gentleman and slave pass'; adding, 'As he is not well, it is a pity to stop him here.'"[101] Again, Ellen's "sick" body tricks them into aiding them in their escape.

People "believe" Ellen's body because she convinces them to do so. She must cover all signs that would tell who she really is; she cannot write, see, or even, at times hear. All means of communication, therefore, are concealed and others must rely on her appearance to define her identity. This is not simply a case of dressing like a man; it is the case of becoming a man in a life or death situation. Furthermore, if Ellen fails to convince others that she is a *white* man, it would mean death as well. She must completely cross the boundaries from her own body into the body that will allow her freedom. She spends several days in a state of transition— inhabiting a white man's body with her husband as her slave and thus eliminating the female presence completely from the story of freedom. Ironically, she must completely disappear in order to appear as a free woman.

When the Crafts arrive in Philadelphia on Christmas morning of 1848, they are led to the home of the Ivins, Quakers whose daughters later try to teach the Crafts to read.[102] Soon after they reach the boarding house,

Ellen "threw off her disguise and assumed her own apparel."[103] Even the landlord was fooled and asked for William's "master," saying "'he knew [Ellen] was not the gentlemen that came with me.'"[104] Ultimately, the disguise is convincing but Ellen cannot appreciate her freedom until she reclaims her own appearance.

While the disguise of a white man allowed Ellen northern movement, it is this appearance as a woman with fair skin that begins to circulate internationally. Sterling writes that former slave and abolitionist William Wells Brown stops by to ask their accompaniment to New England. Brown writes to *Liberator* editor and abolitionist William Lloyd Garrison on January 12, 1849, with their story: "'Here is a wonderful case—read it! SINGULAR ESCAPE.'"[105] He goes on to note: "'They are very intelligent. They are young, Ellen 22, and Wm. 24 years of age. Ellen is truly a heroine.'"[106] Agreeing to go with Brown, the Crafts are called "the Georgia fugitives" as they travel and displayed as couple. "Although the two Williams did all the talking, it was Ellen who aroused the greatest interest. Most northerners had never seen a woman slave before," Sterling writes.[107] She gives the following account of the fascination with Ellen: "After William addressed a meeting in Northborough, there were murmurs in the audience: 'I want to hear his wife.' At first Ellen replied to a few questions; by mid–April she had become a regular part of the program. 'Mrs. Craft gave a very particular account of their escape,' *The Liberator* said. 'It was told in so simple and artless a manner as must have carried conviction to the mind of everyone present.'"[108] R.J.M. Blackett also writes that Ellen's "true" appearance evoked sympathy in European tours.[109] They were in awe that such a beautiful (read: "white"-complexioned) woman could have been treated so poorly. Viewed through Victorian ideals of womanhood, it seems that Ellen Craft was still pressured to claim whiteness as her means of escape.[110] Ellen was urged to "tell truth" and had greater incentive since she wanted her mother to find her. She also wanted to start her new life, however, because of the increasing awareness of her story. She wanted to be able to reap the benefits of freedom as a black woman instead of as the "white slave" that people saw her as.[111]

The story ends with the partial restoration of a scene of "domesticity" for the Crafts. The couple settles at Boston, William as cabinet-maker and Ellen with a needle. Although inhabited by free blacks, the racial scene in Boston was not without problems. Sterling writes that blacks were confined in Boston to one school and denied pews in churches and admission to public entertainment.[112] William had problems getting work and opened a secondhand furniture store; Ellen found work as a seamstress in homes and learned upholstery.[113] William Craft writes that Ellen was "scared" of whites, but perhaps she was scared of who she had to be in order to gain acceptance.[114] Descriptions of this scene provide a fascinating study of roles and appearances. The couple finally "appears" to live a normal life, as their bodies literally inhabit free spaces. Yet, William has difficulty securing work because local artisans are threatened by this African-American outsider. What freedom allows them, however, is the corporeal freedom that slavery did not. William is still able to secure work, and they are finally comfortable with the idea of having children.

During the three years they spent at an agricultural school in Ockham, Surrey, the Crafts bore their first child, Charles Estlin Philips.[115] While learning the educational system at Ockham, the Crafts bettered their own education, and William taught cabinetmaking while Ellen taught needlework.[116] As further evidence of their new mobility, they later opened an import-export goods business in London.[117] After William continued to lecture, they decided to publish the story of their escape and therefore document in print the means by which they acquired selfhood and physical mobility.

William spends several years in Africa as an educator and missionary with the Company of African Merchants in the 1860s. Blackett writes: "During William's absence in Dahomey, Ellen devoted most of her energies to the education of their young family" of four children, which suggests a very important subtext to his account—Ellen is finally free to raise her own children.[118] After Sherman's march through Georgia in 1864, Blackett writes that the military commander at Macon informs Ellen in response to inquiries about her mother (through Wendell Phillips and other American contacts) that her mother is alive and well. Ellen has the money sent to cover her mother's trip to London, and she arrives within a month to reunite with her daughter.[119] The story of freedom is not an individual one, but one about putting broken pieces back together—of families, of stories, of lives. Thus, symbolic "bodies" are also reconstructed as histories are remembered and "*re-membered.*"[120] The story begins with two individuals, develops into the history of a couple, and then includes the history of a family's freedom. With each piece that Craft includes, he establishes a new narrative of freedom that extends across generations and across geographical limitations.

Although the Crafts' escape efforts were preserved by William's memory and by his pen, Blackett states that "little is known about [Ellen's] other activities during these years."[121] He acknowledges, however, that she raised money for freedmen and was a "leading spirit in the formation of a ladies' auxiliary and Foreign Freedmen's Aid Society."[122] She also worked to gain support amongst the British for a girls' school in Sierra Leone and got involved in the Women's Suffrage Association.[123] As if this were not enough, Ellen joins her husband William after his return from Dahomey in a trip to London to honor William Lloyd Garrison, and to Paris to participate in a reunion of the international abolitionist movement.[124]

The final piece to the story about the Crafts' mobility is their move back South. The reason Blackett gives is that the company with which William worked in Africa wanted repayment of his debts. Since the family had used most of their money to finance the trip, they had to sell the family home in late 1867 with no consistent source of income.[125] The solution, however, offered a very different kind of productivity. They planned to buy a plantation in Georgia to be run cooperatively by freedmen, a move which would "free the former slaves from the contract-labor system and help them to become independent farmers."[126] After nineteen years away, the Crafts return to Boston to prepare for their trip to Georgia with three of their then five children in tow.[127] They spend seven months finding their old abolitionist friends and speaking with them of their plans in order to raise money.[128]

It is significant that some of the most important parts of Ellen Craft's story occur after the narrative officially ends. It is after the publication of the book that freedom occurs on a broad level, after its circulation begins that the Crafts are able to return to their original site to create new memories and legacies. Blackett writes that "the choice of Georgia was more than just sentimental ... it may even have been motivated, as Phillips implied, by a misplaced urge to thumb their noses at a plantocracy that had for so long denied them their liberty." Whatever the reasons, however, both William and Ellen dedicate much of their lives and work to the progress of freedmen once they return to the south.

After their arrival in Georgia, the Crafts moved to a plantation called Hickory Hill across the state line in South Carolina.[129] Blackett describes their planting of crops and the two schools that Ellen and her daughter ran on the plantation. One was for children during the day, and another for adults at night.[130] Sadly, a band of night riders set fire to the house in fall of 1870 and destroyed their crop.[131] However, the Crafts then moved to Savannah, then Woodville (a plantation twenty miles away from Savannah), where they took out a three-year lease on a farm.[132]

Although Ellen described Woodville as "a miserable hole, dirty and full of rats; snakes running all over the house," where they had a poor initial crop of cotton that nearly depleted their resources, the Crafts stuck it out and tried to buy Woodville.[133] They hosted tenant farmers on their land; the Crafts lent money and gave "seeds, rations, and tools" in exchange for shares of crops.[134] William went to New England in 1873 for a year to raise money, but Ellen kept the property in order in his absence. Blackett writes that "buildings were repaired and fences mended with the aid of families she had attracted as tenants," Ellen also renovated a barn, where she moved the school which doubled as a church on Sundays.[135] Her son Brougham arrived in December 1873 to run the school so that Ellen could improve the Sabbath school: "The freedmen's response to the school was more than Ellen could have anticipated.... Blacks in Ways Station took every advantage of the school at Woodville. By the end of 1873, there were twenty to thirty students."[136] William got much of the funding that they needed from subscriptions and loans and even got books donated to the school by Harper & Brothers in New York[137]; meanwhile, Ellen continued to run the plantation. They improved the frame of the schoolhouse in 1874, which allowed room for more students. Although they faced opposition from some white's threatened by the loss of "control" over blacks, Blackett notes that "by 1875, the school was the finest for whites or blacks in the entire county."[138]

The Crafts' experiment was not without problems. The crops were never large enough to support the tenants, who also had to work elsewhere. Rent was used to maintain the plantation and the school, and they continued to face threats from neighbors who were concerned with the potential for black laborers to gain power.[139] However, despite these threats Ellen continued to "move" about: she "traveled around the area in her buggy, administering to the medical needs of the people, prodding them to send their children to school, and teaching the women sewing and other 'domestic arts.'"[140] She invested in creating both homes and institutions as productive spaces for African Americans to reconstruct themselves in freedom.

Ellen's success was unfortunately hindered by legal problems. When William was accused of using money collected for Woodville for personal use, a charge which took the Crafts into court and cost additional money, the Crafts' success underwent a sharp decline.[141] Support for Woodville dried up and the Craft children moved away to find jobs. Blackett writes that there are few records of what the Crafts did after 1878, although it is documented that they were able to repay some of their loans and even purchase additional land (that they later had to mortgage for credit).[142] Ellen's part in this story concludes with her death. Blackett writes: "Ellen died in 1891, and William lost the one person whose strength and determination had sustained their efforts at Woodville through the most trying times.... Ellen's death also coincided with a return to the economic, social, and political uncertainties of the years immediately after the end of Reconstruction."[143] These "uncertainties" include the rise of Jim Crow laws, financial panics, and lynch mobs.[144]

Blackett ends Ellen's story as William began it, as a determined woman who sustains herself and her family through trying times. Despite the less than happy ending of Ellen's story, her life leaves a legacy of success. She is largely responsible for the freedom of herself and her husband, she speaks truth to many in other countries in order to inform them of the treacherous plight of slaves, and she "crafts" a new narrative on the space of a plantation that allows for the collective support and education of former slaves. As William authors one part of their story after freedom, traveling to secure resources for their enterprise, Ellen significantly carries on the work of the school itself. Her story continues to be one of physical labor and physical movement, from renovating the schoolhouse to moving through the community to teach and to make sure people know of the opportunity to send their children to school. Although the book does not detail any medical training for Ellen, we learn that she also helps them maintain their bodies. This is symbolic, as attention is paid to Ellen's own body throughout the narrative. Ellen reclaims her position of womanhood, then makes it possible for the freedmen to effect and maintain their liberation through education and self-directed labor.

Framing Free Bodies

As a legally free woman and as a previously enslaved woman (respectively), Charlotte Forten and Ellen Craft provide two very different perspectives of freedom. At the heart of both stories, however, is a desire for physical manifestations of what freedom represents. It is not enough merely to "be" free; one must also be able to exert evidence of freedom. That is, one must be able to "do" what one could not do before legal or figurative liberation. For Forten, freedom offers the chance to teach others what she has spent years studying, the freedom to put her intellectual upbringing into practice. For Craft, freedom allows her to live in a particular location, the southern region of the United States as a free woman rather than as a slave, as an educator, and as a manager of her own household. Through their experiences, both of these women had to find ways to exert or legitimize their status as free women. It was not just the law that made them so; Craft had to go against the laws that prohibited slaves to move freely across state lines in order to gain free status. Instead, these women and others created their own discourses of emancipation.

Through the "ambivalent legacy" of freedom, I ask how women represent themselves as free by means of both physical and cultural representations. Hartman specifically analyzes an "economy of bodies." During slavery, she argues, "the absolute dominion of the master, predicated on the annexation of the captive body and its standing as the 'sign and surrogate' of the master's body, yielded to an economy of bodies, yoked and harnessed, through the exercise of autonomy, self-interest, and consent."[145] After slavery, she writes, "although no longer the extension and instrument of the master's absolute right or dominion, the laboring black body remained a medium of others' power and representation."[146] Hartman uses this model to argue that the newly emancipated could not enjoy the full idea of freedom because they were restricted by behavioral codes, but I argue that the women in this case study manipulated the master-slave determined economy of bodies to create their own definitions of freedom within a national discourse. They determined the terms on which freedom was issued—the costs and even the locations, and figured out how they could participate in liberatory processes or journeys.

Transforming their circumstances involved going beyond a restrictive environment to places where they felt free; it also involved literal or figurative transformation of their bodies. Forten was no longer the educated middle-class northerner—she became the educat*ing* temporary southerner (although she tried her hardest to maintain claim to her former state in her narrative). Craft literally became another "body" in order to free herself but then assumed a new form of freedom both within her house and in her community. Furthermore, there was a body she could not assume as a slave that she could as a free woman—that of a mother, and later, that of an educator.

Forten tries to preserve her "self" by creating a separately defined other, but she eventually becomes part of a black southern body politic as she attaches herself to a common mission of progress for freedmen and women. Likewise, Craft leaves her adopted status of free northerner to return to the site where others remain in the condition she left. Both utilize the means of education to help bring others out of enslavement. Education, then, becomes an addition to legal emancipation that allows an "emancipatory figuration of blackness." The fact that these women lead with their minds *and* hands—inhabiting classrooms of freedmen rather than domestic households of white men—allows a less ambivalent means of freedom. The classroom space, in effect, allows a more liberating form of domesticity; all bodies in the space are working toward a productive end—literally to produce students who are engaging knowledge. For these women, personal transformations in consciousness then translate to potential transformations in identity and status for numbers of African Americans.

Chapter Three

Elizabeth Keckley and Freedom's Labor

Within a decade after Forten circulates her story in the media and the Crafts also publish the details of their journey, Elizabeth Keckley's narrative, *Behind the Scenes: or, Thirty Years a Slave, and Four Years in the White House* (1868) appears in print. In past and present representations, the story of Elizabeth Keckley has often been shadowed by the memory of Mary Todd Lincoln, wife of the sixteenth United States President Abraham Lincoln, who Keckley represents as part of her text but not the complete narrative. Currently, Keckley's text and accounts of the consternation it caused in its release of details about the Lincoln family are found in collections of Lincoln memorabilia and she is even represented as a family associate and confidante in the 2012 film *Lincoln*. As such, the texts that do discuss Keckley predominantly describe her relationship to Mrs. Lincoln.[1] As slaves were defined by more than their enforced servitude, however, Elizabeth Keckley (who, after buying her freedom, had free administration over her labor as a seamstress) was defined by more than even her work for her most famous clients. Keckley's "thirty years as a slave" (calculated as 23 years by historians[2]) is as much a part of the way she positions herself as American historian and firsthand witness as are her references to a well-known national address. As narrator, Keckley locates her own story and that of the freed men and women that come after her within a familiar historical context. This strategy not only helps bring African American histories to light but also fills in gaps in national accounts of prominent figures and events during the Civil War period.

Although Keckley's text was published in 1868, there are still few critical commentaries that exist. This is likely due to the text's disappearance from the public eye after it became a source of controversy for the Lincolns and their supporters. Recent texts such as Jennifer Fleischner's *Mrs. Lin-

coln and Mrs. Keckly (2003) and, for youth, Becky Rutberg's *Mary Lincoln's Dressmaker* (1995) have offered updated biographies on Keckley but little critical commentary on her work as narrative. Xiomara Santamarina's chapter on Keckley in *Belabored Professions: Narratives of African American Working Womanhood* is one of few recent publications about Keckley that incorporates analysis of Keckley's literary project with her biographical information. Each of these books, to their credit, makes some progress toward reintroducing Keckley's narrative to a reading public. However, by replacing her story with their retellings, the biographies could also diminish the power of Keckley's voice as primary narrator.

Keckley's freedom is the freedom to contract and control her labor, to command authority as a woman on her own terms instead of those of a spouse, and to help improve the lives of freedmen and freedwomen. With the insight that comes from her position amongst each group on which she reports (former slave, independent laborer, promoter of racial uplift), Keckley crafts a narrative best represented by her metaphor of going "behind the scenes." More than a mere expose, her narrative illustrates a journey into each of the spaces that influence her life. In her preface, Keckley gives her rationale for taking her readers "behind the scenes": "I have often been asked to write my life, as those who know me know that it has been an eventful one. At last I have acceded to the importunities of my friends, and have hastily sketched some of the striking incidents that go to make up my history."[3] Even from the beginning of her narrative, Keckley allows that she will share events that contribute to *her* history; this is autobiographical material.

Keckley asserts the truth in what she has written *and* her ability to represent multiple sides of American history, adding: "As one of the victims of slavery I drank of the bitter water; but since destiny willed it so, and since I aided in bringing a solemn truth to the surface *as a truth*, perhaps I have no right to complain. Here, as in all things pertaining to life, I can afford to be charitable."[4] Truth-telling is indeed a proclaimed purpose of this narrative as Keckley even allows, "If I have portrayed the dark side of slavery, I also have painted the bright side."[5] Most importantly, she positions herself as an accountable witness who can even transcend her own experience to illustrate national truths. The power of Keckley's narrative lies in her use of both the position from which she came as a slave and that in which she located herself through independent labor. In her comprehensive account, her willingness to "tell" these truths, she can thus

Three. Elizabeth Keckley and Freedom's Labor

provide eyewitness information from multiple domains, from the homes of her masters to the White House.

Behind the Scenes includes a great deal of information about the Lincoln's personal lives, but implicit in even these stories are Keckley's attention to character accounts and her capacity to share what she witnesses during her experiences as a free laborer. It is on the grounds of "truth-telling" that Keckley defends her details of what she observed while employed by Mary Todd Lincoln: "It may be charged that I have written too freely on some questions, especially in regard to Mrs. Lincoln. I do not think so; at least I have been prompted by the purest motive. Mrs. Lincoln, by her own acts, forced herself into notoriety. She stepped beyond the formal lines which hedge about a private life, and invited public criticism."[6] In this statement, Keckley seems to understand the heart of the criticism levied against her— that it is not her narrative itself but rather her voicing of her opinion on one *particular* topic that critics find problematic. In her defense, she returns to her pure motivations to tell the truth. It is Mrs. Lincoln that created an unfavorable perception of *herself*, Keckley argues, by offering private flaws to the public. Keckley only ventures into the public sphere on this topic, she says, in order to "place Mrs. Lincoln in a better light before the world" in both of their best interests: "My own character, as well as the character of Mrs. Lincoln, is at stake, since I have been intimately associated with that lady in the most eventful periods of her life. I have been her confidante, and if evil charges are laid at her door, they must also be laid at mine, since I have been a party to all her movements. To defend myself I must defend the lady that I have served."[7] Keckley's motivation to include Mrs. Lincoln in her story is to place herself in the best light possible.

In these few lines, Keckley not only asserts her authority to "tell," since she has indeed been "a party to all her movements," but also the right to defend her own character from ill repute or associations and to "witness" against or about whites. "Behind the Scenes" is the perfect metaphor for Keckley's venture. Her aim is not to tell all that she knows about her "intimate associations" with Mrs. Lincoln but to lay claim to events that have affected her own life and the lives of her readers. "Why should I not be permitted to lay her secret history bare," Keckley asks, "especially when that history plainly shows that her life, like all lives, has its good side as well as its bad side!"[8] Her accounts of Mrs. Lincoln are, in effect, just additional examples of the many sides to the many stories that Keckley tells.

Keckley's Life

Behind the Scenes illustrates numerous themes of freedom in Keckley's life. With the end of her enslavement comes the ability to write freely of her experiences with her master's family as well as with her later employers. She weaves the histories of free African Americans into national narratives of the presidency and wartime history. Most significantly, she uses her freedom to speak and to write as a position from which to illustrate her own humanity—her character, her life's labors, and her ability to use her testimony to ensure that stories of other freedmen and freedwomen are told. Mary Todd Lincoln is not used to offer recommendation or credibility to Keckley's story; in fact, Keckley asserts that *she* provides this service for Lincoln. References to the Lincolns are instead part of Keckley's strategy to fill in the gaps of American history of African Americans freed before, during, and after the Civil War.

Keckley acknowledges from the beginning of her narrative that she is connected to many different spaces and the histories they hold. Although this is her story, she cannot separate it from details such as the poverty of the Garland family, the daughter and son-in-law of her master Burwell to whom she is loaned and whom she supports with her sewing. She cannot leave out her sewing efforts for future Confederate first lady Varina Davis (who asked her to accompany herself and husband Jefferson Davis when they moved South at the start of the Civil War). Keckley also cannot omit firsthand details of Abraham Lincoln's life and death during her tenure as dressmaker for Mary Todd Lincoln. As significant to Keckley's narrative are accounts of refugees, then freedmen coming to Washington and her work to secure their safety and livelihood during a critical historical juncture. Thus, this text is not solely "about" any of these other parties; it is a means of establishing Keckley's authority and credibility on a variety of subjects.

By writing and publishing a narrative that uses her life as a slave and as a White House employee as a frame within which she relates to her public all that she does and sees, Keckley seizes the position of authority from those who might try to tell who *she* is. Even the documents written by others that attest to her freedom become part of *her* narrative—she positions them where she desires in her story. Keckley commands discourse with an audience that could potentially be very diverse and uses her experience as a lens to comment on national events.

Three. Elizabeth Keckley and Freedom's Labor

In an introduction to *Scenes*, William Andrews asserts that Jacobs' text and Keckley's narrative "serve as bookends of the Civil War" and thus focus on different aspects of black women's experiences.[9] Their methods are similar, however, as they both use the narrative form to reclaim their agency from oppression of slavery and servitude. This is not to say that Keckley consciously emulates Jacobs' work, although it is possible that she had read it.[10] Instead, it is significant that both women, at the beginning and the end of the turbulent decade of the 1860s, use personal narratives to assert their humanity. Keckley, like Jacobs, emphasizes her right to freedom throughout the text and it is from this platform that she positions herself to tell the story of America during her lifetime.

Telling Her Story

The first two chapters of Keckley's autobiography focus on her life as the slave of the Burwell family of Virginia (where she was born) and, later, North Carolina. "My master, Col. A. Burwell, was somewhat unsettled in his business affairs, and while I was an infant he made several removals," she writes.[11] Yet, through residence in many locations at the will of her master, Keckley still considers herself free. "I came to earth free in God-like thought, but fettered in action," she asserts.[12] The mission of her life, then, as expressed in her narrative, is to gain the latter aspect of this freedom. Her literary effort is then dedicated to describing her efforts toward a free life, but she must tell the circumstances from which she came in order to express the value of her liberation.

Keckley's first tours "behind the scenes" are those of her own life in her master's household. Through a series of scenes, Keckley crafts her history as the center of the Burwell's. She is indeed free in thought and seems to use even instances in which she is in another's control to her benefit. Her descriptions of scenes become a metaphor for her ability to see, to tell, and to craft a history that establishes her as a credible witness. As a free woman, she is in a position to shape her narrative toward her own end, and as she does so, she realizes the significance of her past on her present state: "I am now on the shady side of forty, and as I sit alone in my room the brain is busy, and a rapidly moving panorama brings scene after scene before me, some pleasant and others sad; and when I thus greet old familiar faces, I often find myself wondering if I am not living the past over again.... Hour after hour I sit while the scenes are being shifted; and as I gaze upon the past, I realize how crowded with incidents my life has been."[13] Rather than randomly accounting for events, Keckley's narrative chronicles what motivated her to seek freedom, how she did so, and what she did from a position of liberation.

The first stage, like narratives of enslavement written by Frederick Douglass and Harriet Jacobs, shows Keckley's awareness of her restricted state. As a four-year-old, Keckley was charged with the care of a baby and was lashed severely the first time she allowed the baby to fall. Yet her emphasis is not on her punishment, as she simply states "this was the first time I was punished in this cruel way, but not the last."[14] Keckley describes the false promise of family, as her master Mr. Burwell brings the man she calls her "father" to the household before sending him with his own master to the West. "I can remember the scene as if it were but yesterday."[15] Keckley recalls as she describes the misery of having her family broken apart. Through these moments, Keckley only hopes for a better future even if it comes in the afterlife: "We who are crushed to earth with heavy chains, who travel a weary, rugged, thorny road, groping through midnight darkness on earth, earn our right to enjoy the sunshine in the great hereafter."[16] In each moment of pain, Keckley is ever looking forward even when she cannot see what will come next.

Other scenes of violence in her childhood include being flogged by a schoolmaster in North Carolina whose abuse she challenges, saying "Nobody has a right to whip me but my own master, and nobody shall do so if I can prevent it."[17] When he does so nonetheless, cutting into her flesh with a rawhide, she immediately demands an explanation from her master, who assaults her as well. Her response is significant, as she perceives the philosophical injustice as well as the physical harm. "My spirit rebelled against the unjustness that had been inflicted upon me, and though I tried to smother my anger and to forgive those who had been so cruel to me, it was impossible."[18] In Keckley's reflection, this is the turning point as her spirit drives her toward freedom. She will struggle again with Bingham before he is finally subdued by his conscience, then must fight with Burwell again before he reverts to peace as well.

These, Keckley's "revolting scenes," do not even compose the worst moment of her narrative. Like other slaves before her, her appearance becomes a source of abuse as she is sexually assaulted:

I was regarded as fair-looking for one of my race, and for four years

Three. Elizabeth Keckley and Freedom's Labor

a white man—I spare the world his name—had base designs upon me. I do not care to dwell upon this subject, for it is one that is fraught with pain. Suffice it to say, that he persecuted me for four years, and I—I—became a mother.... If my poor boy ever suffered any humiliating pangs on account of birth, he could not blame his mother, for God knows that she did not wish to give him life; he must blame the edicts of that society which deemed it no crime to undermine the virtue of girls in my then position.[19]

Like Jacobs, Keckley feels a sense of honesty toward her readers, and although rape and pregnancy have significant effects on her life, she chooses not to dwell on them. Keckley reveals these details in efforts to tell the truth. In the same statement, Keckley attempts to excuse her son from a less than noble birth for which she had no responsibility. Keckley makes clear the power dynamic to which she is subject and the means by which she and her son are victimized.

As soon as she makes this revelation about social immorality, however, Keckley quickly moves to her next narrative of life in Hillsboro, North Carolina, where she is ironically asked to sew dresses and serve as attendant to several weddings:

There have been six weddings since October; the most respectable one was about a fortnight ago; I was asked to be the first attendant, but, as usual with all my expectations, I was disappointed, for on the wedding-day I felt more like being locked up in a three-cornered box than attending a wedding.[20]

Perhaps these "failed expectations" are results of her inability to participate in these weddings as the honoree. Keckley can only associate with this plateau of womanhood through her work. She is made to support the Garlands, the family of one of her master's daughters, by sewing for "the best ladies in St. Louis."[21] Keckley initially offers her services as a community dressmaker in order to allow her mother to stay in the home, as she fears the work will wear on her. With this labor, however, even as a slave, Keckley gains a reputation as a seamstress and dress-maker. "When my reputation was once established I never lacked for orders," Keckley states in a brief rhetorical move that shows her understanding of the possession of her labor.[22]

Keckley knows that she is not the primary beneficiary of her work, as she embarks upon this "career" because she has to help her master's family. She understands, however, that she commands her craft. Her artistry contributes to her standing in the community, which shows that Keckley considers herself as more than a means of forced labor. Additionally, Keckley understands the economic value of her labor, as she calculates the practical evidence of her success: "With my needle I kept bread in the mouths of seventeen persons for two years and five months," she writes.[23] She is able to do, by her own hand, what her new master cannot do with his own labor—support a family for an extended period of time.

Keckley illustrates that her masters and their social networks depend on her labor to the extent that they literally could not live without her. With her hand, and therefore her finances, she provides the very food that seventeen people eat for over two years. This understanding of the economic power of the slave, articulated by Frederick Douglass in 1845, becomes the cornerstone to her text.[24] Keckley ultimately illustrates what it meant for an enslaved woman to understand both her economic impact and how she could take control of her status, and the motif of craft comes to shape and permeate Keckley's narrative. If she can sew a bridesmaid's dress and sell her dressmaking services to support others, she can sew for her own financial benefit. This is ultimately the turning point that motivates her to secure her freedom and serves as a reflection on the transition from being physically owned to representing her freedom within society and on the page.

Telling Her Story

In an introduction to *Scenes*, William Andrews asserts that Harriet Jacobs' *Incidents in the Life of a Slave Girl* (1861) and Keckley's narrative "serve as bookends of the Civil War" and thus focus on different aspects of black women's experiences.[25] Their methods are similar, however, as they both use the narrative form to reclaim their agency from oppression of slavery and servitude. Keckley, like Jacobs, emphasizes her right to freedom throughout the text and it is from this platform that she positions herself to tell the story of America during her lifetime.

The rarely-discussed first two chapters of Keckley's autobiography focus on her life as the slave of the Burwell family of Virginia (where she was born) and, later, North Carolina. "My master, Col. A. Burwell, was somewhat unsettled in his business affairs, and while I was an infant he made several removals," she writes.[26] Yet, through residence in many loca-

Three. Elizabeth Keckley and Freedom's Labor

tions at the will of her master, Keckley still considers herself free. She asserts: "I came to earth free in God-like thought, but fettered in action."[27] The mission of her life, as expressed in her narrative, is to gain the latter aspect of this freedom. Her literary effort is then dedicated to describing her efforts toward a free life, but she must tell the circumstances from which she came in order to express the value of her liberation.

Keckley's narrative chronicles what motivated her to seek freedom, how she did so, and what she did from a position of liberation. As a four year old, Keckley was charged with the care of a baby and was lashed severely the first time she allowed the baby to fall. Yet her emphasis is not on her punishment, as she simply states "this was the first time I was punished in this cruel way, but not the last."[28] Keckley describes the false promise of family, as her master Mr. Burwell brings the man she calls her "father" to the household before sending him with his own master to the West. "I can remember the scene as if it were but yesterday," Keckley recalls as she describes the misery of having her family broken apart.[29] Through these moments, Keckley only hopes for a better future even if it comes in the afterlife: "We who are crushed to earth with heavy chains, who travel a weary, rugged, thorny road, groping through midnight darkness on earth, earn our right to enjoy the sunshine in the great hereafter" (10). In each moment of pain, Keckley is ever looking forward even when she cannot see what will come next.

Other scenes of violence in her childhood include being flogged by a schoolmaster in North Carolina whose abuse she challenges, saying, "Nobody has a right to whip me but my own master, and nobody shall do so if I can prevent it."[30] When he does so nonetheless, cutting into her flesh with a rawhide, she immediately demands an explanation from her master, who assaults her as well. Her response is significant, as she perceives the philosophical injustice as well as the physical harm. "My spirit rebelled against the unjustness that had been inflicted upon me, and though I tried to smother my anger and to forgive those who had been so cruel to me, it was impossible."[31] I argue that this, in Keckley's reflection, is the turning point as her spirit drives her toward freedom. She will struggle again with Bingham before he is finally subdued by his conscience, then must fight with Burwell again before he reverts to peace as well.

Keckley's "revolting scenes" do not even compose the worst moments of her narrative. Like many other enslaved persons before her, her appearance becomes a source of abuse as she is sexually assaulted:

> I was regarded as fair-looking for one of my race, and for four years a white man—I spare the world his name—had base designs upon me. I do not care to dwell upon this subject, for it is one that is fraught with pain. Suffice it to say, that he persecuted me for four years, and I—I—became a mother.... If my poor boy ever suffered any humiliating pangs on account of birth, he could not blame his mother, for God knows that she did not wish to give him life; he must blame the edicts of that society which deemed it no crime to undermine the virtue of girls in my then position.[32]

Like Jacobs, Keckley feels a sense of honesty toward her readers, and although rape and pregnancy have significant effects on her life, she chooses not to dwell on them. Keckley reveals these details in efforts to tell the truth. In the same statement, Keckley attempts to excuse her son from a less than noble birth for which she had no responsibility. Keckley makes clear the power dynamic to which she is subject and the means by which she and her son are victimized.

After bearing her son, after dedicating her life to the comfort of others with no financial benefit, Keckley realizes that she can never hold the status of pure and untainted womanhood that the brides she sews for in Hillsboro, North Carolina, assume.[33] They, if not wealthy, are not slaves and reap the benefits of freedom (including the elevated status of womanhood) that Keckley cannot. Keckley can only associate with this plateau of womanhood through her work. She is made to support the Garlands, the family of one of her master's daughters, by sewing for "the best ladies in St. Louis."[34] Keckley initially offers her services as a community dressmaker in order to allow her mother to stay in the home, as she fears the work will wear on her. With this labor, however, even as a slave, Keckley gains a reputation as a seamstress and dress-maker. "When my reputation was once established I never lacked for orders, " Keckley states in a brief rhetorical move that shows her understanding of the possession of her labor.[35] She knows that she is not the primary beneficiary of her work, as she embarks upon this "career" because she has to help her master's family. She understands, however, that she commands her craft. Her artistry contributes to her standing in the community, which shows that Keckley considers herself as more than a means of forced labor.

Additionally, Keckley understands the economic value of her labor, as she calculates the practical evidence of her success: "With my needle I kept bread in the mouths of seventeen persons for two years and five months," she writes.[36] She is able to do, by her own hand, what her new master cannot do with his own labor—support a family for an extended period of time.

Keckley illustrates that her masters and their social networks depend on her labor to the extent that they literally could not live without her. With her hand, and therefore her finances, she provides the very food that seventeen people eat for over two years. This understanding of the economic power of the slave, articulated by Frederick Douglass in 1845, becomes the cornerstone to her text.[37] Keckley ultimately illustrates what it meant for an enslaved woman to understand both her economic impact and how she could take control of her status, and the motif of craft comes to shape and permeate Keckley's narrative. If she can sew a bridesmaid's dress and sell her dressmaking services to support others, she can sew for her own financial benefit. This is ultimately the turning point that motivates her to secure her freedom.

Economics of Freedom

In *Belabored Professions*, Xiomara Santamarina discusses the utopian possibilities of work for Keckley: "Keckley forged a new space for black femininity that improbably straddled ... the overlapping but incompatible domains of antebellum womanhood and labor."[38] She goes on to state that "her autobiography displays a collaborative aspect that points to her southern, enslaved history and to how she saw her work as contributing productively to, and participating in, her clients' elite womanhood."[39] Santamarina uses Keckley's command of her freedom as a marker of upward mobility. Labor offers utopian possibilities, she argues, because Keckley sees her work as a contribution to society.[40] Santamarina uses these stories as a way to support black female agency through labor against theoretical claims "about the oppositional relationship of black identity to work."[41] They are about more, however, than proving that black women can gain agency through work. They are about a reversal of who controls the labor, a move which both benefits from and allows for a type of agency for the laborer.

Keckley uses the results of her labor—the number of people she is able to support—as a means of calculating what she is worth, then measures the social status her labor allows for them against her own. "While I was working so hard that others might live in comparative comfort, and move in those circles of society to which their birth gave them entrance, the thought often occurred to me whether I was really worth my salt or not; and then perhaps the lips curled with a bitter sneer,"[42] Keckley writes. Such reflections confirm that she understands her immense financial value and then draws upon her calculations to formulate her plan for freedom.

She initially refuses to consider the proposal of a man referred to only as "Mr. Keckley" on the grounds that she cannot bear the thought of bringing children into slavery—"of adding one single recruit to the millions bound to hopeless servitude."[43] In other words, she will contribute no more uncompensated labor to slave owning families. This is her impetus to propose to buy the freedom of herself and her son. Even after her proposal is denied, she states: "I would not be put off thus, for hope pointed to a freer, brighter life in the future. Why should my son be held in slavery?... By the laws of God and nature, as interpreted by man, one-half of my boy was free, and why should not this fair birthright of freedom remove the curse from the other half—raise it into the bright, joyous sunshine of liberty?"[44] Keckley's account of her economic value translates into the legacy that she will leave through her son. If she should not suffer from the burden of slavery, she suggests, her son, who is already "half free," should definitely not be thus oppressed.

Keckley persists in this quest for freedom by refusing the suggestion of her master that she take the quarter he offers and ferry herself and her son to freedom on the other side of the river. "It is the cheapest way that I know of to accomplish what you desire,'" Garland says.[45] Keckley does not want "cheap" and illegal freedom, however, refuting, "I can cross the river any day, as you well know, and have frequently done so, but will never leave you in such a manner. By the laws of the land I am your slave—you are my master, and I will only be free by such a means as the laws of the country provide.'"[46] What Keckley demands in this conversation is the economic sanction of her freedom, the confirmation that it can never be revoked once the price is paid. She gets what she asks for, as her master later tells her "that I had served his family faithfully; that I deserved my freedom, and that he would take $1200 for myself and boy."[47] Keckley forces her master to do what she does through her years of labor—to assess her value to the family, to put a price on the labor she provides—and the result of his consideration becomes "joyful intelligence" for her. She invokes such a phrase not because he puts a price on the bodies of herself and her son, but because her labor has been recognized in a tangible way that will secure her freedom.

After this contract is articulated, Keckley writes that she "consents" to marry. Even before the settlement is paid, she demonstrates her self-ownership in offering herself to another. She briefly describes her wedding in front of family and guests in the parlor and specifies that she was "given away" by Garland and the same pastor "who had solemnized the bridals of Mr. G's own children" served as officiant.[48] These are further examples of the family's recognition of her and her recognition of her own humanity. This discussion is hardly about the marriage, as she argues that Mr. Keckley proved to be "a burden instead of a helpmate": "More than all," she continues, "I learned that he was a slave instead of a free man as he represented himself to be."[49] If marriage was to be Keckley's evidence of her own freedom, she could not afford to compromise it at the hands of someone who does not possess similar liberties. Freedom, not marriage, is the ultimate goal for her.

While her married life occupies minimal content in her narrative, Keckley's work to secure her freedom plays a central role. The contradictions of Keckley's life as a slave are evident in criticism of the text. In *Mrs. Lincoln and Mrs. Keckly* [sic], Jennifer Fleischner writes that Lizzy was a slave for 23 years for her original master's son-in-law, Hugh Garland. Fleischner states: "if Lizzy ever experienced something like happiness as a slave, it was with the Garlands."[50] "Happiness" is a highly subjective term in this case; Keckley documents physical and sexual abuse while with her former family, the Burwells, yet this does not mean that she was "happy" with the Garlands. This shows the contradiction of identity to which an enslaved person was subject. For example, Keckley resents bringing the child of the Burwells' associate Alexander Kirkland into the world because she knows that he will be a slave, but in order to reclaim him she gives him the name of the black man her mother married (George Pleasant Hobbs was not Keckley's biological father but loved her as his child).[51]

Keckley endures her labor for her master's family while still trying to maintain her own sense of selfhood. As she connected her son to her black stepfather, she draws inspiration and connection to community from the free black populations in the areas in which she lives. With this inspiration, she inscribes herself in social networks in Petersburg, Virginia, and St. Louis. Encouraged by their success, Keckley requests to be placed in social circulation to support the Garlands so that her mother does not have to endure the stress of work and travel, but in this move she negotiates mobility for herself as well.

The free black population in Petersburg was mostly made up of "unmarried, self-supporting women."[52] These women were heads of households and supported themselves as "washers, ironers, seamstresses, house servants, and cooks"; some were also midwives, nurses, doctors, storekeepers, and proprietors. Keckley drew inspiration from her association with these women. Fleischner claims: "In these working- and middle-class black women Lizzy could see the possibilities beyond slavery for someone like her. With the taste of autonomy new in her mouth—never before had she had so much freedom of movement or of thought as here in Petersburg—she began hungering for more."[53] Fleischner describes Keckley's possibility of being hired out as her key to transcending her status as an enslaved woman: "For even then, she must have been anticipating a time when she might buy her own freedom, as her slave father wished to do and others she knew had done. In Petersburg she had seen how much money an ambitious black woman could make, and she knew that the money she kept, after handing over the portion her master would demand, could be put toward buying herself" (126). Fleischner analyzes Keckley's establishment of her career as such: "Being hired out would mean more independence and autonomy: walking to and from jobs alone and regulating her own time. Most important, it would be a chance to establish relationships outside of the slavery household. This would be the key to freedom."[54] It is in this instance that Keckley uses her social skills to gain economic prowess. She sees other women who are just like her except by law and this, along with the money that she has to hand to her master for no work he has done, becomes motivation for her as well. By circulating amongst the free black communities in St. Louis, Fleischner asserts, "Lizzy could enter the 'second class' of blacks," i.e., those who are not independently wealthy but who are self-reliant.[55] Keckley also masters the art of networking with these ladies for whom she sews, who will later contribute money to her campaign for freedom.

Keckley turns an initially undesirable situation—having to work in the community to support the family that owns her—into an opportunity to increase the value of her labor. She places herself into social networks as the provider of goods and gains the respect and dependence of others through her work. Although most of the money goes to the Garlands, she gains an understanding of her economic worth. She knows how much money she brings in specifically with her handiwork. Once Keckley understands this value, she can determine how to release herself from one economy—the institution of slavery, into another—free labor. She then converts her social credit (which she already recognizes the value of) into real money.

Keckley's Price: Negotiating Freedom

For Keckley, gaining freedom is a delicate negotiation. Keckley first secures a price of $1200 from Hugh Garland for herself and her son. After Garland's death, a Mr. Burwell comes from Mississippi to settle the estate and says that he would allow her to raise the necessary amount for her freedom. She plans to go to New York and raise funds and is told by Mrs. Garland that she must get six signatures that would vouch for her return and pay the amount if she did not. The sixth man, however, does not believe that she will return, which disturbs her. Keckley would prefer "slavery, eternal slavery rather than be regarded with distrust by those whose respect I esteemed."[56] Again, Keckley demonstrates that her character is paramount, but in the end this character and her economic value yield a compromise.

One of Keckley's patrons pledges to raise the money amongst friends in St. Louis. In a combination of kindness and a sense of debt to Keckley, Mrs. Le Bourgois states: "I have two hundred dollars put away for a present; am indebted to you one hundred dollars; mother owes you fifty dollars, and will add another fifty to it."[57] This money is not only a gift but also a confirmation of Keckley's merit. Others contribute accordingly. As Keckley has earned her social credit, she does not want anyone to be able to *take* credit for its result. In order to free herself on their economic terms, she wants to play by the rules of their economy. She earns the money to make a purchase and her freedom is her receipt. Fleischner argues that purchasing herself "was not only logical, it also fit her character.... She was a pragmatist, not an idealist, and, as one who had to fight for it, she prized respectability. In fact, paying for herself would be a measure of self-reliance and success and, therefore, a source of pride."[58] Freedom becomes the ultimate purchase that Keckley can make with her own money, money that comes both directly and indirectly as a result of her labor.

Anne Garland, who officially releases Keckley after her husband's death, recognizes Keckley as a tradeswoman in her documentation of her freedom: "Know all men that I, Anne P. Garland, of the County and City of St. Louis, State of Missouri, for and in consideration of the sum of $1200, to me in hand paid this day in cash, hereby emancipate my negro woman Lizzie, and her son George; the said Lizzie ... is of light complexion, about 37 years of age, by trade a dress-maker."[59] This is ultimately the external recognition that Keckley needs of her subjectivity. The community has recognized the value of her trade and her mistress recognizes her as a laborer independent of the Garland household. Once she has achieved this recognition, Keckley is free in action, word, and deed. She can then turn her eye to the plight of others in oppressive situations.

Santamarina also discusses on the way in which Keckley gleans social value from material value: "In *Behind the Scenes*, Keckley depicts the social relations of dressmaking as a crucial site for mediating the nation's postbellum anxieties over the role ex-slaves and free blacks were to play in a changing economy and society."[60] She continues: "Although southerners who sought to reassert their authority over their former slaves promoted stereotypes of freedmen as lazy and unwilling to work, Keckley spoke to the productive possibilities of black laborers."[61] Keckley foresees her freedom and her intellectual ability from the beginning of this text, and her vision of freedom is only enhanced when she becomes a black career woman. This vision is the theme that comes to permeate the rest of Keckley's text. In the lines of her different reflections, Keckley makes evident the significance of freedom for former slaves. She first describes her journey toward personal freedom and then uses her position as free woman to reverse the model of blacks as marginal figures.

The three chapters Keckley writes on her life as a slave are only a small fraction of the fifteen chapters of the book. These chapters have often been ignored by those who have reviewed the book (often for purposes of recording Lincoln history). What, then, is the ultimate significance of the inclusion of this section? Santamarina argues that Keckley's optimism distinguishes this early description of "thirty years a slave": "What makes Keckley's slave narrative so distinctive, however, is her explicit refusal to represent slave life as unremittingly dark."[62] This is not, however, a denial of the horrors of slavery. In order to build the story of her life of freedom, I believe Keckley's realization of her own potential is the light that is reflected through her text. Santamarina states, "she demonstrates how her role in the creation of status justifies her view of herself as a member-participant in the paternalistic slaveholding 'family.'"[63] At the very least, through the Garlands she realizes that she is an invaluable

Three. Elizabeth Keckley and Freedom's Labor

member of the household because she contributes to its value. Santamarina uses the metaphor that Keckley "claims credit" in a system of obligations—she bases her value on the privilege her work allows others. This, she adds, translates into her work as a dressmaker—she helps white women maintain their status and can therefore identify with white elite femininity.

Keckley also makes her patrons realize what she already knows—that her value far exceeds any price that they could put upon her. This is why Garland initially suggests that she escape and why Mrs. Le Bourgeois later "loans" her the money; they know that even as a slave, she has realized the value of freedom and consciously claimed it for herself.

After securing her freedom, Keckley's literary flourishes emerge. This is the moment in the narrative at which she represents her life most effusively: "Free, free! What a glorious ring to the word. Free! The bitter heart-struggle was over. Free! The soul could go out to heaven and to God with no chains to clog its flight or pull it down. Free!"[64] Freedom has many meanings in this description. It is a word, the results of a struggle, and a means of changing the whole purview of the natural earth for Keckley. Finally, it is the cohesion of man's law, woman's work, and God's grace. Keckley concludes the chapter with official documentation—receipts signed by the donors, which she calls "the history of [her] emancipation" (24). The chapter ends in testimony by nine white men and women, including her former mistress, the Commissioner of Missouri, the clerk of the St. Louis Circuit Court, and, finally, the Recorder of the State of Missouri, County of St. Louis that her price of $1200 has been "paid." This is the only time in the narrative besides the letters appended from Mary Todd Lincoln that Keckley allows another person's words to stand in the place of her own.

By having these witnesses quoted verbatim in her narrative, Keckley suggests that the only authority others have is to confirm her freedom. She, however, is the agent of this freedom, which she asserts in the first line of Chapter Four: "The twelve hundred dollars with which I purchased the freedom of myself and son I consented to accept only as a loan. I went to work in earnest, and in a short time paid every cent that was so kindly advanced by my lady patrons of St. Louis."[65] Keckley's narrative of the freedom process has four significant phases: negotiating the price of freedom, securing the finances, obtaining legal documentation, and reimbursing her donors. Collectively, these stages demonstrate Keckley's business acumen and self-sufficiency; although her enslavement was immoral, she wants to clear any sense of debt. This history is what her narrative has built up to. The stories of the Burwells and the Garlands have been but details of her former life as a slave (as I will argue about the Lincolns playing such a role in her life as a free woman).

Keckley's description of obtaining freedom with the help of the society she serves is a metaphor for building the audience she hopes to reach. After she purchases her freedom, Keckley uses the letters written on her behalf as evidence. These letters become hers to use as she wishes; once documented in her story she is in control of their content. Keckley then uses her words to document the stories of others who are trying to become free, and the description of the intimacies she enjoys with her employers in Washington (including Jefferson and Varina Davis and the Lincoln family) seem to frame her community interests.

After she chronicles the purchase of herself and her son from Anne Garland, the focus of Keckley's story becomes her increased mobility and assistance to others. The fourth chapter of the narrative chronicles the first stages of her life as a free woman; this portion of the text is literally the beginning of her "freedom narrative." The first stage in her freedom narrative is to establish her independence from her husband, who she believes detracts from her physical and emotional well being:

> All this time my husband was a source of trouble to me, and a burden. Too close occupation with my needle had its effects upon my health, and feeling exhausted with work, I determined to make a change. I had a conversation with Mr. Keckley; informed him that since he persisted in dissipation we must separate; that I was going North, and that I should never live with him again, at least until I had good evidence of his reform. He was rapidly debasing himself, and although I was willing to work for him, I was not willing to share his degradation [28].

Keckley's refusal to associate herself with her husband's depravity is the first personal assertion of freedom she makes. She has a vision for what her new life would allow that is threatened by her husband's path to ruin. Just as she allows a final word from her former owner, a word that says she is free, she allows a conclusion to the story of her life with Mr. Keckley: "My husband is now sleeping in his grave, and in the silent grave I would bury all unpleasant memories of him" (29). She could have chosen to erase him completely from the narrative, as it is her story, but the brief moments in which he is mentioned offer significant life lessons. As mentioned earlier, she initially rejects his proposal on the grounds that their

Three. Elizabeth Keckley and Freedom's Labor

kids would not be free. Then, she marries him after her freedom has been promised (i.e., on her own terms). Finally, his alcoholism and her realization that he was never a free man give her grounds to change her feelings toward him. Before death ultimately separates them, Keckley has liberated herself from a person who does not contribute to her sense of freedom. Freedom for Elizabeth Keckley is a legal matter but an emotional one as well.

In Keckley's new independent life, Santamarina argues, dressmaking is recognized as a commercially valued skill; with it, she also inserts herself into a network of femininity as that recognition comes at the hands of white female clients.[66] I propose that while Keckley's livelihood does depend on that recognition, she significantly understands the ways in which her white female clients depend on her and secures her authority with this knowledge. Santamarina concludes that these interracial relationships also demonstrate the conflict between Keckley's roles in the "public" marketplace and "private" spaces of white womanhood; she is embedded in both but only accepted by some in the former role.

The narrative suggests that Keckley's acceptance is not of greatest importance. She makes the decisions when and where she shall work and establishes her own terms. Keckley even dismisses clients who will not cooperate with these terms. Santamarina contends that "text and reception show how symbolic conflict erupts when dominated, 'domestic,' and even 'loyal' black labor is literally and figuratively emancipated, moving out of its subordinate role 'behind the scenes' to take the nation's center stage."[67] I add that Keckley's accounts of conflict within the various domestic realms in which she works, along with the conflict that accompanies the release of her book, only attests to the fact that she is significant enough to be the source of contention. Keckley asserts her freedom to circulate in the highest echelons of society, to speak and to "tell" amongst these spheres, and garners attention in return.

Freedom and Politics

After she resolves the concerns of her past, Keckley begins her narrative of physical mobility. She "tak[es] the cars direct" from St. Louis to Baltimore in 1860, leaving the final place of her enslavement for good (29). This simple turn of phrase is significant; it suggests that she makes no literal or figurative stops on her way to her first "free" place of residence. What she does there, also described in just a few lines, is as important to the narrative: "I stopped six weeks, attempting to realize a sum of money by forming classes of young colored women, and teaching them my system of cutting and fitting dresses" (Keckley 29). In a short period of time, Keckley moves from slave labor to free labor to educator. This begins the theme of uplift she develops in her text. Keckley teaches for financial reasons, but the idea that she chooses black women as her pupils demonstrates her responsibility to make sure that her work is continued. She teaches them a skill and thus ensures the continuity of her craft and method of self-sufficiency through independent labor. In the end, her scheme earns her little money and she leaves Baltimore "with scarcely money enough to pay [her] fare to Washington" (29), but she leaves her first legacy as a free woman to her students.

Washington then becomes the primary location of her freedom. Keckley describes her efforts to obtain work immediately at a rate of "two dollars and a half per day," then finding that she must obtain a license to remain in the city (29). She writes that "[she] also had to have some one vouch to the authorities that [she] was a free woman" (29). At this point, similar to the way in which she secured her freedom, Keckley draws upon her social credit again:

> My means were too scanty, and my profession too precarious to warrant my purchasing [a] license. In my perplexity I called on a lady for whom I was sewing, Miss Ringold, a member of Gen. Mason's family, from Virginia. I stated my case, and she kindly volunteered to render me all the assistance in her power. She called on Mayor Burritt with me, and Miss Ringold succeeded in making an arrangement for me to remain in Washington without paying the sum required for a license; moreover, I was not to be molested [30].

This narrative describes Keckley's ability to use her resources even in Washington. She uses her work and her network as currency, and apparently it is sufficient exchange for her license and her security. As a result of remaining in Washington, Keckley increases her social and industrial collateral by securing work from Varina Davis, wife of then-Senator Jefferson Davis, and, later, wives of other political figures, including Mary Todd Lincoln.

Keckley also garners a new aspect of freedom as the modiste for these women—the ability to determine the terms on which she works. As a slave laborer for the Burwells, then the Garlands, she gives no account of refusing work. However, in her "freedom narrative" Keckley shares the account of deciding not to go to work for Varina Davis in the South after secession. Her discussion of the ensuing Civil War with the wife of the future Confederate president is a historical moment within itself:

> "Who will go to war?" I asked.
> "The North and South," was her ready reply. "The Southern people will not submit to the humiliating demands of the Abolition party; they will fight first."
> "And which do you think will whip?"
> "The South, of course. The South is impulsive, is in earnest, and the Southern soldiers will fight to conquer. The North will yield, when it sees the South is in earnest, rather than engage in a long and bloody war" [31].

Although Varina Davis' prediction is proven wrong, Keckley's documentation of this conversation both makes her a character in Civil War prehistory and a historian of it. Keckley has no concrete evidence against Varina Davis's prediction, but she chooses to believe an alternate ending is possible. Keckely is then able to document the way that the war plays out as she and others are affected.

Mrs. Davis wishes to take Keckley South and "take good care of [her]," predicting that "colored people" will be mistreated by Northern people who believe that they are the cause of the war (32). After considering the proposal, however, Keckley decides to stay in Washington: "I knew the North to be strong, and believed that the people would fight for the flag that they pretended to venerate so highly.... A show of war from the South, I felt, would lead to actual war in the North; and with the two sections bitterly arrayed against one another, I preferred to cast my lot with the people of the North" (32). Keckley again displays her agency in her narrative. She thoughtfully considers the statements of her employer (significantly giving no response to the wish of Mrs. Davis to "care for her"), and in the end, her decision demonstrates her political intellect and commitment. Keckley asserts herself as a Northerner and dedicates herself to her new neighbors. At this moment, she metaphorically establishes her residence in free territory.

She will go on to have a final word on the Davis's role in the War. She empathizes with Davis after the bloodshed and death of the war: "The years have brought many changes; and in view of these terrible changes even I, who was once a slave, who have been punished with the cruel lash, who have experienced the heart and soul tortures of a slave's life, can say to Mr. Jefferson Davis, 'Peace! You have suffered! Go in peace'" (32). This is neither empathy with the Southern agenda in the War nor support of the secession or the institutions that the South fights to keep. It is the ability to feel the suffering of another as a human. Ironically, Keckley is in this moment in a better position than Davis, but as a former slave she can sympathize with his misery. Keckley is also embedded in memories of Davis, as she realizes by viewing a wax figure of him at a Chicago fair that she sewed the chintz wrapper in which he was memorialized.[68] Although the item on the wax figure is not the one in which Davis is reportedly captured, Keckley adds, her role in the story and as historian is still valid: "The dress on the wax figure at the fair in Chicago unquestionably was one of the chintz wrappers that I made for Mrs. Davis in January, 1860, in Washington; and I infer, since it was not found on the body of the fugitive President of the South, it was taken from the trunks of Mrs. Davis, captured at the same time" (33).

Keckley's conclusion to the Davis narrative symbolically features her as an agent. She is inscribed in their history as dressmaker before the War but distant from Confederate failure. Her conversation with Varina Davis in which she chooses to remain in the North even makes Keckley a political agent as she consciously aligns herself with the winning side. Keckley metaphorically circulates with her work—both her sewing and her writing allow her to position herself from many angles to give comprehensive understandings of events that shape her time.

Once she secures work for Mrs. Lincoln, Keckley also begins to layer what she sees in the White House with her own story. In this case, she is affiliated with the "victorious" side but is also privy to the uncertainty within the home of the Union's leader.

> News from the front was never more cheering…. As I would look out my window almost every day, I could see the artillery going past on its way to the open space of ground, to fire a salute in honor of some new victory. From every point came glorious news of the success of the soldiers that fought for the Union. And yet, in their private chamber, away from the curious eyes of the world, the President and his wife wore sad, anxious faces [70].

This is a primary example of the type of layering Keckley does in her narrative. In this moment, she stages what she sees everyday at her window with the news she hears about the war and, finally, what she sees with her own eyes in the home of the President. These representations of knowledge show that her perspective is more comprehensive than most about the complexity of the war.

Three. Elizabeth Keckley and Freedom's Labor

She also adds the layer of African American narratives to her stories of the presidential administration and the Civil War. In a discussion of Lincoln's second inauguration, Keckley writes of how orders were issued to keep "colored people" from attending the event but Frederick Douglass was recognized by a member of Congress and brought directly to meet Lincoln.[69] This then becomes the story of Lincoln's introduction to Douglass, whom he later relied upon for advice about what to do with the newly freed men and women.

A most significant eyewitness account Keckley shares describes the day the war ends. She is working on a dress with the wife of Secretary Harlan when she sees artillery pass her window: "as it was on its way to fire a salute, I inferred that good news had been received at the War Department. My reception-room was on one side of the street, and my work-room on the other side. Inquiring the cause of the demonstration, we were told that Richmond had fallen" (72). This is another comprehensive account in which Keckley's work allows her to see premonitions of good news and receive a firsthand account at her worksite of the source of the celebration. The location of her workplace across the street, additionally, gives her greater access to details of the event: "I ran across to my work-room, and on entering it, discovered that the girls in my employ also had heard the good news. They were particularly elated, as it was reported that the rebel capital had surrendered to colored troops" (72). Keckley uses this opportunity to connect all the stories of the diverse groups with which she interacts. Mrs. Harlan is present and they rejoice together; she finds out that African Americans are responsible for the surrender and as an employer, is able to give the girls she employs a holiday to celebrate. In this moment, all of her worlds conjoin and she is at the center as narrator, integral character, and agent.

Keckley concludes her story of the surrender with her invitation by Mrs. Lincoln to City Point to confirm the surrender. As it is near her old home of Petersburg, Keckley is pleased to join her as a free woman. She uses this as an opportunity to reflect on her journey: "Alas! How many changes had taken place since my eye had wandered over the classic fields of dear old Virginia! ... I wondered if I should catch a glimpse of a familiar face; I wondered what had become of those I once knew.... I wondered, now that Richmond had fallen, and Virginia been restored to the clustering stars of the Union, if the people would come together in the bonds of peace" (73). Her reflections seem more like those of a political philosopher than of one who is hardly considered to be a citizen. Again, her personal interest is evident as she wonders about those who she knows. Her interest in the state of the nation is also apparent. I argue that this is another moment in which her past and her present, two very different worlds, are inseparable. She was a slave in Virginia who returns as a free woman. Before, she represented her master's household, now she represents herself with the sponsorship of the President. Each of these positions affects her opinion of the fragile political state, but she knows that her liberty is in this moment irrevocable.

Keckley writes that she enters the Capitol with the Presidential party, a scene which she observes as "a desolate appearance—desks broken, and papers scattered promiscuously in the hurried flight of the Confederate Congress" (73). This story of Confederate exodus significantly ends as *her* story. She picks up papers which coincidently include "the resolution prohibiting all free colored people from entering the State of Virginia" (73). In a scene that displays both irony and triumph, Keckley sits in the chairs of the Confederate administrators and even visits the home of Jefferson Davis. She literally and figuratively inhabits their spaces—they are absent, while she is present, and Keckley gets to tell the story. She also silences their histories in favor of her own. By treading these steps and ultimately rewriting these stories, Keckley gains access and authority in spaces that were formerly closed to her and other African Americans. She concludes the chapter by saying that "this was one of the most delightful trips of my life, and I always revert to it with feelings of genuine pleasure" (Keckley 76). Thus, their exit allows for her entrance without restriction or oppression. The failure of the Congress to uphold an moral agenda, in her opinion, allows for the execution of freedom by other hands. I argue that Keckley rewrites the story of the surrender where she is the principal figure, and she is able to tell the stories of all sides. She has, again, seized a position of authority and literally reconstructs the agency in her tale.

In chronicling the story of freedom for blacks in America, Keckley also documents a period of great transition:

> In the summer of 1862, freedmen began to flock into Washington from Maryland and Virginia. They came with a great hope in their hearts, and with all their worldly goods on their backs. Fresh from the bonds of slavery, fresh from the benighted regions of the plantation, they came to the Capital looking for liberty, and many of them not knowing it when they found it. Many good friends reached forth kind hands, but the North is not warm and impulsive [50].

Three. Elizabeth Keckley and Freedom's Labor

From a position of freedom that came just years before, Keckley discusses the false expectations of what freedom would bring for those who came after her. She records what they look for and do not find—their own negotiation of what freedom means. Keckley writes here with knowledge and perception. She continues: "Poor dusky children of slavery, men and women of my own race—the transition from slavery to freedom was too sudden for you! The bright dreams were too rudely dispelled; you were not prepared for the new life that opened before you, and the great masses of the North learned to look upon your helplessness with indifference—learned to speak of you as an idle, dependent race" (50). She understands that out of no fault of their own except their standards for their new lives, the newly free are disregarded and broken by what the North actually offers.

These discrepancies between what the freedmen need and what is available to them motivate Keckley to act for their benefit. After seeing a festival for the benefit of sick and wounded soldiers, Keckley decides: "If the white people can give festivals to raise funds for the relief of suffering soldiers, why should not the well-to-do colored people go to work to do something for the benefit of suffering blacks" (51). "I could not rest," she concludes, and she immediately makes a suggestion in the "colored church" that a "society of colored people be formed to labor for the benefit of the unfortunate freedmen" (51). Thus, she forms the "Contraband Relief Association" with forty initial members.

Her initiation of this organization is evidence of Keckley's realization of the possibilities of her free status. Not only does she now hold a different position in society, but she now commands enough influence to help relieve the distress of these "poor dusky children of slavery." Finally, Keckley can again draw upon her networks—this time for their benefit rather than her own. Mrs. Lincoln subscribes to the Association, as do prominent blacks in Boston and New York (including the Rev. Henry Highland Garnet, then-pastor of New York's Shiloh Church).[70] Frederick Douglass significantly contributes $200 (the same amount as the Lincoln's initial donation) and lectures for the organization as well. Money even comes from anti-slavery societies in England and Scotland, and Keckley is re-elected President of the Association.[71]

Keckley is able to distinguish the illusions of freedom from the work that one actually has to do to ensure progress. "Some of the freedmen and freedwomen had exaggerated ideas of liberty. To them, it was a beautiful vision, a land of sunshine, rest and glorious promise. They flocked to Washington, and since their extravagant hopes were not realized it was but natural that many of them should bitterly feel their disappointment" (62), she writes. Keckley continues: "the emancipated slaves, in coming North, left old associations behind them, and the love for the past was so strong that they could not find much beauty in the new life so suddenly opened to them" (62). These people, huddled in camps, declare to Keckley that they would rather go back to slavery than enjoy the freedom of the North.[72] Keckley also describes, however, those who "went to work with commendable energy, and planned with remarkable forethought" (63) building cabins, cultivating land, and creating schools in what became known as "Freedmen's Village." She cites stories of twelve girls who find employment in the Washington schools as evidence of their success.

In these stories of securing relief for the freedmen and their efforts for themselves, Keckley continues to make black histories central to her documentation of the Civil War. She offers several eyewitness accounts of events that would not have been recorded in much of the news, such as Frederick Douglass' meetings with Lincoln. Douglass, Keckley reports, is received with kindness and later becomes a source of much advice to Lincoln on how to integrate blacks into society after slavery formally ends. She gives an account of the fall of Richmond to black troops, a detail which would likely have been omitted in accounts of the Confederate surrender (Keckley 72). Keckley emphasizes the presence of blacks—the visual image of a "sea" that they made at Lincoln's inauguration in addition to individual accounts of significant actions and interactions that she sees.[73]

Keckley's role in Lincoln history *and* American history is not that of an ordinary historian. She simultaneously accounts for her life experiences and how she affects and is affected by others. She not only describes significant events, but she also discusses her involvement in them. Her descriptions of Mrs. Lincoln include her dependence when her son dies, how she only wants Keckley around when her husband dies, and how she refuses to leave Washington without Keckley (finally depending on her to raise money from selling her wardrobe—popularly called the "Old Clothes Scandal"). It is unlikely that Keckley's interest in offering such descriptions is only to provide information about Lincoln, although she probably foresaw the value of this "inside" information to the public. Keckley uses this opportunity to capitalize on her freedom—freedom to tell and to withhold whatever information she pleases, freedom to command interactions with those who find her indispensable. She secures her visibility and the visibility of other former slaves by taking readers behind the scenes of her life. A primary example of her insight is her account of Abraham Lincoln's death. She describes being sent for by Mary Todd Lincoln when Lincoln dies and her memories of her last encounter with him.[74] She recalls Lincoln as the "Moses of [her] people" (84), in this instance witnessing a side of him that others did not see. I argue that readers cannot separate the Lincolns' history from the others she discusses, even in such descriptions as brushing President Lincoln's hair, because they are all part of Keckley's life story.[75]

In her conclusion to her work with the Lincolns, Keckley describes Mrs. Lincoln's resistance to being helped by blacks such as Douglass and Garnet even after she is admittedly poor. Having created significant debt by buying clothes she could not afford during her husband's administration, Mary Todd Lincoln was put in an even greater state of poverty after his death. The greatest irony in this tale, and the one that provokes the most anger and embarrassment in its revelation is that Lincoln requests Keckley's assistance in selling these clothes. The "Old Clothes Scandal" is described in newspapers as well as biographical accounts of the Lincoln family. A fact Keckley emphasizes, however, is her donation of Lincoln memorabilia to Wilberforce University.[76] That Keckley is in the position to help this black school with the donation of Lincoln's "cloak, bonnet, comb, brush ... the glove worn [by Lincoln] at [his] first reception after the second inaugural, and Mr. Lincoln's over-shoes" (all things given to her by the family), even as she helps Mrs. Lincoln in her dire financial situation, shows her ultimate triumph.[77]

Life After Lincoln: Writing Her Story, Redefining History

Without discussing her work with the Lincoln family in detail, I emphasize the ways in which Keckley's masters and clients prior to Mary Todd Lincoln ultimately depend on and allow her to work on her own terms and develop her own understanding of what it means to be a free woman. After she ceases her work for Mrs. Lincoln after President Lincoln's death (and her involvement in what came to be known as the "Old

Clothes Scandal" in which she tried to help Mrs. Lincoln sell her dresses for additional income), she sews briefly for the daughters of Lincoln's successor President Johnson. She ends employment with them after they request her to work outside of her workroom, which she refuses to do.[78]

Keckley's narrative ends with her account of establishing her self-sufficiency and final authority. She secures a pension from Congress after her son's death in the War, asserting her humanity with motivation from of one of her former patrons: "I disliked the idea very much, and told her so—told her that I did not want to make money out of his death. She explained away all of my objections—argued that Congress had made an appropriation for the specific purpose of giving a pension to every widow who should lose an only son in the war, and insisted that I should have my rights."[79] Although Keckley does not even want to pursue the pension, the fact that others, including a member of the House from Illinois, believe that she should have it establishes her rights as equivalent to other (white) mothers who lose their children. Keckley is technically not a war widow, as her son's father was a white man with whom she never held a relationship, but the loss of her only son is recognized by the state is the same way. Thus, the story of bearing her only child is revisited and, in a sense, resolved. Keckley refused initially to bring enslaved children into the world and ensures that George's legacy is perpetuated under the law.

Keckley uses her enslavement as a stepping-stone for her freedom but never separates herself from her past. When her story is removed from that of the Lincolns, it can be seen as a story of many people, as Keckley assumes the freedom to represent America. As a final word, Keckley's return to the Garlands signifies the rewriting and the refinishing of history. As she visits City Point, the site of the exodus of the Confederate Congress, she visits Vicksburg and Rude's Hill, Virginia (the home of another Garland daughter) as a free woman and even rebukes her former mistress for not providing her with "the advantages of a good education."[80] She has proved her progress and self-sufficiency and can meet with them on common ground as a free woman.

Keckley also visits the Garland children in Vicksburg, Mississippi, and her former home in St. Louis. When her Northern friends question how she can visit these scenes of enslavement, much less with any kind words, Keckley expresses that "the past is a mirror that reflects the chief incidents of my life. To surrender it is to surrender the greatest part of my existence."[81] She depends on her past to help her determine her future—the liberty that she desires in labor and in social interactions.

Rather than seeing herself only as part of the Lincoln story (although she quotes deliberately the moments in which Mrs. Lincoln refers to her as her "best" or "dearest" friend), Keckley uses that story as a layer of her narrative experience. It becomes part of the foundation on which she builds her discussion of the turmoil in America during the Civil War with specific references to the plights of black refugees, then freedmen and freedwomen. Like Jacobs' descriptions of the Nat Turner revolt and its aftermath in her own household, Keckley issues her own versions of then-current events but writes them specifically from her perspective; she is part of, not removed from these histories. She is at once former slave who can see the struggles of those trying to realize freedom and a self-made member of the black middle class whose network includes such figures as Frederick Douglass and Henry Highland Garnet.[82]

Keckley's focus on Mary Lincoln's dependence on her through Lincoln's tenure in the White House and his death seems to be her way of demonstrating, as in her first masters' households, how a family she serves cannot do without her. As the author of her own narrative, Keckley escapes subordinate status in the story that is told—yes, she is charged with "insubordination" and breaking codes of private confidence, but this is the result of having assumed her prerogative as a writer (a direct effect of her freedom). Keckley departs from the reliance on others to vouch for her in order to vouch for her own authority and credibility. To this end, perhaps being considered a "gossip" was not the worst thing that Keckley could have endured, as famous figures become part of Keckley's story rather than imprisoning her in theirs. Ultimately, Keckley's ability to use the White House as a location in which her own freedom is displayed and the freedoms of others are realized is the primary success of her text. As in her handiwork, she crafts these stories deliberately, and her own life story becomes symbolic of the visibility she tries to give to other freedom stories.

Keckley understands her own delicate position between the truth and those details about life in postbellum America that some of its inhabitants would rather keep a secret. She argues: "If I have portrayed the dark side of slavery, I also have painted the bright side," but with the end of Keckley's enslavement by her own initiative comes the ability to write freely of her experiences with her master's family as well as with her later employers.[83] She weaves the histories of free African Americans into national narratives of the presidency and wartime history. Most significantly, she uses her freedom to speak and to write as a position from which to illustrate her own humanity—her character, her life's labors, and her ability to use her testimony to ensure that stories of other freedmen and freedwomen are told. References to the Lincolns become part of Keckley's strategy to fill in historical gaps of African Americans freed before, during, and after the Civil War.

To whom is Keckley's text addressed? Is it to Mrs. Lincoln's critics, and if so, what can be made of the portions of the book before her work with the Lincoln family is even introduced—the narrative of her life as a slave? Santamarina argues that Keckley publicized her labor in the White House in order to clear Mrs. Lincoln's name and even that Keckley's description of her role as Mrs. Lincoln's "modiste" was intended to "champion" "her much-maligned former employer" (141). I do not disagree with this explanation. The question remains unanswered, however, why Keckley would write primarily for the sake of protecting a public figure to which she owed little more than a portion of her livelihood. Was Mrs. Lincoln as dear to Keckley as she claims Keckley was to her, or is there another agenda in this text?

It is at this point that I depart from Santamarina's focus on Keckley as a source of labor for these families; she argues that "Keckley's racial deference to the family ... bridges the gap between social inferiority and interdependence to assume a sentimental aspect involving the loyal and devoted personal (black) servant" (154). Why, I ask, cannot Keckley be considered in control? Rather than her dependence on the family for this social value, the focus of the rest of the book seems to be on Mary Lincoln's dependence on her through Lincoln's tenure in the White House and his death. While Santamarina argues that this is a form of "admitting [black women] into a form of recognized participation in political effect" (155), of claiming her privilege as "'one of the family'" I argue that this is instead Keckley's way of showing yet again how the family she serves cannot do without her.

Keckley's narrative style had the potential to draw a diverse audience from its initial publication. Some would read to see what credibility a black woman could have to tell about the private life of a prominent white family; many readers would then become indignant that a black woman would reveal what they thought were the "secrets" of a prestigious family.

Three. Elizabeth Keckley and Freedom's Labor

I believe many of these responses were means of discrediting Keckley as both a free black female entrepreneur and narrator of multiple life stories—her own and those with whom she interacted. By making her narrative inclusive of histories of white northern political figures as well as of southern slave masters, from recently freed slaves to those already in the black middle class at the time of its publication, Keckley masterfully drew a crowd through which, intentionally or not, she could illustrate what freedom meant for African Americans in the nineteenth century. I argue that the story of the Lincolns becomes a tool to draw attention to the story of freedom but is not Keckley's main focus. Implicitly, Keckley's association with them (as well as the wives of Jefferson Davis and Stephen Douglas and the daughters of President Andrew Johnson, whom she also dressed) makes her visible to the same dubious readers who would then use their attentions to discredit her work. Whether such publicity was positive or negative, however, Keckley's readership could not avoid the stories of the freedom struggle within her text. Descriptions of the Lincoln household become the basis of a palimpsest in which refugees and freedmen coming to Washington occupy the center. Ultimately, Keckley's ability to use the former to feature the latter is the primary success of her text. As in her handiwork, she crafts these stories deliberately, and her own life story becomes symbolic of the visibility she tries to give to other freedom stories.

As the author of her own narrative, Keckley escapes subordinate status in the story that is told—yes, she is charged with "insubordination" and breaking codes of private confidence, but this is the result of having assumed her prerogative as a writer (a direct effect of freedom). Santamarina determines that Keckley makes a mistake in "outing" Mrs. Lincoln: "The scenes of work, intimacy, trust, and rhetorical authority that Keckley goes to such lengths to describe in her text show that she mistakenly assumed that because all her employers vouched for her she could vouch for herself" (158). I do not believe, however, that such an assumption was a mistake. Keckley departs from the reliance on others to vouch for her in order to vouch for her own authority and credibility. To this end, perhaps being considered a gossip was not the worst thing that Keckley could have endured. These accusations are reflections of the fact that people read and considered the content of the book; that Keckley was visible as a writer. These famous figures become part of Keckley's story rather than imprisoning her in theirs.

Some critiques of Keckley's project have focused on the resistance of her reading public to her shared accounts (especially of Mrs. Lincoln). Santamarina argues that Keckley becomes the sole witness to the grief of "intimate labor" (155), as black women are admitted into recognized participation but then condemned as gossips (156). Such reviews condemn Keckley as "angry," illicit, and "unveiling."[84] In her biographical account of the lives of Mary Todd Lincoln and Elizabeth Keckley, Jennifer Fleischner adds that "Lizzy" was thought to violate "Victorian codes of friendship and privacy" and those of "race, gender, and class" (317); she was therefore thought of as "treacherous" and "desecrating." This book was even thought to demonstrate dangerous consequences of educating black and Irish working classes. Fleischner writes: "this response came from Northern reviewers who felt uncomfortable being confronted with a black seamstress who was obviously more than a 'faithful negro servant,' who was in fact a free black woman, with autonomy and authority, who moved between a free white and a *free* black middle class" (317).

This line of criticism, that the reception of Keckley's book was evidence that she could not narrate her own attributes, misses the point of what this text is able to do. An example is Santamarina's statement "Although one might view *Behind the Scenes* as an autobiographical 'good card' that succeeds in bypassing the mediation of Keckley's employers, the text's reception then and now suggests that Keckley's subordinate position vis-à-vis her clients provided her with more 'credit' than was or is extended to her by her reading audience'" (159). In her eyes, Keckley's credit comes from her own ability and not the reliance on her readership or anyone else to recognize her. At the point at which her text circulates, she has secured a position that demands people's attentions.

Although many tried to discount Keckley's work, the Lincoln's son Robert included, perhaps the most vitriolic attack on Keckley's text was a publication by an anonymous author in the same year as *Behind the Scenes*. The book, mockingly entitled *Behind the Seams; By a Nigger Woman Who Took in Work from Mrs. Lincoln and Mrs. Davis* was released by the National News Company in New York and sold as ten-cent pamphlets.[85]

Jennifer Fleischner has noted its publication, but no Keckley critic has engaged with the ways in which this author attempts to denigrate her character. I find the author's methods significant because the attempts to ridicule her show that he or she has seriously engaged her text. Many details are recalled in order to poke fun at the idea that Keckley would

Three. Elizabeth Keckley and Freedom's Labor

even consider herself a valid author, but the lampooner has obviously read Keckley's text word for word. This shows that even those who criticize her found something interesting (or threatening) enough to combat. The fact that the Lincoln's son Robert even tried to get the book removed from circulation shows its content was to be reckoned with.

Behind the Seams is posed as a challenge to the authority Keckley tries to assert in her text. Its title objectifies her by replacing her name as author with "a nigger woman who took in work from Mrs. Lincoln and Mrs. Davis." Not only does this description call her out of her name, but it reduces her value to those for whom she performed domestic labor. The title does not even specify the type of work she does; it is only concerned with positioning her as servant.

The content of the parody gets worse. It begins "My name is Betsey Kickley, and I am a most extraordinary nigger" and asserts that the narrator writes "for my own benefit in a pecuniary point of view, as I am hard up." The author initially reduces Keckley's narrative attempts to stereotypes, mocking both her race and her talent. The preface continues: "I am going to try an experiment and see if I can't make more money by writing a book than by taking in sewing." While I have argued that Keckley's narrative was written more for the sake of telling her involvement in such events as the Lincoln presidency than making money, this text suggests that her only purpose was to profit from Mrs. Lincoln's misfortune (an assertion that is refuted by her defense of Mrs. Lincoln's character). *Behind the Seams* continues in an effort to defend the Confederate actions. It reads: "I am a romantic nigger, and although I was a slave for thirty years; I do not blame the Southern people, nor hold them responsible. I only blame the God of nature and the fathers who framed the Constitution for the United Sates. I forgive them, too, however, as I am all right now, having been transformed from a nigger slave who took in sewing in the South, into a free nigger writing a book in the North" (preface). By having this narrator speak as a black woman who excuses slavery as the fault of God and the founding fathers of America, and not the Southern people, the author displaces the guilt that readers of Keckley's text might experience as a result of her treatment and forgiving spirit. Although Keckley does revisit the family of her former master and mistress on friendly terms, it is because she has established herself in a place of power wherein she does not depend on them for any of her happiness. This text does something different—it makes Keckley subordinate even in her freedom.

Besides detracting from her writing, *Behind the Seams* repeatedly attempts to "undress" Keckley's character even from its title; it attempts to make "Kickley" [sic] reveal what the author believes is her true self. First, it alleges that Keckley only succeeds by "wearing the clothes" of others: "I am an independent nigger, and it's no body's business what I write, so I made up my mind that if I could find a publisher who would engineer my book, I'd try the thing on as I used to do with Mrs. Lincoln's dresses" (preface). This parody not only suggests that Keckley's book is not a serious undertaking but also that she is using its content without permission—it is neither an endeavor that "fits" her nor that belongs to her in this evaluation.

Behind the Seams will not let Keckley move from the position of inferiority due to her beginnings as a slave. It mocks her history, "I was born a nigger and a slave. My parents were slaves and niggers" (5), and the position to which she has risen, "I was a stupid nigger when young, though I have since turned out to be a great authoress" (5). The text also mocks her mother's grief when her father is sent away from the Burwell plantation: "We never saw him any more, but entertain confident expectations of meeting 'the old un' sooner or later or the other side of Jawdam [sic]. My mother cried a great deal when the 'old un' (I'm quoting my bosom friend Dickens) left" (5). In this moment, *Behind the Seams* mocks the belief many slaves held in reuniting with loved ones and the sentimentality Keckley expresses on the separation from the man she knows as her father. He relegates her emotion to imitation of Victorian writing rather than a product of her own reflections.

Besides its vitriolic language, perhaps the most incisive aspect of *Behind the Seams* is its refusal to recognize the violence and sexual assault Keckley describes. The author calls whippings inflicted on her "matinee performances" (7) and, as an ultimate insult, mocks her claims of rape by the friend of the Burwells. The account is instead written that "I was virtuous and modest, like Caesar's wife, and refused him, but he bothered me with his attentions for four years, when I struck my colors, and capitulated. The result of the capitulation was that I-I-I-I-I-became a mother. A fine mulatto baby was the result of my surrender at indiscretion" (7). As if it is not enough to discredit her work, this author attacks her character. The text alleges that Keckley surrenders to this man rather than being taken by force and that the baby was the product of her indiscretion rather than an attack. This is another means of this critique to challenge

Three. Elizabeth Keckley and Freedom's Labor

Keckley's credibility, a theme which persists throughout the remainder of the publication. Once the author announces her relocation to St. Louis with the Garlands, the text suggests that Keckley has relinquished all virtue despite her industriousness: "With my needle I kept bread and biscuits in the mouths of seventeen persons, for two years and five months. Thus it was that I became a modiste, though I could hardly be called modest any longer, on account of that *sans ceremonie* marriage" (7). The parodist mocks Keckley's trade and literally strips her of her virtue. As if physical and sexual violence is not horrible enough, it is suggested that Keckley can never achieve a position of respectability.

Finally, *Behind the Seams* mocks Keckley's attempts to marry and become a free woman, likely suggesting that she can never hold the same position or social status of white women. Her marriage to Keckley is reduced to the description that a "nigger man" fell in love with her while she was snickering and married her; her freedom is associated with wanting to become a slave owner: "Having lived in the South so long, and becoming imbued with the idea that nigger property would pay handsomely, I proposed to become a slave owner and so wanted to buy a couple of niggers from Mr. Garland. I offered him twelve hundred dollars for my son and myself, and felt that I then would have a legal right to call the former my own" (8). Thus, she never becomes "free" in this description—instead she becomes a slave owner while remaining the slave.

The text even mocks Keckley's elaborations on her own freedom; in every assertion, she is still a "nigger":

> I was a FREE nigger!! My son and myself were free.
> A FREE nigger!!! What a big thing on a skating pond.
> A FREE nigger! The earth wore a brighter look, and the stars sang Yankee Doodle.
> A FREE nigger! Bully for me, and bully for you, and thrice bully for the dear good lady who made me so. Heaven bless this good Southern lady. I love her, and I love the South for her sake; and so I shall not be ungrateful, and I never shall write a book full of no-such-things about the Southern people ... [9].

In this assessment, Keckley's freedom is made into a lighthearted joke and her agency is removed, as it is attributed solely to her mistress for "making" her free. It also reduces her agency in helping the black refugees and makes light of their plight; indeed, its mention of them is only one paragraph while they take up much of her attention in the actual narrative: "In the summer of 1862 a large number of runaway niggers came to Washington in search of liberty, and money or work—and found rather too much of the first commodity and too little of the others.... They soon became so hard up, that I got some nigger societies to raise the wind for them. We raised the wind a little, but it did not blow a regular greenback gale" (12). By choosing to focus on the limits of Keckley's success rather than the immense efforts of the Contraband Relief Agency, the author again removes the spirit of collaborative progress that is present in Keckley's actual narrative.

The parody reduces Keckley's characters to stereotypes. Elsewhere in the story are mentions of "Frederick Douglass, nigger" (15), descriptions of Keckley's laughter as the only sign of emotion she shows, descriptions of the White House furniture being stolen by the "niggers" when Mrs. Lincoln leaves the White House (15), and a reference from Tad Lincoln during a spelling lesson that a picture he sees is "either a large monkey or a small nigger, I can't tell exactly because one is so much like both, I cant tell tother from which." Keckley's response is that "When I think of this incident, I always show my teeth" (16). This text, in effect, does not only "undress" Keckley in a derogatory manner but dehumanizes all blacks in attempts to discredit their character completely.

Any reader of this text is left with a picture of Keckley as nothing more than Mrs. Lincoln's "bosom" lackey, an ordinary woman who tries to profit from having learned to read and write and of all blacks typecast as "niggers"—the narrators attempt to denigrate an entire group of people. The book closes: "I write books and I take in sewing.... Publishers and ladies please take notice. Terms moderate" as if the book is solely and pecuniary effort. Finally, the "narrator" does not even write her name: it is signed "Betsey Kickley, (Nigger) × Her mark" as if someone else has been her amanuensis. "Kickley" reports regret for writing about Lincoln, as "Mr. Lincoln was, truly, a great and good man, and I almost feel ashamed of myself when I think of what I have still before me to write in this book, in relation to his widow; especially when I reflect that in order to make my book pay, both myself and the publisher, I shall be compelled, at times, to draw the long bow a little, even in speaking of my dear bosom friend, Mrs. Lincoln" (13).

Against what is alleged by this parody, I argue that self-recommendation is not the sole purpose of Keckley's text. Instead, I believe that Keckley is establishing the point from which she offers herself as witness. She does not define her audience, perhaps in belief that her story is for everyone. The

Three. Elizabeth Keckley and Freedom's Labor

text tells how a domestic slave earned her freedom through social mobility, then uses her visible platform to tell the story of freedom for others. In so doing, Keckley creates a model for personal freedom that extends from individual to collective agency. In her own journey, she is ever conscious about opportunities that exist for her gain—the ability to control one's labor and to craft one's story both literally and metaphorically. Others demand her work, and she is then able to offer her assistance to refugees, former slaves, and even Mrs. Lincoln. Her work with the Lincolns is a reflection of the position she attained and not just means of securing social credit.

Keckley wrote a response to her critics in the *New York Citizen* on April 25, 1868, that challenged them to decide who actually scandalized Lincoln's name. "Was it because 'my skin is dark and that I was once a slave' that I am being 'denounced?' she asked. 'As I was born to servitude, it was not fault of mine that I was a slave; and, as I honestly purchased my freedom, may I not be permitted to express, now and then, an opinion becoming a free woman?'" (in Fleischner, 317). I argue in this line of reasoning that expressing her opinion as "a free woman" was Keckley's motivation from the beginning. Others disagreed with her assumption of the privilege to share particular insider accounts (those of prominent people and legendary events), but they could not contest her right to do so. Fleischner argues: "For Elizabeth Keckly, who was self-conscious about her lack of education, writing was a daring assertion of self" (316), and I add that she made that self known through her relationships with others. Keckley's memories of her life in slavery and activism of her later years are inherently connected. Her experience as a slave motivates her to seize her own destiny as a free woman, but in doing so, she maintains agency in the domestic sphere. Keckley's labor as a dressmaker makes her a witness to what goes on inside her clients' homes, but as an independent worker, she is not subject to silence.

In the end, Keckley's role as American historian and her exposure "behind the scenes" of the Lincoln tenure in the White House was covered up in American history. The angry headlines disappeared by June 1868, and Keckley's book ultimately sold few copies. Keckley and others believed that the Lincolns' son Robert suppressed its sale. Mary Todd Lincoln was left feeling betrayed by the publication of twenty-four letters she had sent to Keckley, letters that Keckley says publisher James Redpath had promised not to print.[86] Redpath was, Fleischner writes, "a former antislavery journalist and war correspondent" but "also an energetic propagandist and promoter" who "must have seen the possibilities for sales in publishing this insider's view of the White House." Partially as a result of Redpath's attempts at self-promotion, Mary Todd Lincoln expelled Keckley from her life, angrily dismissing her in a letter as "'the colored historian.'"[87] This description, ironically, is one of the greatest compliments to Keckley's work. By asserting her freedom to write her own life story, she could position the lives of others who needed such attention within its lines. Some of Keckley's subjects, namely Mary Todd Lincoln, resented the public interest, but others, such as the recently freed blacks in America, needed it to secure resources during uncertain Civil War and postbellum conditions.

Keckley's awareness of her personal freedom transcends to promotion of national freedom. In the accounts of those who condemned her work, Keckley is the metaphorical "slave" of the Lincolns who overstepped her boundaries by telling their secrets, but Keckley has already written herself out of the confines of subservience to her later employees. She illustrates, first in her years as a slave and then in her years as a free woman, her negotiations of her own freedom. In the end, she orchestrates her own mobility in both circumstances and illustrates what it means to live as a person who is both legally and inherently free. The union of these stories into a singular narrative positions Keckley as an authority on both slavery and freedom. Freedom for Elizabeth Keckley is not just freedom of her physical being. It is freedom to profit from the circulation of her work *and* freedom to move through any space that she pleases.

Finally, Keckley's freedom is accompanied by the ability to relate what she sees and act when she can for the benefit of others. Once she has secured her own freedom, she wants to help others to experience the same state of security. In the moment that Keckley dedicates her time and resources to aid "suffering blacks," Keckley has not only asserted her freedom but also asserted a higher position on the social hierarchy; she includes herself in the class of the "well-to-do colored people."[88] Her assertion of her status here is also representative of the point in the narrative from which she speaks. She is upwardly mobile but ever mindful of the position from which she came. Freedom is represented in this text by Keckley's ability to seize the power of representation from others. When she ceases to be known as "Garland's Lizzie," she gains and establishes significant means of authority.

Three. Elizabeth Keckley and Freedom's Labor

Michael Berthold's argument that *Behind the Scenes* is "still profoundly about [Keckley's] self" suggests that the text becomes a venue for Keckley's construction *and* defense of "self," as she both relates to community and reflects on her own character. As more than a continuum of the more well known slave narrative tradition, narratives of freedom written by Keckley and others depart from the dependence on authority by others in attempts to tell their own stories unassisted. Reading Keckley's narrative as a narrative of freedom shows her ability to depart literally and figuratively from unfavorable circumstances. Thus, Frances Smith Foster's argument that Keckley's post-emancipation publication made the text less relevant as an anti-slavery text than others, such as that of her "soldier sister" Harriet Jacobs, can be adapted.[89]

Santamarina writes: "As a transitional, postbellum text that combines slave narrative and political memoir, *Behind the Scenes* moves away from the concerns of the slave narrative and focuses mainly on demonstrating how a slave woman might recast the coercions of slave labor so as to produce herself as an empowered agent, rather than solely as a victim of bondage" (143). My intervention suggests, however, that the shift from the concerns of the slave narrative then become the concerns of a new genre, a narrative of freedom.

The layers of stories that Keckley imposes on one another are many— the story of her life, those of the Burwells and Garlands, stories of the Davis family and the Lincoln family, those of the black refugees and freedman that come to Washington, stories of her interactions with Frederick Douglass and Henry Highland Garnet. The union of these stories into a singular narrative is a metaphor for Keckley's project. She positions herself as authority in many aspects of American life. Keckley is protagonist, agent, and historian, and in each of these tales she shows her connections in diverse realms of society. Freedom for Elizabeth Keckley is not just freedom of her physical being. It is freedom to profit from the circulation of her work *and* freedom to move through any space that she pleases.

Keckley inverts the social hierarchy as she describes her journey from "thirty years a slave" to a valued White House employee. She becomes the speaker of the "last word" on both her master's family and Mary Todd Lincoln. Through these narratives, Keckley asserts that this is her story but she has access to many experiences—all of those with whom she has been affiliated, from slaves to public figures. By composing her own narrative, Keckley ensures that she is never imprisoned within the margins of history. Those considered on the outside of society—former slaves, black women included—become central figures in the narrative. Although she has been reduced in some criticism to merely another domestic figure in a famous household, as long as Keckley's words remain she is an authority on presidential and Civil War history as well as personal and collective freedom from the institution of slavery.

Keckley offers a different mission for texts published after the Civil War. In her brief account of her experience under enslavement and more extensive testimony of her life in freedom as a successful dressmaker with notable clients, Keckley illustrates what it means to live as a person who is both legally free and materially productive. By composing her own narrative, Keckley ensures that she transcends the margins of the history she records. Those considered on the outside of society—former slaves, black women included—become central figures in the narrative. Although she has been reduced in some criticism to merely another domestic figure in a famous household, as long as Keckley's words remain she is an authority on presidential and Civil War history as well as personal and collective freedom from the institution of slavery.

CHAPTER FOUR

"Fiction"ing Freedom
Frances Ellen Watkins Harper's Novelistic Tradition

In the years that led into the twentieth century, ideas about racial progress after Emancipation were also circulated through fiction in addition to through newspapers, essays, speeches, journals, and poetry. Rather than being opposed to "true" narratives in our considerations of genre, fiction is an important way of revealing truths through literature. The work of Frances Ellen Watkins Harper, among other nineteenth-century African American intellectuals, produces fictionalized subjects that also serve as intellectual figures. This type of scholarship grounds the types of work that fiction was used to do in early African American writing—it extends conversations from newspapers and other forums to inform audiences using a different method of communication. While my reading is not definitive as to one type of work that fiction does, identifying the work of fiction in nineteenth-century narrative discourse can help make more evident the types of texts that gain visibility after the Reconstruction period.

In the narratives with which Harper is concerned, fiction functions to highlight stories that have not been told by existing media at the time of their publication. The boundaries between purely invented material and already existing stories (from newspapers, speeches, and oral histories), however, are indistinct. The source of the material matters less than its effect. Thus, diverse means of developing more honest, accurate, or representative perspectives of African American lives are represented through fiction.

African American novels also function as histories; they allow changing versions of black subjectivity through the charting of experiences across historical periods. These novels do not have fixed spectrums, but instead represent glimpses of specific characters at particular points in time. The characters can be from many sources but are then used by the authors to represent crucial human experiences. In the case of nineteenth-century African American literature, authors often conflated numerous stories and experiences onto a few characters to show the breadth and depth of ontological challenges during slavery and freedom.

Between the years of 1867 and 1869, Frances Ellen Watkins Harper embarked on a tour of the Southern states of South Carolina, Georgia, Alabama, and Tennessee.[1] As she lectured throughout the region on topics such as temperance, education, domestic improvements, suffrage, and "reconciliation" between races during a critical period in American history, Harper represented the possibilities that Reconstruction could bring.[2] Although she lived her entire life as a free woman and benefited from formal education, Harper never distanced herself from the concerns of those who had been enslaved.

Many details about Harper's life are limited, and Frances Smith Foster writes that most of the known information is derived from her abolitionist friend William Still's *The Underground Railroad*, published in 1871.[3] It is known, however, that her early life was not one of complete privilege. Harper was born to free parents in Maryland but orphaned at an early age.[4] Her uncle, the Reverend William Watkins, a "fervent abolitionist, a community leader, and a highly regarded teacher," took her in and made sure that she received an education.[5] His school, the William Watkins Academy for Negro Youth, emphasized biblical studies, classics, and oratory skills. Watkins himself contributed to William Garrison's paper *The Liberator* and may have helped Harper publish her early work.[6]

Harper attended school until the age of thirteen, at which point she gained employment as a domestic worker for bookstore owners. Between sewing and caring for the Armstrong children, Harper read from the store's stock and wrote her earliest volume of poetry, *Forest Leaves* (1846), of which no known copies exist.[7] Harper's early life is significant because she used her access to educational resources to develop herself as an intellectual figure and a public scholar.

Her work as a teacher, first at Union Theological Seminary in Ohio (after her uncle moved to Canada) and then in Little York, Pennsylvania, forced her to reflect on the condition of those in her home state of Maryland; as she remained voluntarily exiled, legislation was passed in 1853 that those entering from the free states in the North could be captured and sold.[8] Even as a free woman by birth, Harper risked harassment if she were to visit her friends or family in Baltimore. Troubled by the restrictive and dubious nature of freedom, Harper continued to write and publish poetry in response to her concerns. *Forest Leaves* in 1846 was followed by *Poems on Miscellaneous Subjects* (published in 1854 and reprinted in 1857). She also reflected upon Harriet Beecher Stowe's *Uncle Tom's Cabin* through poetry in *Frederick Douglass' Paper* and the *Liberator*.[9] After moving to Massachusetts, where she launched her speaking career in 1854 in New Bedford, then Maine, where she gained employment with the Maine Anti-Slavery Society, it became evident that Harper was a force in both oratory and the written word.[10]

The issues that Harper discussed in her poetry soon came to light in fiction, and Harper published the first short story by a black woman in 1859. In "The Two Offers," she illustrates physical and metaphorical freedom as two cousins trace their life paths; one marries an excessive gambler and ends up dying, perhaps of heartbreak. The other chooses life as an unmarried woman and intellectual figure and gains triumph from authority over her own life. Harper allows this character (Janette) to utilize her freedom to live and to write on her own terms much in the way she did in her own life. She suggests that women must have their intellectual needs met; physical love is not enough. In this same span from her first book in 1846 through what Melba J. Boyd calls the "first reputable novel by a black woman in 1892" (*Iola Leroy*), Harper published three serialized novels in *Christian Recorder* in 1859, 1877, 1888.[11] Throughout her career as a writer and teacher, Harper continued to lecture throughout the United States and Canada.[12]

Frances Ellen Watkins Harper's work is increasingly recognized and discussed, as Frances Smith Foster discussed her work in two books and published her serialized novels (*Minnie's Sacrifice*, *Sowing and Reaping*, and *Trial and Triumph*) in 1994. Maryemma Graham has published a complete volume of her work but writes in her introduction that there is more work to be done on Harper's texts. In critical terms, Melba Joyce Boyd writes that she is an artist and activist whose insight "constitutes a viable ideological framework for contemporary radical thought."[13] Many critics choose to focus on her poetry, perhaps because it constitutes the earliest and longest spanning genre in her work.[14] Other scholars and critics such as Ann du Cille have discussed the marriage plots incorporated in her work, and Hazel Carby uses Harper and other novelists as a way to rethink cultural politics of black women.

In this chapter, I read the way Frances Ellen Watkins Harper represents the freed woman's role in reconstructing her community through fiction. As she concludes in "Two Offers," "true happiness" is found for women in "full development and right culture of [their] whole natures."[15] Both her shorter novel *Minnie's Sacrifice*, which appeared in the *Christian Recorder* in 1869, and her longer and most-well known novel, *Iola Leroy*, feature mixed-race female characters who are raised as white women and have to decide how to live their lives once they discover they are black. *Iola Leroy* is historical fiction, as it features post–Emancipation issues such as the reconnecting of families, but more generally, what black people should do "on the threshold of a new era."[16] In Iola's decision to "teach in the Sunday-school, help in the church, [and] hold mothers' meetings to help these boys and girls to grow up to be good men and women,'" Harper's text is a fictional account about the virtues of education and proof that black women can be instrumental race leaders.[17]

I argue that Harper's novels present ways to imagine or idealize the effects of emancipation in a different form than other genres she undertakes (including lectures and poetry), but the subjectivities represented in her novels and other genres are cyclical and intertwined. Using the methodology of Hazel Carby's *Reconstructing Womanhood*, in which she uses fiction to rethink the cultural politics of black women while she documents their emergence as novelists, I investigate the manner in which Harper represents freedom through fiction and analyze the connection between nineteenth-century African American novels and preceding works.[18]

Representing Race

> When I found out that I was colored, I made up my mind that I would neither be pitied nor patronized by my former friends; but that I would live out my own individuality and do for my race, as a colored woman, what I never could accomplish as a white woman.[19]

Sacrifice and education are the means articulated in Frances Ellen Watkins Harper's fiction for women to take up the responsibility of racial leadership. Both Minnie and Iola choose to educate fellow members of their race as their contribution to African American progress. Once they discover their racial origins, they invest themselves in promulgating knowledge in a very passionate way; they literally implant the seeds of racial elevation.

Marriage is an important theme in Harper's work, but it is not the only means to building a legacy. Her first short story, "Two Offers" (1859), which appeared in the *Anglo-African Magazine,* characterizes a woman who is torn between two offers of marriage and finds through advice given by her "pale intellectual" cousin that "true happiness consists not so much in the fruition of our wishes as in the regulation of desires and the full development and right culture of our whole natures."[20] *Iola Leroy* also features a woman who initially chooses not to marry in addition to a couple that decides, through marriage, to dedicate themselves to racial uplift. It seems through these examples that marriage is not the only context in which collective work can be done in the African American community; instead, women can also "wed" themselves to the race itself. Both Minnie and Iola marry (although Iola resists for much of the text out of obligation to helping freed slaves), but Harper focuses on how they see themselves in a relationship with their communities in addition to their husbands.

Minnie marries a man who has also changed his sympathies after discovering that he is black and dedicates herself to his uplift and that of others. As Louis fights for the Union army, an allusion to the historical moment in which the text is published, Minnie is a dutiful and supportive wife: "She tried to beguile him with the news of the neighborhood, and to inspire him with bright hopes for the future; that future in which they should clasp hands again and find their duty and their pleasure in living for the welfare and happiness of our race, as Minnie would often say."[21] She revels in the opportunity to have a role in building up "a race upon whose brows God had poured the chrism of a new era—a race newly anointed with freedom."[22] Minnie's inspiration to her husband, then to the freedmen she teaches in cabins, gives her life meaning. Harper writes: "Oh, how the enthusiasm of her young soul gathered around that work! She felt it was no mean nor common privilege to be the pioneer of a new civilization."[23]

After the war, Minnie uses the status she has entered as racial advocate to urge a place for black women in the political sphere. On the issue of suffrage, she argues:

> "But, Louis, is it not the negro woman's hour also? Has she not as many rights and claims as the negro man?"

> "Well, perhaps she has, but darling, you cannot better the condition of the colored men without helping the colored women. What elevates him helps her."
>
> "All that may be true, but I cannot recognize that the negro man is the only one who has pressing claims at this hour. To-day our government needs woman's conscience as well as man's judgment."[24]

Minnie develops a tradition of service that keeps Louis connected to the race even after her death. She has traveled throughout Negro cabins inspiring people to educate themselves, obtain land, and prepare for challenges ahead; she has advocated on behalf of black men and women alike. The conclusion of the story is the lesson that Minnie learns, that the "greatest want" of black people is earnest women who build up the race.

Minnie is both intellectual and activist in Harper's portrayal, and she is used as an example of the work that Harper tried to do herself as she made speeches across America: "While I confess ... that Minnie has only lived and died in my imagination, may I not modestly ask that the lesson of Minnie shall have its place among the educational ideas for the advancement of our race?"[25] The representation of Minnie is an intellectual enterprise in this text, as Harper uses an "imaginary" figure to show the effects of female commitment and dedication to working for racial progress. Harper is also specific in how she sees this work playing out—first, the woman must identify herself as part of a collective body; Minnie, like Iola decades later, "sacrifices" the possibility of white privilege to suffer the plight of racial oppression. Then, the woman must, through education, present a way out. In a lengthy conclusion, Harper argues:

> The lesson of Minnie's sacrifice is this, that it is braver to suffer with one's own branch of the human race,—to feel, that the weaker and the more despised they are, the closer we will cling to them, for the sake of helping them, than to attempt to creep out of all identity with them in their feebleness, for the sake of mere personal advantages, and to do this at the expense of self-respect, and a true manhood, and a truly dignified womanhood, that with whatever gifts we possess, whether they be genius, culture, wealth or social position, we can best serve the interests of our race by a generous and loving diffusion...[26]

Diffusion is an interesting metaphor here, for it represents the inability to separate oneself from the mass, to be at once in multiple places and have influence in multiple spheres. Harper suggests one must cling to her race and use her talents to serve them rather than denying community for personal elevation. Education becomes the gift with which Harper endows her female characters, and it is evidenced by an unshakable commitment to spreading knowledge to others. As in Douglass's texts, education is the best way to escape bondage; even in Harper's post–Emancipation work, it is used by the women to enhance life of free African Americans.

Iola Leroy then becomes a culmination of the possibilities of female intellectual influence. Like Minnie, the education Iola receives in the text is not for her own benefit, but so that she can reach and teach others. Also set in the Reconstruction period, Iola dedicates herself immediately after Emancipation to becoming a teacher in one of the country's new schools for black people. Iola refuses to marry a white doctor for this reason: "My life work is planned. I intend on spending my future among the colored people of the South ... they need me; and I am sure when I taught among them that they were very grateful for my services."[27] Iola, like Minnie, places the integration of her efforts into black Southern life above opportunities that can be afforded her through individual union. Although Iola marries Dr. Latimer in the end, the text suggests that a woman must be fully confident of her own abilities and aware of possibilities to help her community before joining efforts with somebody else.[28] By interpreting Iola's lessons as Harper's lessons (Carby parallels the lives of the fictional character and her author), one can see the virtues and visibility of black female intellectualism.

In what is perhaps an allusion to what Harper accomplishes through Iola Leroy, Dr. Latimer encourages Iola to write a book "to inspire men and women with a deeper sense of justice and humanity."[29] When Iola resists, fearful that she has neither time nor money to undertake such a task, Latimer responds, "'Miss Leroy, out of the race must come its own thinkers and writers.'"[30] Harper, through Latimer, suggests through this exchange that Iola Leroy would make an appropriate subject for a book as well, for Harper does write such a text. Harper is consistent, as the possibility for women to emerge as racial leaders is as evident in the 1850s and 1860s as in 1892. Iola Leroy, like her creator Frances Ellen Watkins Harper, is educated but also educator, and both set standards for teaching and community work.[31]

"True reconstruction" is issued in this text as "the surrender of the best brain and heart of the country to build, above the wastes of war, more stately temples of thought and action."[32] The unity of "thought" and "action" are key; as long as one is willing to use both to promote uplift, there are no gender boundaries as to who can reconstruct the nation. The best "brain and heart of the country," Harper suggests, can be found in black women just as well, if not moreso, than in anybody else. Harper's characters Minnie and Iola are perhaps representative of Frederick Douglass's intellectualism and Martin Delany's activism—they draw upon their own knowledge to implement the importance of learning, thereby connecting their individual pasts with a collective future. Racial progress comes from more than just ethnic identification in Harper's fiction; it involves a dedication to cultivating free minds in addition to maintaining free bodies.

Intellectual Bodies at Work

Harper demonstrates the types of intellectual investments and race work that early African American fiction can produce through individual subjects.[33] She constructs intellectualism in different ways, including how someone comes to knowledge, how one incorporates intelligence into activism, or how a subject promotes educational undertakings. These texts are also examples of how authors weave beliefs and morals into fiction—they suggest that racial progress must be a mutual effort, but it can also be stimulated by just one person.[34] Harper uses individual subjects as a bridge to reflect and improve cultural concerns such as restraints of slavery and implications of "freedom" in America, issues that threaten the subjects as well as the communities in which they are situated.[35] In order to achieve this end, however, a mission of racial progress is written on a single body.

Early African American fiction performed a similar type of work to other genres that preceded it; although it is read as another form than newspapers, essays, or speeches, for example, it was also used by nineteenth-century authors to understand both the changes and the challenges of the period in which they lived. As Harper has her characters cite lines from her own speeches, texts are used within texts in early African American novels to create conversations amongst genres on similar issues. Early African American novelists also create intellectual figures with which to do this work. They proclaim the work of a black leader on the basis of gender, educational status, and critical perspective. Even through fiction, black subjects are part of an intellectual project. The insertion of fictional narratives into the objectives of African American intellectual work further articulates how racial progress was defined, initiated, or accomplished in order to project specific goals toward a desired readership.

Four. "Fiction"ing Freedom

Examining some of the figures featured in the fiction of Frances Ellen Watkins Harper demonstrates means of addressing black communities, whether to inspire them to seek freedom before Emancipation or to educate freedmen afterward. I ask, what are the types of characters that emerge as racial leaders in these texts, and on what terms? Who become the "race women" and how are their missions carried out? I analyze the methods by which Harper as an early novelist and also active black abolitionist, journalist, and educator, turned novels into political and instructional messages. *Iola Leroy*, I argue, was heavily influenced by her early efforts to promote social change. Harper's novels are not only as a continuum of work she published in newspapers and other media but also serve as agents for progress in their own right through the creation of fictionalized race leaders.

Early African American fiction was also never completely distinct from other genres used to do political work. Significantly, many African American novelists first published their creative work in newspapers along with, or in addition to, their essays. Frances Ellen Watkins Harper published poetry, essays, and fiction in the *Liberator*, *Frederick Douglass' Paper*, the *Anti-Slavery Bugle*, and the *New York Anglo-African* before publishing her first novel.[36] Newspaper publications served as outlets for a great deal of African American writing because of the broad audiences they generated, and fiction also influenced conversations about slavery, emigration, family life, and other political and domestic matters within the African America population in the United States.

Reading Communities

Early African American novels draw from a notion of reading as a way to create communal racial identities. Benedict Anderson's *Imagined Communities* speaks to the ways that "nationality," and "nationalism" are cultural artifacts created and sustained by a nation defined as "an imagined political community."[37] "Nationalism has to be understood by aligning it, not with self-consciously held political ideologies, but with the large cultural systems that preceded it, out of which—as well as against which—it came into being."[38] Forms of material culture in African American communities represent these cultural systems. Newspapers, then novels promote nationalism by making stories available to a wide public, a public that is then connected by virtue of access to common texts. By tracing various histories of print capitalism, Anderson establishes newspapers as key in creating reading publics that became "imagined communities," and, ultimately, "nations." A "cultural product" in effect became responsible for the ability for "rapidly growing numbers of people to think about themselves, and to relate themselves to others, in profoundly new ways."[39] The role of newspapers after Emancipation is to serve as a common text that all are, literally free to read. African American national identity is established, then preserved, by the ability of African American communities both to read and to tell their own stories.

Iola Leroy tells the story of separated, then reunited families and former slaves who try to find the best use of their efforts in reconstructing black communities. Newspapers in this case are used to chronicle the national histories that the novel includes, those of Emancipation and Reconstruction the development of African American educational institutions, as well as the personal histories—victories of being able to read of one's freedom, for example. As in *Clotel*, both the newspapers and narratives within the novel's context work together to tell a story; the narrative attends to development of subjects that are excluded from journals. Newspapers historicize the text, but the narrative is needed to tell more background information, and in this case, elaborate on the roles that black people assume in the "new era" after slavery ends.

Although all of the slaves in the community cannot read, the newspaper serves the entire community in the text. It gives Robert, as reader, the ability to serve as both storyteller and witness; he lives, sees, and tells the history of slavery and freedom. Robert hides papers that he is supposed to sell to boarders, and uses them to "let some of the fellow-servants know how things were going on"; ironically, his "ole Miss" "would let [him] read anyone of [her books] except a novel."[40] Harper, however, connects the value of the newspaper and the novel. Her text can be thought of as a closer look at the stories of the war and Emancipation that newspapers represent.

Before Iola, the daughter of a slave woman and white man, is remanded into slavery, she is against abolition: "I don't think these Abolitionists have any right to meddle in our affairs. I believe they are prejudiced against us, and want to get our property. I read about them in the papers when I was at home."[41] After she is freed, Iola, who finds out that she is Robert's niece, tells him of her plans to find her mother: "I will advertise for her in the papers, hunt for her in the churches," she says.[42] In an ironic scenario that the novel portrays, Iola represents both "white" reader who uses the newspaper to maintain racial division and the black freed slave who draws from a community of black readers to reconstruct her family. The significance of the multiple intertextual allusions found in these texts to my project is that the presence of newspapers within the novels elucidates the relationship among white readers, black readers, and stories involving African American characters. In some texts (especially earlier ones), newspapers are ways for whites to read about subjects on which blacks are silenced, despite how inaccurate such reports may be. In others, black readers also have access to these stories, but in neither case do the newspapers express the complexities of African American lives. Novels then become chronicles of lived histories; the presence of newspapers draws attention of readers to the ability of another genre, the novel, to offer alternate, more accurate, or more complete histories.

Harper "fictions" history through the characters she creates, the relation of her work to her life, and the opportunities for progress that she offers through her plots. In an interview about "The History of Sexuality," published in *Power/Knowledge*, Michel Foucault refutes the idea that "fiction" and "truth" can be easily identified as separate entities. He writes: "I am well aware that I have never written anything but fictions. I do not mean to say, however, that truth is therefore absent."[43] Instead, Foucault argues, fiction both functions as and is a function of truth; "truth" can actually be accessed from fictive, or invented, circumstances or discourse: "It seems to me that the possibility exists for fiction to function in truth, for a fictional discourse to induce effects of truth, and for bringing it about that a true discourse engenders or 'manufactures' something that does not as yet exist, that is, 'fictions' it."[44] Fiction for Foucault is not an abstract discourse but one that can, instead reveal ideas that have not yet been accessed by other means. In this analysis, various forms of fiction serve to create truths, specifically more accurate representations of African American subjects than those already in circulation in the second half of the nineteenth century.

These authors still, however, engage with history and politics—the effects of slavery, Emancipation, and Reconstruction on black individual and collective subjectivity. Foucault argues, "One 'fictions' history on the basis of a political reality that makes it true, one 'fictions' a politics not yet in existence on the basis of a historical truth," suggesting that one "fictions," or "invents," or "creates" histories and politics on the basis of political and historical truths.[45] Harper writes from already-existing political and historical contexts but uses fiction to write themselves and/or the subjects they create into these contexts.

The trope of the racial leader is not particular to men, however, as Iola Leroy, Minnie (from Harper's shorter novel *Minnie's Sacrifice*), and Annette (from Harper's third novella *Trial and Triumph*) also emerge to represent the best that free blacks have to offer—educators and leaders willing to guide their communities through crucial periods in history.

The material form of the novel allows the inclusion of various forms of histories (including newspaper articles and the reprint of the author's own speeches, as become words of Iola Leroy) to enhance the subjects it represents. Early African American novels still, however, function as histories. They allow changing versions of black subjectivity through the charting of experiences across historical periods. The novel does not have a fixed purview or spectrum but represents a glimpse of particular characters at particular points in time. The characters can be from many sources but are then used by the authors to represent critical human experiences. In the case of nineteenth-century African American literature, authors often conflated numerous stories and experiences onto a few characters to show the breadth and depth of ontological challenges during slavery and freedom.

How, then, do fictional texts (specifically novels) serve as historical interventions in literary history? Harper published poetry, essays, and fiction in the *Liberator, Frederick Douglass' Paper*, the *Anti-Slavery Bugle*, and the *New York Anglo-African* before publishing her first novel.[46] William Wells Brown used his fugitive and abolitionist status to establish himself as journalist in Britain and America before he became a novelist. Newspaper publications served as outlets for a great deal of African American writing because of the broad audiences they generated, so short fiction came to participate in conversations about slavery, emigration, family life, and other political and domestic matters within the African America population in the United States.

As the political climate changed in the 1850s due to events such as the Compromise of 1850 and the Fugitive Slave Law, the number of publications of newspapers, and therefore publications in newspapers, rose in numbers.[47] Significantly, as Dickson Bruce describes, newspapers such as Frederick Douglass' responded to literary texts such as Harriet Beecher

Stowe's *Uncle Tom's Cabin* through reviews. Douglass saw the novel's publication as a political event with the potential to affect debates over slavery.[48] I call upon these examples of abolitionist writing to show the predecessors for historically-concerned novels in the years leading up to the publication of African American novels. Harper, Brown, Douglass, and Delany (whose Blake was serialized first in the *Anglo-African Magazine*, then in the *Weekly Anglo-African*) used newspapers to promote their own abolitionist agendas and respond to the cultural climate of the United States; they then utilized this media to contribute fiction to the communities created by newspaper circulation.[49]

In *To Wake the Nations*, Eric Sundquist challenges canonicity by looking at less celebrated works in "American race literature." He writes, "In the case of both white and black authors, the key is to understand the authorial context, the historical moment and reigning cultural pressures, even the deliberate strategies employed for producing signs of both racial consciousness and racial antagonism" (9). It is not enough to simply note that these authors were publishing fiction in addition to their abolitionist work. I am interested in developing the notion of what types of work these novels did with their subject matter—the means by which they sought to impact African Americans in addition to the means by which they were published. When Iola Leroy expresses her desire to become an educator of freed slaves after the war, uttering verbatim words from Frances Ellen Watkins Harper's speeches "Colored Women of America" (1878) and "Duty to Dependent Races" (1891), the novel becomes both fact and fiction.[50] Its significance lies not in which words are "real" or invented but in the idea that a subject exists within a historical context that promotes African American education and community work.

Sundquist adds, "Any reconstruction of American literature depends not just on acknowledging the importance and place of neglected authors but on reconceptualizing the extent of textuality, the cultural and historical integuments that bind any work irrevocably to a time, a geography, and an array of social and aesthetic practices" (20). He specifically examines the narratives of Frederick Douglass and other male authors as he seeks to place race at the center of American experience. By the time Harper published *Iola Leroy*, many other men and women had achieved her status of freedom; they were now comrades in utilizing resources for collective improvement. Just prior to her final novel, Harper used *Trial and Triumph* (1888–1889) to advocate for temperance and education. The moral is that the race needs educated mothers and that the home is the primary place for instruction. The protagonist Annette is the child of a mother who has no self-control but, endowed with intellect, she goes to the South to teach and therefore gains an opportunity to be both "friend and sister" to the freedmen.[51] As a biographical parallel, Harper participated in the World's Congress of Representative Women in 1893 as part of the Columbian Exposition in Chicago along with Anna Julia Cooper, Fannie Barrier Williams, Fannie Jackson Coppin, Sarah J. Early, and Hallie Quinn Brown. These women joined together to fight for representation and take part in the quest for suffrage.[52]

Harper's novels and novella possibly join the body of what Michele Mitchell calls "prescriptive literature": "bound" texts (including tracts, manuals, pamphlets, and sermons" that made it easier to reach audiences.[53] Authors used them, Mitchell argues, to reach parents, who then reproduced good habits in their children as the literal meaning of "reproduction" took effect.[54] Harper's fiction, then was an example of the connection between stories and realized freedom. From her own observations and adaptation of the emerging genre of fiction within the African American literary tradition, Harper inscribed what freedom could mean for those who had the power to imagine it.

Chapter Five

Reflections on Freedom, or Freedom Retold

"We look back, not to become inflated with conceit because of the depths from which we have arisen, but that we may learn wisdom from experience."[1]

"Looking back" on stories of women who wrote themselves into not only public, but national discourse, illustrates some of the many obstacles that had to be overcome in the transition from oppression to liberation. Keckley was part of a genre of post-emancipation black women writers, but she also significantly "looked back" to include her own personal history under the institution of enslavement. Decades after the institution was ended formally by government legislation, Anna Julia Cooper and Lucy Craft Laney established the foundation for national uplift to continue through teaching, which became both a popular and an instrumental profession for black women. In addition to reflecting on their own life experiences in essays and speeches, Cooper and Laney used their knowledge to teach others how to make the most of their opportunities of freedom in both educational and domestic settings.

Cooper's only published book, *A Voice from the South* (1892), set the standard for women's involvement in racial progress after Emancipation. Laney did not publish a book manuscript but gave several speeches and published essays on what women (and especially mothers) could do to raise productive children in the first generation after emancipation. Through their efforts to promote the possibilities that freedom held from classrooms to households, educators Anna Julia Cooper and Lucy Craft Laney also created and transformed African American women's literary history.

Although she is largely absent from discussion of literature, Laney, who founded Haines Industrial and Normal Institute in Augusta, Georgia, in 1886, established her influence especially throughout the southern United States. She directly influenced educator Mary McLeod Bethune (who apprenticed at Haines) to start Bethune-Cookman College. Additionally, Laney established the first black kindergarten and the first nursing school for black women in Augusta, Georgia. Her efforts were noted by many, including W.E.B. Du Bois and Booker T. Washington. Instead of discussing her interaction with her more famous peers or a particular text that either Laney or Cooper authored, instead I am interested in the stories these women used (including their own) to disseminate the language of liberation and specifically the written, rhetorical, and lived strategies these educators used to strengthen their respective learning communities.

Both men and women took on these challenges as they strived for increased mobility. Narratives of reconstruction (in both its historical and metaphorical senses) witnessed and written by the very people undergoing significant transformation reveal much about individual and national history. When stories by and about black women are incorporated into the history of reconstruction, we are able to see that some of the strongest efforts, especially through education, were made by them.[2]

In 1901, W.E.B. Du Bois reflected on the problems with government-prescribed reconstruction efforts by The Freedmen's Bureau in an article published in the *Atlantic Monthly*:

> What shall be done with slaves? Peremptory military commands, this way and that, could not answer the query; the Emancipation Proclamation seemed but to broaden and intensify the difficulties; and so at last there arose in the South a government of men called the Freedmen's Bureau, which lasted, legally, from 1865 to 1872, but in a sense from 1861 to 1876, and which sought to settle the Negro problems in the United States of America.[3]

Du Bois studies this seemingly ambitious "government of men" in his essay, focusing on "the occasion of its rise, the character of its work, and its final success and failure ... as one of the most singular and interesting of the attempts made by a great nation to grapple with vast problems of race and social condition."[4] He makes it clear early on, however, that his study is not an optimistic one.

Du Bois initially paints a picture of the fugitive slaves that penetrated Northern army lines as "old men, and thin..., women with frightened eyes, dragging whimpering, hungry children; men and girls, stalwart and gaunt"—hardly the picture of the triumphant and free family unit.[5] Those arriving in 1861, when slaves of Missouri rebels were declared free, came

Five. Reflections on Freedom, or Freedom Retold

as self-declared freemen, deserted and captured populations.[6] This, Du Bois argues, is the beginning of the Freedmen's Bureau as these men, women, and children had to be provided for; they "welcomed" the "contrabands" as military laborers, a group whose number grew as time went on, until Lincoln officially emancipated the slaves of rebels in January of 1863. Du Bois states that the need to answer the officers' questions of "'What must be done with slaves arriving almost daily?'" led (Edward) Pierce of Boston to establish the ground for the Bureau.[7] Pierce founded the Port Royal experiment in which Charlotte Forten participated and started Freedmen's Aid Societies.

First, Du Bois writes, men were enlisted as soldiers or hired as laborers, as women and children were guarded in camps. Then, various organizations (including the American Missionary Association, National Freedmen's Relief Association, and American Freedmen's Union), started Freedmen's Aid Societies.[8] The need for aid beyond what these organizations did was, Du Bois described, "no ordinary matter of temporary relief, but a national crisis ... a labor problem of vast dimensions."[9] There were problems of idleness due to lack or disorganization of work efforts and no guaranteed distribution of pay, which caused demoralization amongst the freedmen.[10] Eventually, governments developed amongst the many geographic areas to redress grievances and establish school systems. General Saxton succeeded Pierce in South Carolina and sold and leased abandoned land while receiving thousands of camp followers in General Sherman's march.[11]

What Du Bois' account does not include, however, is a description of the women who weren't among the soldiers and laborers. This is, perhaps, because the focus of the Freedmen's Bureau was on the men who headed families. As the Bureau developed, efforts were taken to provide land on which the men could live and work. Congress attempted to establish a "Bureau for Freedmen" in the War Department in 1864 to allow for "'general superintendence of all freedmen'"—establishing regulations, leasing lands, adjusting wages, and representing them in civil and military courts. This bill was defeated in the Senate and replaced in 1865 as a "'Bureau of Refugees, Freedmen, and Abandoned Lands.'"[12] The bill was to extend one year past the "War of Rebellion," in which time the Secretary of War could issue "rations, clothing, and fuel" and sell and lease land to ex-slaves in forty-acre parcels. This bill, Du Bois argues, allowed the government to "assume charge of the emancipated Negro as the ward of the nation," but now remained black men "emasculated by a peculiarly complete system of slavery," and now forced to work amidst the "stricken, embittered population of their former masters."[13] If the men were emasculated, one might ask, what happened to the women who also lost aspects of self in the transition from plantations to contraband camps? One can only speculate, as their plights remained absent from national narratives.

Du Bois traces the history of the Bureau through General Oliver Howard (appointed May 1865), under whose regime new commissioners were appointed and cooperation with benevolent societies continued. The new commissioners were to "make the destitute self-supporting," "act as courts of law," "establish the institution of marriage among ex-slaves, and keep records; see that freedmen were free to choose their employers, and help in making fair contracts for them," but the problems of the past with distributing land and jobs persisted.[14] Du Bois states that three things worked that year—much suffering was relieved, 7000 fugitives were established on farms, and the "crusade of the New England schoolma'am" was inaugurated, but the mission still seemed too great to overcome the many problems that freedmen experienced.

Du Bois discusses the final form of the Freedmen's Bureau through the act of 1866, which extended its existence to July of 1868, authorized additional commissioners, sold forfeited lands to freedmen and Confederate public property for Negro schools.[15] The freed slave, however, was still described by Du Bois as "crouched," "bewildered between friend and foe."[16] The black man, he argues, had emerged from slavery which "classed [him] and the ox together" after which the cleft between whites and blacks grew. The figures who remain, however, in Du Bois' analysis are "a gray-haired gentleman ... who stood at last, in the evening of life, a blighted, ruined form, with hate in his eyes" and "a form hovering dark and mother-like, her awful face black with the mists of centuries, [who] had aforetime bent in love over her white master's cradle, rocked his sons and daughters to sleep ... ay, too, had laid herself low to his lust and borne a tawny man child to the world, only to see her dark boy's limbs scattered to the winds ... "[17] After this lengthy description, which traces the failings of the Bureau's service to the black man, how is it possible that only the white man and the black woman remain? Furthermore, how is this dynamic significant to Du Bois' analysis?

The irony of this replacement of the figure of the black man with the black woman is indicative also of the figures who are eventually at the forefront in the other narratives discussed. Despite the way in which the race gets to this point, the woman is charged with bringing them out. As he concludes his essay, Du Bois asserts that the "greatest success" of the Freedmen's Bureau was establishing the free school among Negroes and free elementary education throughout the South. Although the opposition to Negro education was great in the South, Du Bois states that "Fisk, Atlanta, Howard, and Hampton were founded in these days" and 750,000 of the six million dollars expended over five years for education came from the freedmen themselves. Successful Reconstruction efforts were credited to hard work, the "aid of philanthropists and the eager striving of black men."[18] The work of black women, such as Laney, is also evidence of success. She did not just educate young pupils, but created a kindergarten that was modeled throughout the country. She did not just establish a school, but one with a classically based college preparatory curriculum for a range of ages. During the time that many noted African American colleges were established, Laney also incorporated similar curricula into elementary through high school classrooms.[19]

Neither Cooper nor Laney is frequently mentioned amongst the "Women's Era" writing of the 1890s, perhaps because their writing was not considered "popular" literature. Mary Helen Washington writes, however, that without women like Cooper and her contemporaries, we would know little about nineteenth-century black women's lives, "and yet the black intellectual tradition, until very recently, has virtually ignored them and devalued their scholarship as clearly subordinate to that produced by black men."[20] Washington asserts that these women were activists AND intellectuals, "more committed to the idea of uplift than to their own personal advancement, partly because they could not isolate themselves from the problems of poor black women" (1). Both Cooper and Laney dedicated their lives to what Cooper called "education of the underprivileged'" and therefore also to the development of black feminist thought.[21]

Lucy Craft Laney: From Slavery to Scholarship

Out of many well-known black female educators, including Mary McLeod Bethune, Nannie Helen Burroughs, and Charlotte Hawkins Brown, Lucy Craft Laney was the only one to have been previously enslaved and to have been born before Emancipation was formally decreed.[22] Laney was a model for those who came after her of how to reach people in the highest and lowest social echelons. These women communicated with each other through various means (including letters), and Laney even taught both Bethune and later her son Albertus at her school in Augusta, Georgia. Audrey McCluskey writes of these educators: "As the first post-slavery generation of educated black women, they are also linked by their views on the role of education in uplifting the race and in gaining respect and acceptance for their maligned black sisters."[23] Freedom by means such as skilled trade and physical relocation has been discussed, but Laney continues the tradition established by women such as Charlotte Forten and Ellen Craft of promoting freedom through education. As McCluskey argues, these educators "have remained on the margins of history, invoked as examples of black female achievement but accorded little in-depth scholarly attention."[24] She calls them a "visible sisterhood of purpose" and I add that Laney helped define that purpose to motivate and elevate by establishing educational training institutions for children and for nurses.[25]

Laney was born into slavery in Macon, Georgia; her father, who was a minister and a carpenter, bought his family's freedom and reunited them.[26] Laney was encouraged to pursue an education and graduated ranked first in her class from Atlanta University in 1873.[27] She taught in Georgia's public schools for years before opening Haines Normal and Industrial Institute in Augusta, Georgia in 1886.[28] During this span, Reconstruction ended and black Americans were faced with more opposition due to the removal of troops from the South. They were charged with continuing to reconstruct their own communities with little outside or governmental support. Laney succeeded in this task, however, drawing over thirty teachers and nine hundred pupils to Haines by 1914.[29] This was an incredibly difficult task, especially given the South's difficulty in emerging from Reconstruction.

From the late 1800s through the early 1900s, Augusta was the home of a relatively visible and successful black middle class. The population included William J. White, who founded Augusta Baptist Institute in the city (which later became Morehouse College in Atlanta, Georgia).[30] In addition to teaching and mentoring Bethune, Laney would go on to teach John Hope, who became first black president of Atlanta University in 1929.[31] Laney's activism also extended beyond Augusta. After participating in Du Bois's Atlanta University Conferences, Farmer's Conferences in Tuskegee that began in 1890, and becoming active in National Association

Five. Reflections on Freedom, or Freedom Retold

of Colored Women organized in 1896, she was eventually invited by Du Bois to the Amenia Conference in 1916 (which described as an "interracial conclave of leaders assembled to discuss future of the race."[32]

The Farmers' Conferences became the Hampton-Tuskegee Negro conferences, which were concentrated in rural communities, while the Atlanta Conference highlighted urban issues such as poverty, low wages, and the rate of mortality for blacks. It led to some of the first social science studies on city-dwelling blacks in which Du Bois used Laney as investigator. "Her report to the First Atlanta conference in 1896 was on the 'Causes of Excessive Mortality: Poverty' and described conditions of blacks under city 'settlements'—mothers working extensive hours and fathers laboring for little pay, with both denied opportunities for decent employment."[33] Laney addressed the problems of parents who were employed outside of the home and still unable to provide sufficient time or financial resources for their children.

Laney did not only describe the problems in black communities, but she also offered solutions. At the Second Atlanta Conference, Laney presented topics such as "Mothers' Meetings," "Need of Day Nurseries," and "Need of Kindergartens" to the Women's Meeting attendees. McCluskey writes: "Each speaker proposed some special way in which African American women could or should be more useful to their communities. Dubbed the 'mothers' meetings,' these became the media for bringing effective instruction and practical strategies to the masses in matters religious and moral."[34] Laney also endorsed the idea in the conference of "day nurseries" for children while mothers worked, which likely led to her establishment of the first kindergarten for black children in Georgia.

Laney called motherhood "the greatest joy" and proclaimed that the race needs "'manly, God-fearing husbands'" and "'womanly, God-fearing wives.'"[35] As an observer, educator and scholar, Laney's rhetoric focused on religion, marriage and the maternal role as she discussed ways to enhance the institutions that withstood slavery and could potentially grow much stronger in freedom. She is also proof that everyone had a role to play in building up the community, from men and women improving their own domestic environments to other individuals supporting collective efforts of uplift.

If, in Jacobs' words, freedom did not come in the "usual way" with marriage, Laney's version did not include marriage or her own children. Yet, Laney's concern was with uplifting the entire race through her work.

Audrey Thomas McCluskey writes that Laney did not seek the spotlight and shunned romantic attraction. Richard R. Wright, Sr., Laney's Atlanta University classmate and a high school principal in Augusta, Georgia, called her "'the loveliest, most energetic and attractive brown skin girl he had ever met.'"[36] She publicly resisted his advances, although she is rumored to have had a relationship with him that even her friends were warned not to disclose. Du Bois referred to Laney as "'the vestal virgin who kept the fires of Negro education fiercely flaming,'" which shows that her motivation was not limited to her own romantic or domestic circumstances.[37] She engages a larger plight that establishes her as both activist and visionary. McCluskey states, "Despite her unmarried status, her advocacy of home life bestowed a halo of spiritual motherhood upon Laney.... She believed that it was largely the job of black mothers to eliminate the class-based gap between the educated and the masses."[38] If eliminating the class gap was the task of black mothers, then it was the task of black teachers, in Laney's perception, to spread this word to them. She inspired mothers to nurture their children as she did the same for them. Ironically, she fit the description of a teacher, as many school systems required them to be single.[39] However, Laney used her "unattached" position to navigate discursively among women and men, including Booker T. Washington and Du Bois.

Laney was a friend of Margaret Murray Washington, third wife to Booker T. Washington, but also had much in common with Mr. Washington. Laney chartered Haines Institute in 1886, only five years after Washington (then married to first wife Olivia Davidson Washington) founded Tuskegee.[40] Laney's model of a preparatory institution did not mirror Washington's, however, as she offered more academic than industrial courses. Mary McCleod Bethune apprenticed with Laney in 1896 before opening her own school in Daytona in 1904.[41] Du Bois, who admired Laney for her "principled, uncompromising advocacy on behalf of black people," visited Haines in 1917 to lecture on difference between industrial education and preparation of the "talented tenth" for race leadership. In an editorial in *The Crisis*, he wrote: "'There is fighting in Augusta ... a lone, little black woman waging war, not only against entrenched prejudice ... but also with traitors and hypocrites in her own race; men who know how to work with tourists for tidy sums by cringing and kowtowing. Yet, Lucy Laney triumphs even when her school is poor and half equipped.'"[42] Laney is recognized for overcoming on her own, but the community for which she works is also her greatest resource.

Education—something that black Americans were increasingly gaining access to and that could promote change in the home and in the community—was instrumental in most of Laney's proposals. Her early conference talks culminated in the 1899 "Burden of the Educated Colored Woman" at the Hampton Negro conference, where she addressed the need for more black women in teaching positions. The "educated colored woman," Laney argued, had different challenges to deal with than her white counterparts. In "The Burden of the Educated Colored Woman," Laney argues that the effects of slavery, in which "the foundation of right training and good government, the basic rock of all true culture the home … was not only neglected but utterly disregarded," still persist.[43] There was "no time in the institution," she argues for "mother's molding" and "woman's care."[44] Thus, despite the work of Phillis Wheatley and Sojourner Truth, "whose work and lives should have taught, or at least suggested to their instructors, the capabilities and possibilities of their dusky slave pupils," the leaders of the oppressive institution failed to find the best methods of development for boys and girls.[45]

For 250 years, Laney argues, marriages were illegal for blacks in southern states.[46] No attention was given to "homes and to home making," which are integral in child education and development.[47] The results of this failure to secure clean and safe domestic environments brought about "intellectual and moral death."[48] Thus, the burden for teachers was first a practical one, to spread knowledge of hygiene among people who had never been thus informed. Additional needs are to support men who have been accused unjustly of crimes and are therefore serving extended sentences. Both men and women must bear the burden of prejudice in both North and South, but Laney asserts, "No one suffers under the weight of this burden as the educated Negro woman does; and she must help to lift it."[49] As a formerly enslaved woman who used education to locate herself amongst the best and brightest minds of her time, Laney's insight into what an educated black woman should do was both personal and practical advice.

As a member of the group that suffered most, in Laney's words—likely because she could see and understand the opportunities that she had to work harder for, if she gained at all—Laney then charges black women with making others aware of opportunities and helping them advance. The black woman does this, Laney states, by serving as a physician to diagnose and prescribe a cure. "We would prescribe," she says, "home better homes, clean homes, pure homes; schools better schools; more culture; more thrift; and work in large doses." "Can woman do this work?" she asks, then answers, "She can; and she must do her part, and her part is by no means small."⁵⁰

The work with which she challenges black women as they move ahead as free people and into the twentieth century was to teach young children:

> Negro women of culture, as kindergartners and primary teachers have a rare opportunity to lend a hand to the lifting of these burdens, for here they may instill lessons of cleanliness, truthfulness, loving kindness, love for nature, and love for Nature's God. Here they may daily start aright hundreds of our children; here, too, they may save years of time in the education of the child; and may save many lives from shame and crime...⁵¹

Although rhetoric of African American uplift had been heard in other narratives by the time of Laney's speech, the morals she encourages black women, especially teachers, to instill, set a precedent for the progress of an entire younger generation. If these women "of culture" can "daily start aright" these children, they can put them on a strong educational path and prevent them from succumbing to crime. There is also pervasive rhetoric of respectability—with a good start, they can also be kept from shaming themselves and their families who have such high hopes for their opportunities.

Only years removed from an enslaved status herself, a formally educated Lucy Craft Laney analyzes the hindrances of Negro families from reaching their full potential and prescribes the women, especially in the role of teachers of young students, as the answer to instilling right moral guidelines. She uses this address, also published as an essay in the *Report of the Hampton Negro Conference* in July 1899, as a means to reflect on the challenges black people have faced but also as a means of projecting a brighter future. She metaphorically reconstructs a scene in which from a very young age, children are given hope and opportunities for success. By providing this support, black women are charged with a purpose and given the mission to help these children. The reconstruction of the black household comes from the entire family—the women in teaching life lessons and saving lives from "shame and crime," the men in the work that they do to support their families, and the children in becoming a new generation instilled with "cleanliness, truthfulness, loving kindness, love for nature, and love for Nature's God."⁵²

Five. Reflections on Freedom, or Freedom Retold

Educational models established by black women were able to develop students in ways that other institutions alone could not. Laney was very interested in improving the quality of domestic life (which was thought of primarily as the women's sphere) but believed such improvement would change African American lives overall. Thus, she encouraged marriage in order to establish secure homes although she chose a different path for herself. In her own childhood, both parents provided income, and Laney learned to read with her mother while her father became ordained in the Presbyterian church in Macon.[53] As an adult, Laney promoted black control of schools in addition to homes, control which depended on access to education.

The Freedmen's Bureau expired by limitation in 1869, except for the educational department (which ended in 1872, when Howard's work with the Bureau ceased) and the bounty department (which was transferred to a different office). Du Bois concludes with a eulogy on the "passing of a great human institution before its work is done" by arguing that "the legacy of the Freedmen's Bureau is the heavy heritage of this generation."[54] He ends his reflection on the Freedmen's Bureau with the prophetic statement that will begin his *Souls of Black Folk* two years later, "The problem of the twentieth century is the problem of the color line," announcing even in the first year of the century that racial issues will persist.[55] Even in his foresight, the question still remained as to the status of the woman throughout this strife. Du Bois offers one narrative of Reconstruction by tracing the history of the Freedmen's Bureau. His "freedman," however, was literally a man; women's perspectives were largely absent. Du Bois provides an organizational analysis for the failure to incorporate men into the nation, but the failure to provide for women is implicit as well.

Cooper and Laney offer another perspective by documenting the work of the woman after Emancipation. Laney's efforts were a combination of government and religious resources and her belief that the community would be perceptive to changes that would benefit them. Like many other institutions during the life of the Freedmen's Bureau, Laney would later receive funding from the American Missionary Association. She was initially denied the money she needed but persisted until her request was honored. She also, however, raised much of her own funding for Haines Institute.

As education became the central aim for the male leaders (having a system of public education became a prerequisite for readmission to the

Union), any previous tendencies toward relief-based aid disappeared.[56] Problems in reform were already occurring among organizations; the American Freedmen's Union Commission faced competition with the American Missionary Association over the mission of Reconstruction (the AMA, by virtue of its name, was invested in religious regeneration amongst freedmen), but in the end the AFUC failed to establish a public education system that included blacks and ceased operation in 1869.[57] The challenges already faced in reform became even greater obstacles to white women (and then, inherently black women), who tried to participate in Reconstruction.[58] Even in the 1866 Southern Homestead Act by Congress, most people could not afford inferior land and underwriting. For some black Americans to take up Sojourner Truth's proposal and move to a region they had never seen was a sign of her incredible efforts of promotion. Thus, reconstruction also occurred as people physically relocated and recreated their communities.

Emancipated black Americans merged various models of Reconstruction efforts as they created plans for gradual success. They worked within legal, educational, and domestic discourses in order to ensure democratic participation for themselves and their families. Literature also served as a means for having their voices heard. If, as Laney advocated, the educated Negro women could "teach Black Babies," the model established in the classroom could become replicated in homes.

Teaching Texts

Laney's report to the Hampton Negro Conference can be considered in a volume of texts used to educate—hers educates an audience of teachers and professionals on the status of black households and classrooms. There were also, however, an increasing number of texts used to teach freedmen how to improve themselves and raise their children after slavery. Comparing the examples of Laney, a former slave who expanded her opportunities through education, Cooper, a free black female educator, and white writers such as Lydia Maria Child who were more immediately removed from the subjectivity of slavery, demonstrates the diverse notions of what "teaching" after emancipation meant.

Child's collection, entitled *The Freedmen's Book*, would have been one used for the purpose of educating former slaves in such settings as

Five. Reflections on Freedom, or Freedom Retold

classrooms established by freedmen's aid and missionary societies. The intended message would also propose uplift from within African American communities, but the underlying assumption was that former slaves had few skills that would make them prosperous as free men and women. The address is at times infantilizing and it can be perceived that even some well-meaning abolitionist-turned reconstructionists believed that former slaves were incapable of being self-sufficient and therefore remained completely dependent on them.

In reality, many states refused to support freedmen schools and Northerners became increasingly resistant to any appearances of "charity" to the freedmen. Despite the fact, as Du Bois discussed, that freedmen contributed to their own schools through labor and whatever financial contributions they could secure, both men and some women expressed disdain for "giving" the freedmen anything.[59] Those women who advocated relief were criticized, but most organized activity ended by 1870 in general (except for the New England Freedmen's Aid Society, which continued to advocate Northern intervention and funding until 1876).[60] This was due to funding issues but also a lack of success in getting Southern states to endorse or aid their own public education systems, which did not become consistent during the tenure of the aid societies. Nevertheless, however, organizations such as the AFUC proclaimed success with no credit to the work done by the constituents they claimed to serve.[61]

One topic that Child and other missionaries and abolitionists shared was emphasis on caring for souls of children. The potential of freedmen to teach their children, however, was questioned. Books and methods that were used to teach freedmen often focused more on behavior than on academic knowledge. They were in line with codes (about employment) and preventing idleness rather than on encouraging excellence in the classroom. *The Freedmen's Book* that Child edited was one of these texts written to improve the "habits" of former slaves. In her own essay on "education," Child writes:

> It is hard for children born in Slavery to grow up spiritually straight and healthy, because they are trodden on when they are little. Being constantly treated unjustly, they cannot learn to be just. Their parents have no power to protect them from evil influences. They cannot prevent their continually seeing cruel and indecent actions, and hearing profane and dirty words. Heretofore, you could not educate your children, either morally or intellectually. But now that you are freemen, responsibility rests upon you. You will be answerable before God for the influence you exert over the young souls intrusted to your care. You may be too ignorant to

teach them much book-learning, and you may be too poor to spend much money for their education, but you can set them a pure and good example by your conduct and conversation.[62]

While lessons on conduct were necessary for any child, the assumption that former slaves could not teach and that children could not appreciate "book-learning" were those that African American teachers had to work against. Child's doctrine gives black parents the responsibility of educating their children but not the means to lead them in any way through a formal education process.

Texts such as Child's offered a neo-missionary approach by "teaching" freedmen the spiritual lessons that had already gotten many of them through difficult times as slaves. "This you should try your utmost to do, and should pray to the Heavenly Father to help you; for it is a very solemn duty, this rearing of young souls for eternity. That you yourselves have had a stunted growth, from being trodden upon when you were little, will doubtless make you more careful not to tread upon them."[63] Yet, one can look to texts such as Douglass' and Jacobs' to appreciate the capacity for self-teaching and passing on knowledge even under difficult circumstances.

One of Child's lessons was to "unbreak" children of lying, to which she argues that "Slaves, all the world, are generally much addicted" for fear of being flogged for mischief. She adds that "Slave-children" must also be broken of physical violence: "Slave-children, being in the habit of seeing a great deal of beating, early form the habit of kicking and banging each other when they are angry, and of abusing poor helpless animals intrusted [sic] to their care. On all such occasions parents should say to them: 'Those are the ways of Slavery. We expect better things of free children.'"[64] Ironically, the very behaviors Child believes children must be taught or dissuaded from—violence and deceit—are those practices that were exhibited by many slave masters. Such comments suggest not only the burden of behavior being placed in the hands of the very people whose children were never completely in their control to begin with. Despite the misplacement of blame, however, black teachers did not shirk the opportunity to set moral examples. Child believed that "moral education" was more important to children of former slaves than "reading and writing and ciphering," but Laney and others showed the ability to teach both.[65] Literary examples can also be used to show the ways that lessons were disseminated.

Laney as "Mother" and Cooper's Curricula

Lucy Craft Laney died on October 23, 1933, at her Philips Street home in Augusta, Georgia, and it is said ten thousand people attended her funeral service.[66] On the day of her funeral, Lucy Craft Laney was referred to as the "mother of the children of the people" by then-Howard University President Mordecai Johnson. In her efforts, Laney tried to prepare students for secondary school through a strong primary foundation. Supported by the Presbyterian Church, Haines provided students with both religious and secular fundamentals that established them amongst the best scholars in the country. As these children's "mother," she made sure that their education at Haines Normal and Industrial Institute was comprehensive and even mirrored the education that some of the pupils would go on to receive in college.

The *Red and Black* yearbook of 1923, a copy of which still remains intact at the Lucy Craft Laney Museum in Augusta, lists the topics taught between Primary grades and high school as Latin, English, History, Bible, Bookkeeping and Stenography, Science, Dramatics, French, Sewing, Teachers Training, and Music. School activities cited in the annual include Declamation, a pageant, a play, Junior-Senior reception, Baccalaureate, recitals, and oratorical contests. The "History of the School" in the book's introduction discusses the immense growth of the school from its founding in 1886: "Haines School has been recognized by educators the country over as the best preparatory school in the South. Graduates from this Institution enter many of the leading colleges of the country on their diplomas. At present the school has an enrollment of 842 pupils and 24 teachers."[67] This same history claims that Miss Laney "has worked untiringly for the Moral and Spiritual uplift of the Youth America" since its founding as well and, along with Assistant Principal Miss Mary C. Jackson, "built a school which is known throughout the length and breadth of the United States and in Foreign Lands."[68]

As Laney provides a study for what African American women should do for the children of their communities (embodying the fictional model provided by Harper in *Minnie's Sacrifice* and *Iola Leroy*, discussed in Chapter 4), Anna Julia Cooper writes what she observes in the African American community after Emancipation into a case study for *A Voice from the South*. Her voice is just one voice, but it becomes omniscient as it reflects on the need for a space for Black women in social development. Cooper is documentarian, historian, teacher, and guide as she presents life lessons and offers plans for the future.

In "Our Raison D'Etre," the opening to her 1892 collection *A Voice from the South*, Anna Julia Cooper argues strongly for the representation of African American women by themselves. She writes: "The 'other side' has not been represented by one who 'lives there.' And not many can more sensibly realize and more accurately tell the weight and the fret of the 'long dull pain' than the open-eyed but hitherto voiceless Black Woman of America."[69] With the phrase "open-eyed," Cooper offers an insightful metaphor in her description of the black woman. As Keckley watched the goings-on of the Lincoln household, witnessing things others would never have been able to, as Ellen Craft watched the white men around her with enough detail that she could imitate their every gesture, Cooper suggests that black women both experience and see the concerns and issues of America in a way that those of other races and genders do not.

Cooper does not go as far to accuse others of misrepresentation; she states: "As our Caucasian barristers are not to blame if they cannot quite put themselves in the dark man's place, neither should the dark man be wholly expected fully and adequately to reproduce the exact Voice of the Black Woman"; instead, her argument acknowledges the absence in accuracy without black women's input.[70] Cooper raises her own voice to make this acknowledgment. As she establishes her voice, she also brings light to areas that were left unseen.

Cooper offers what she calls "broken utterances" with the hope that they can "in any way help to a clearer vision and a truer pulse-beat in studying our Nation's Problem" (assumedly race relations).[71] Her essays, however, are both eloquent and well-supported. The first, "Womanhood a Vital Element in the Regeneration and Progress of a Race," is a case study of women's involvement in historical moments. It initially reads as a course on civilization, beginning: "The two sources from which, perhaps, modern civilization has derived its noble and ennobling ideal of woman are Christianity and the Feudal System."[72] Cooper establishes the history of women's capability to a time as early as her audience can possibly remember, thus suggesting that before any of them lived women played an essential role.

Cooper continues: "Our satisfaction in American institutions rests not on the fruition we now enjoy, but springs rather from the possibilities and promise that are inherent in the system, though as yet, perhaps, far in the future."[73] She marks an interesting dichotomy that connects the past with the future and leaves the present as a time to be moved past. Thus, she suggests that there is current dissatisfaction with American institutions but that the "inherent possibility" of the past could be recreated. She writes: "We have not yet reached our ideal in American civilization.... But there can be no doubt that here in America is the arena in which the next triumph of civilization is to be won; and here too we find promise abundant and possibilities infinite."[74] By setting America as the stage in her text for the "next triumph of civilization," Cooper both creates excitement about what the country could be and establishes herself as an authority for how such promise can be realized. From its very beginning, therefore, Cooper becomes a consultant on civilization and a guide to its improvement.

Before specifically mentioning women of color, Cooper argues that the "hope for our country primarily and fundamentally rests" on "the homelife and on the influence of good women in those homes" and even quotes Ralph Waldo Emerson that "'a sufficient measure of civilization is the influence of good women.'"[75] To return to the title of her essay, it is obvious that she is arguing for the recognition of womanhood in rebuilding and moving "a race" forward, but in her initial examples she makes women's visibility an issue for the human race in general. Cooper supports this argument with evidence of regard for women in European civilization and also with the Gospel of Jesus Christ, which preached "reverence for woman as woman regardless of rank, wealth, or culture."[76]

Cooper then presents a lesson plan for evaluating women through the perspective of the Gospel. She argues that "throughout his life and in his death [Christ] has given to men a rule and guide for the estimation of woman as an equal, and a helper, as a friend, and as a sacred charge to be sheltered and cared for with a brother's love and sympathy...," which defines women as a gift from God for a purpose and charges men with care and kindness. She then emphasizes that women develop the history of the church through their Christian influence.[77] Finally, Cooper summarizes that "the position of woman in society determines the vital elements of its regeneration and progress ... not because woman is better or stronger or wiser than man, but from the nature of the case, because it is she who must first form the man by directing the earliest impulses of his character."[78] Thus, this essay becomes a lesson on Christianity, civilization, and human character that places woman at the center of each. As a teacher,

Cooper provides evidence needed to make these cases, and it would be difficult to argue against her most effective case studies—history and religion.

Although she instructs her readers on past practices, Cooper does not let the past serve as the sole voice of reason. After establishing the means necessary to improve "a race," she charges women with using their God-given responsibilities to do so. She writes: "Woman, Mother,—your responsibility is one that might make angels tremble and fear to take hold! To trifle with it, to ignore or misuse it, is to treat lightly the most sacred and solemn trust ever confided by God to human kind."[79] She does not leave the men completely responsible for not recognizing women's gifts and talents; women must make their influence known. Thus, Cooper's lessons are addressed to a diverse audience—to all men who have not realized the influence of women in the history of the country's most powerful institutions and to women who have not asserted themselves in improving humankind.

Life Lessons and Moving Forward

Cooper makes the critical move to issues of progress within the African American race at this juncture by adding her argument to that of Dr. Alexander Crummell, a son of an enslaved father and free mother who became a priest, missionary, and nationalist. Cooper writes:

> I would beg, [however, with the Doctor (Crummell's) permission,] to add my plea for the Colored Girls of the South; that large, bright, promising fatally beautiful class that stand shivering like a delicate plantlet before the fury of tempestuous elements, so full of promise and possibilities, yet so sure of destruction.... Oh, save them, help them, shield, train, develop, teach, inspire them!... There is material in them well worth your while, the hope in germ of a staunch, helpful, regenerating womanhood on which, primarily, rests the foundation stones of our future as a race.[80]

As Cooper reflects on the past of American civilization in order to prove the necessity of women's work, she then reflects on the progress of African Americans since slavery. "The race is just twenty-one removed from the conception and experience of a chattel, just at the age of ruddy manhood. It is well enough to pause a moment for retrospection, introspection, and prospection."[81] Cooper uses this reflection to draw inspira-

Five. Reflections on Freedom, or Freedom Retold

tion based on scientific and emotional rhetoric. As she calls men to recognize women in her early arguments, she challenges other races to recognize African Americans as a productive race despite biological stereotypes: "There is something to encourage and inspire us in the advancement of individuals since their emancipation from slavery. It at least proves that there is nothing irretrievably wrong in the shape of the black man's skull, and that under given circumstances his development, downward, or upward, will be similar to that of other average human beings."[82] Cooper adds the elements of biology and natural selection to her argument; she makes a similar argument for equality due to the fact that given similar circumstances, the black man can produce in a manner similar to anyone else.

Cooper also argues that reflection should not be the dominant mode of planning; the race must actively move forward: "But this survey of the failures or achievements of the past, the difficulties and embarrassments of the present, and the mingled hopes and fears for the future, must not degenerate into mere dreaming nor consume the time which belongs to the practical and the effective handling of the crucial questions of the hour; and there can be no issue more vital and momentous than this of the womanhood of the race."[83] Without hesitation, Cooper asserts that the most important issue in making progress is allowing women to take their place in actively creating a brighter future for black men, women, and children.

Cooper finally places her concerns on the agenda with three strategic moves. First, she makes a discursive shift from physical to emotional matters: "Here is the vulnerable point, not in the heel, but at the heart of the young Achilles; and here must the defenses be strengthened and the watch redoubled."[84] With this transition she changes the focus of the audience to internal matters, strengthening from within in order to promote overall progress. She then suggests that the method of change is to move away from the past, which was not of the "American Negro's" design: "We are the heirs of a past which was not our fathers' moulding. 'Every man the arbiter of his own destiny' was not true for the American Negro of the past: and it is no fault of his that he finds himself to-day the inheritor of a manhood and womanhood impoverished and debased by two centuries and more of compression and degradation."[85] Cooper suggests that black Americans cannot help the past that they inherited, one that is rife with "degradation," but that they can recreate and regenerate their race. This ability to change, she argues, cannot be carried out but for the black woman: "Now the fundamental agency under God in the regeneration, the re-training of the race, as well as the ground work and starting point of its progress upward, must be the black woman."[86] In line with the argument later made by Lucy Craft Laney, Cooper says Black women must retrain the race to make it what is supposed to be.

The physical work once linked to men is no longer solely their responsibility. Cooper writes: "with all the wrongs and neglects of her past, with all the weakness, the debasement, the moral thralldom of her present, the black woman of to-day stands mute and wondering at the Herculean task devolving upon her. But the cycles wait for her. No other hand can move the lever. She must be loosed from her bands and set to work."[87] At this point, physical work of lifting the race is now responsibility of woman. But *others* must "loose," or permit her to do the task that is hers alone.

The essay ends with making concrete the need for women's efforts. Cooper argues: "Our meager and superficial results from past efforts prove their futility; and every attempt to elevate the Negro ... cannot but prove abortive unless so directed as to utilize the indispensable agency of an elevated and trained womanhood."[88] Returning to her internal revolution, she states: "A race cannot be purified from without.... We must go to the root and see that that is sound and healthy and vigorous; and not deceive ourselves with waxen flowers and painted leaves of mock chlorophyll."[89] It is not enough that others can see the accomplishments of African Americans from the surface (the "mock chlorophyll"); the race has to be healed and made healthy from its very root.

Cooper concludes that the work to be done is not based on individual efforts but on the improvement in the "parts" of the race that have been underrepresented and underused: "We too often mistake individuals' honor for race development and so are ready to substitute pretty accomplishments for sound sense and earnest purpose."[90] She states, "A race is but a total of families. The nation is the aggregate of its homes. As the whole is sum of all its parts, so the character of the parts will determine the characteristics of the whole."[91] This is the time, she offers, in which women will have their chance to work in the classroom and in the home to improve the nation.

In Cooper's analysis, reconstruction means the rebuilding of communities with the woman given the opportunity to lead. It extends beyond the legal reconstitution of the South and looks into the future in a way that that plan did not. By incorporating the black woman's role, she offers, the silence that has been inflicted on her can be broken. This includes the silence of mistreatment and abuse in slavery and the silence of being omitted from public discourse after slavery. In her opening, written at Tawawa Chimney Corner, Cooper writes:

> One muffled strain in the Silent South, a jarring chord and a vague and uncomprehended cadenza has been and still is the Negro. And of that muffled chord, the one mute and voiceless note has been the sadly expectant Black Woman,
>   An infant crying in the night,
>   An infant crying for the light;
>   And with no language—but a cry.[92]

Cooper likens the Black Woman to an infant—making her desires heard but still with room to develop in her means of expression. In her demands for women's inclusion in the rebuilding of the African American race after slavery, Cooper gives words to the cry she defines. Thus, the chord of progress can be heard more clearly.

The ideas expressed in *Voice from the South* perhaps propel Cooper to address the World Congress of Representative Women at Chicago's 1893 Columbian Exposition.[93] Like Laney, Cooper also promoted a "rigorous, classically based curriculum" at M Street School in D.C. (Cooper also offered industrial education). Cooper would continue to proclaim ideas of women's empowerment through the turn of the nineteenth century. In "Colored Women as Wage-Earners," published in the Southern Woman and Hampton School Record in 1899, Cooper remarked on marriage as "contractual relationship" in which the wife should earn part of her husband's wage because of her duties at home.[94] Although these ideas were newer in her time, they would draw interest as black women came to define themselves in the twentieth century due to the fact that many African Americans earned no wage at all just decades before.

African American women's narratives of reconstruction tell us the ways in which they promote their own versions of progress in addition to the ways they were connected in this endeavor. Cooper and Laney, both teachers themselves, make it their purpose to establish legacies of freedom on many levels. They are concerned with reconstructing African American children's lives within the classroom, but also in effect the lives of their families and in their homes. More than teaching one particular text, they issue curricula for living free lives.

These case studies offer the option that the curricula these women issue is the actual text. They use what they have done and learned to create a practical dictum for how to be. Documented in print, their lived experiences become literary history that is circulated to others who are emerging from institutional and metaphorical bondage. As in slavery, when status was determined by the mother, these "mothers" of the race take it upon themselves to pass information. Although neither Laney nor Cooper had their own children, they both metaphorically attempt to transfer the status of freedom to the next generation. Thus, freedom, knowledge, and consciousness can then be transferred without blood.

Laney actively creates a curriculum to promote a bright future for Southern students. Cooper positions herself in the past and creates a textbook for planning future efforts of progress. These and other women create a curriculum of freedom that circulates by means of formal education but has distinct applications for African Americans. This transfer of information through print sets a precedent for circulation of ideas into the twentieth century, including themes of uplift, respectability, and empowerment.

Epilogue
Freedom's Promise: Coming of Age Narratives in African America

For Harriet Jacobs, life was divided into the period before and after the age of fourteen, which she defined as the point when her master recognizes her as a woman. Jacobs wrote, "My mother's mistress was the daughter of my grandmother's mistress. She was the foster sister of my mother; they were both nourished at my grandmother's breast.... They played together as children; and, when they became older, my mother was a most faithful servant to her whiter foster sister."[1] Play, in this instance, was what demonstrated both the connection and the division between her enslaved mother and her mother's mistress to Jacobs. Although both women were nursed by Jacobs's grandmother—her mother's mother—and both played together as children, raised almost as sisters, age then established the division between slavery and freedom as her mother becomes her mistress's servant.

In her relationship with her own mistress, Jacobs wrote that her mistress was kind and would even sew by her side. She stated: "When she thought I was tired, she would send me out to run and jump" again positioning play as a "break" from labor.[2] However, Jacobs quickly iterated that "those were happy days, too happy to last" as she then divulged a narrative of attempts to escape sexual abuse from her master as she approaches her fourteenth year.[3] For Jacobs, "play" was also an imitation of freedom once she learned that the reality of slavery, first for her mother, and then for her, sets in.

She was, at adolescence, then unable to continue to "make-believe" that her childhood is innocent and equal to white children in the same way as before because reality destroys her play. Jacobs used "play" to identify problems such as not being the same color or having the same social status as her young mistress, which she then had to negotiate in real life (first within the institution of slavery and then through a quest for actual freedom). Analyzing the cultures of play specifically amongst girls-turned-women offers an alternative to the narratives of vulnerable womanhood that represent the genre. A modern context connects the ability of both men and women to see how play allowed them to work through circumstances of restriction and oppression.

In *Scenes of Subjection*, Saidiya Hartman specifically analyzes the vexed notion of "play" as it relates to activities in which enslaved persons participated: "Not only was pleasure posed in contrast to labor, but the negation or ambivalence of pleasure was to be explained by the yoking of the captive body to the will, whims, and exploits of the owner and by the constancy of the slave's unmet yearnings, whether for food or for freedom."[4] I argue that interpretations of a constructed reality then led to "assimilation" to an actual reality and the demands that accompanied that reality. For example, Frederick Douglass understood himself as first a "child" and then a "man" in each of his narratives (beginning with *Narrative of the Life of Frederick Douglass, an American Slave* in 1845 and continuing with *My Bondage and My Freedom* in 1855). This transition related not only to age, but to a feeling of control over his identity. This framework of the restrictive nature of pleasure also comes from Douglass's analysis of holidays as "the most effective means in the hands of the slaveholder in keeping down the spirit of insurrection … as conductors, or safety-valves, to carry off the rebellious spirit of enslaved humanity."[5] Without them, he argued, slaves would give in to desperation. In this text, slavemasters were both initiators of and partakers in this degradation—they played the "game" of freedom on the slaves only to remove any possibility of a victory for the other players.

An understanding of instrumental play provides readers of these texts with the tools to explore the possibility of transcending slavery that was realized even before the authors' narratives turned toward freedom. These moments set up the audience for understanding the narrators' desires for and realization of freedom. Furthermore, play served as a rehearsal for freedom as it allowed the narrating subjects to make sense of the world.

Defining Child's Play in Narratives of Enslavement

Historians often discuss the roles of men and women under the institution of slavery, but the plight of children (before they have come into defined gender roles as we understand them) is discussed less frequently.

Freedom's Promise

Perhaps this is because in many cases, there was not differentiation between an adult male and younger male and an adult female and younger female. At a certain age, they were expected to perform the same labor whether those duties were located inside or outside of the home. In some slave narratives, however, the author located himself or herself by a certain age, and that age generally denotes a transition in consciousness. Although the list of "coming of age" narratives of slavery is not conclusive, texts that have become established narratives of gender and enslavement in the African American narrative tradition also discuss these shifts in understanding of one's social status.

In the *Child's World of Make-Believe*, Jerome L. Singer describes the research of Karl Groos in 1901, in which Groos proposed that "play emerges out of natural selection as a form of necessary practice on the part of the child or immature organism for behaviors that are essential to later survival. In this sense, the playful fighting of animals or the rough and tumble play of children and many of the playful courtship activities of animals and children as well are essentially the practice of skills that will later aid their survival."[6] The survival skills that each of these authors are negotiating are those that secure their freedom. Make-believe for Jacobs as a child, for example, turned into her ability to negotiate spending seven years in her grandmother's cramped attic space awaiting her freedom and then playing the role of a sailor in order to escape to freedom. The ultimate goal, then, was the ability of "play" to help the restricted subject learn how to *live*. Hartman discusses this negotiation of enslaved bodies to subjugation through physical labor and amusement:

> Generally, the response of the enslaved to the management and orchestration of "Negro enjoyment" was more complex than a simple rejection of "innocent amusements"; Rather, the sense of operating within and against these closures made the experience of pleasure decidedly ambivalent ... pleasure was less a general form of dominance than a way of naming, by contradistinction, the consumption and possession of the body and black needs and possibilities.[7]

In this assessment, pleasure was used to control by possessing black bodies. However, the argument also allowed that leisure could be a way for enslaved persons to repossess their bodies from those who dominated them by the same means.

To return to Bretherton's argument: "Pretending simulates and transforms routine events from family life, storybooks, and television.... However, the ability to represent these scripts (and their distortions and

Epilogue

transformations) does not emerge fully fledged."[8] Although this analysis incorporates a contemporary media framework, it still addresses the ways in which the subject must transcend the gap of representation. Douglass, for example, could not "become" the master of his own fate without developing an understanding in closer proximity to a culture of enslavement than his childhood consciousness allowed. However, his immediate consciousness (at least in reflection) is one of what enslavement prevented, which was connection to his actual family and inability to grow up in a culture of sanctioned child's play.

Collectively, all of these narratives illustrate examples of "rhetorics of play" discussed by Brian Sutton-Smith in *Ambiguity of Play*. Specifically, the rhetorics of play as "power," "identity," and "the imaginary" theorize the very ways in which these narratives understand and engage the culture of play. Sutton-Smith defines the "rhetoric of play as power" as being "about the use of play as the representation of conflict and as a way to fortify the status of those who control the play or are its heroes."[9] The "rhetoric of play as identity ... [is] usually applied to traditional and community celebrations and festivals [and] occurs when the play tradition is seen as a means of confirming, maintaining, or advancing the power and identity of the community of players."[10] Sutton-Smith argues that "the rhetoric of play as the imaginary, usually applied to playful improvisation of all kinds in literature and elsewhere, idealizes the imagination, flexibility, and creativity of the animal and human play worlds."[11]

These various definitions cover both the "orderly play of girls in their folk games" and the "play of disorder: games of chance, of symbolic inversion, of carnival, of 'deep play,' as well as the 'games people play, 'war toys,' play-fighting, play therapy."[12] Reading play in narratives of enslavement as negotiation of social hierarchy, a means of confirming and advancing power and identity, and as a way to connect the imagined to the actual world help the reader to understand how these texts become a means of understanding and promoting their authors' versions of freedom. Playing roles allows narrating subjects to understand and foresee alternate realities to the ones that they endure. Collectively, these texts demonstrate ways in which play serves as regulation on one hand and on another as a transition to liberation. In each perspective, the significance lies in both who holds and who can interpret the instructions, rules and regulations, i.e., the means to "win."

To connect these narratives, activities of play served both as ways to bring together those "happy days" (as way to have slaves exercise and stay healthy) with reminders of the misery of slavery. This discussion on what play revealed in African American culture, however, did not end with slavery. In Booker T. Washington's 1901 narrative *Up from Slavery*, he articulated how sport was excluded from his own background as he devoted it to work after gaining freedom. He argued: "I was asked not long ago to tell something about the sports and pastimes that I engaged in during my youth. Until that question was asked it had never occurred to me that there was no period of my life that was devoted to play. From the time that I can remember anything, almost every day of my life has been occupied in some kind of labour; though I think I would now be a more useful man if I had had time for sports."[13] Washington equated "sport" not only to freedom, but also to the luxury that he was not allowed throughout his life that began with a period of enslavement. Yet, Washington later stated: "Games I care little for. I have never seen a game of football. In cards I do not know one card from another. A game of old-fashioned marbles with my two boys, once in awhile, is all I care for in this direction. I supposed I would care for games now if I had any time in my youth to give to them, but that was not possible."[14] This statement appears as almost disdain for games in lieu of both time and effort that could be directed somewhere else.

In one argument, Washington essentially thought sports might have made him useful if he were not too busy bringing himself up through work. In the other, Washington seemed more elite in his interests, except for games with his sons. In both, he reflected upon what was not possible for him as a youth because of labor. Yet, he suggested that there is something inherent that might be useful for those with time—fun, even. From the original idea of play as mockery, rules were set in place to regulate the participant's ability to challenge repressive aspects of society. In all of these narratives, however, play was used to negotiate identity, and later, even a socially respectable status for African Americans.

Narratives of the culture of play extended from the earliest known African American narratives through Civil Rights era narratives and into the modern period. Even some of the most memorable moments in my own childhood involved learning and passing down repetitive hand clapping games. Most were accompanied by singing and, at some times, other bodily movements. The most popular children's hand clapping song I remember, "Miss Mary Mack," is also one on which I can find little documentation or history. Some sources suggest that perhaps the song is named after a British ship *Merrimack* or a Confederate ship *Mary Mack*. Other sources cite the

Epilogue

song as "unknown" or just as a common street game. Joanna Cole and Stephanie Calmenson discuss the song in *Miss Mary Mack and Other Street Rhymes*, suggesting a perhaps more urban element to the story of Mary Mack "all dressed in black/with silver buttons/all down her back." However, I remember learning the song in two different versions—one from my mother, who was raised in a southern town in north Georgia, and the other was from classmates as I was also raised in a different small city in a different part of the state. The versions only differ slightly and there are dozens of similar songs and games that define "play" for African American childhood communities, but this reflection connects thematically and contextually to the ways the cultural significance of play is defined for African American boys and girls through centuries of slavery and into freedom.

Imagined and actual freedom is connected through a pattern first identified under an oppressive institution and into the restrictions of rural southern and even urban play. The traditions and ways of looking at play as not only escape but also transformation is critical; play has continued to have a role where processing of development is related not only to adulthood, but to childhood where play "begins" as well. Play serves as confirmation, modeling, and eventually transition into a world in which the narrator has the ability to comprehend and ultimately escape the ways in which he or she is objectified.

As I write this conclusion of a project that has been revised a number of times, originally focusing on narratives of freedom for African American women in the nineteenth century, then shifting to discourse about citizenship, freedom, and nation, and finally centering on how girls and women entered such a discourse, I am shaken by the very public events surrounding young black men in America, specifically, the deaths of Trayvon Martin in Florida (2012), Jonathan Ferrell in my own city of Charlotte, North Carolina (2013), and Michael Brown in Ferguson, Missouri (2014). At least one grand jury decision not to indict the shooter (a policeman, Darren Wilson, in Ferguson) came rather quickly, one case (against Zimmerman, who killed Martin in a neighborhood incident with competing stories), seemed to take forever to come to trial before Zimmerman was acquitted, and the trial for the officer who shot and killed Jonathan Ferrell is at this time stayed.

At the heart of these discussions, still, are the women, who are both living with and writing or speaking about these tragedies. Even with the fathers of these young men vocalizing their pain and frustration, the women who raised and now mourn these sons are the sources of sympathy and empathy for women across America. Martin's mother has been pictured with other mothers of slain children, including the mother of Jordan Davis, who was also killed in Florida in an incident over loud music (name was convicted of attempted manslaughter for shooting other teens in the car but not of murder). People mourn the loss of *our* black boys, for the lost potential, in addition to others ideals these young men would never grow to fulfill. And there can't help but to be a direct connection to the violence against men during the institution of enslavement, being beaten, killed, sold away from their families for any number of real or imagined perceptions of threat. Yes, we mourn for our boys for what they could not become. We mourn for their mothers for the men they will never get to see into adulthood. But what about the girls?

This is not a story of either or, of pick a side. "Bring back our girls" was the cry when over two hundred Nigerian schoolgirls were kidnapped by Boko Haram in April 2014. The "girls" have been located, but still not, to my knowledge, "brought back." The reference to *our* girls begs a question of the possessor and the possessed, in the same way that the young black male victims of violence are *our* boys.

This book then seeks to identify the stories of America's "other" daughters, African American girls and women in eighteenth and nineteenth century literature. Each story in this text is by a self-described or universally understood African American woman author, but I seek to go even further into their stories to get their sense of how they see themselves as girls in their literature even before they wrote themselves as women. At times, these ideas are connected, and at times, girlhood represents a sense of innocence that is marred by the time they reach womanhood. Examining these authors as "girls" in their own reflections, even into adolescence, helps a reading audience see how they came to understand their presence in America, as enslaved and as free women.

In 1885, the Washington Monument was dedicated in Washington, D.C., after 36 years of labor and construction. The following year, 1886, the Statue of Liberty was dedicated in the New York Harbor. By that time, Harper had been writing for over four decades, through the Fourteenth Amendment to the Constitution of 1868, stating, "Section 1. All persons born or naturalized in the United States, and subject to the jurisdiction thereof, are citizens of the United States and of the State wherein they reside. No State shall make or enforce any law which shall abridge the privileges or immunities of citizens of the United States; nor shall any

Epilogue

State deprive any person of life, liberty, or property, without due process of law; nor deny to any person within its jurisdiction the equal protection of the laws," the Fifteenth Amendment ratified in 1870, which declared that "right of citizens of the United States to vote shall not be denied or abridged by the United States or by any state on account of race, color, or previous condition of servitude," and the Civil Rights Act of 1875 that stated that no citizen could be denied equal use of public facilities. Through all of this time, however, black women (and some might argue, women, period), were not recognized as citizens under protection of these laws and privileges. As the Statue of Liberty stood, she was only a representation of what many of America's daughters could not have or do.

The original United States Naturalization Law of March 26, 1790, called "An act to establish an uniform Rule of Naturalization" is said to have provided the first of citizenship in the United States. It states,

> That any Alien being a free white person, who shall have resided within the limits and under the jurisdiction of the United States for the term of two years, may be admitted to become a citizen thereof on application to any common law Court of record in any one of the States wherein he shall have resided for the term of one year at least, and making proof to the satisfaction of such Court that he is a person of good character, and taking the oath or affirmation prescribed by law to support the Constitution of the United States, which Oath or Affirmation such Court shall administer, and the Clerk of such Court shall record such Application, and the proceedings thereon; and thereupon such person shall be considered as a Citizen of the United States.
>
> And the children of such person so naturalized, dwelling within the United States, being under the age of twenty one years at the time of such naturalization, shall also be considered as citizens of the United States. And the children of citizens of the United States that may be born beyond Sea, or out of the limits of the United States, shall be considered as natural born Citizens: Provided, that the right of citizenship shall not descend to persons whose fathers have never been resident in the United States: Provided also, that no person heretofore proscribed by any States, shall be admitted a citizen as aforesaid, except by an Act of the Legislature of the State in which such person was proscribed.

This act addresses those ideals key to the founding of America, including character, but also by its very nature excluded both sons and daughters of African descent (note specifically the connection to paternity when enslaved children followed the status of the mother, the ways enslaved men and women then counted as 3/5 person by the Constitution, and even the reality that one's birth and age had to be documented even to gain admission to the courts).

Paternity could be traced in such laws and acts only in some cases, and in most of them, maternity did not matter. The original "daughters" would have been thought to be the women of the American Revolution and Republic—wives of men who fought wars, signed the founding documents of the country, and who filled in when the men were gone. The secret Society Daughters of America was founded in 1891 as an auxiliary of the Junior Order of United American Mechanics, which decided to form a Daughters of Liberty group after the older Order of United American Mechanics founded the Daughters of Liberty auxiliary for ladies in the 1870s. When the older group objected to the replication by the junior order, they formed the "National Council, Daughters of American," chartered in Allegheny County, Pennsylvania (http://www.joycetice.com/flaghold/flag018.htm).

Originally, the order was open to white American women over sixteen, as well as members of the JOUAM. In 1979, the order was described as open to "'patriotic, white male and female citizens of good moral character, who believe in a supreme being as the creator and preserver of the Universe and who favor the upholding of the American Public School System and the reading of the Holy Bible in the schools thereof, must be opposed to the union of Church and State; must be literate and capable of giving all the secret signs and words of the Order...." (Tri-Counties Genealogy & History). Many stories of the actual daughters have yet to come to light. But even in the metaphorical sense, we can look at Phillis Wheatley as a daughter of America even when not recognized as such. The Daughters of America was still thought to be in existence as late as 1997, when members were still required to endorse the Daughters of America mission statement "to instill a spirit of patriotism into the youth of our land; to place our flag over every schoolhouse; to promote the reading of the Holy Bible therein; and to protest against the immigration of paupers, criminals, and the enemies of our social order."

But what did it mean for black women to be daughters of America, in many cases, illegitimately conceived, unclaimed, and uncared for by prevailing institutions? In order to counteract and contradict the elimination of black men and women from national dialogues during their lifetime, each woman in this study used her status as a black woman (rather free or enslaved, or born to free or enslaved parents) to write them and their families in as well.

In "Representing the Social World in Symbolic Play: Reality and Fantasy," Inge Bretherton refers to Jean Piaget's 1962 notion of "play" as an "essential part in the development of operations ... that alone make the coherent representation of reality possible. Hence, pretending only continues so long as the child cannot effectively accommodate to the real world."[15] In texts written by such noted authors in African American history as Frederick Douglass, Harriet Jacobs, and Booker T. Washington, children's play is discussed as a means of the negotiating the social hierarchy of enslavement. These texts, which are either directly situated within or connected to the genre of slave narratives, also presented games as a means by which enslaved children were made to rehearse their future roles as adult slaves. Through their play, they began to form their adult identities and gain a greater understanding of their social status. In some cases, however, these narratives demonstrated how play occasionally allowed enslaved children to transcend the social hierarchy associated with slavery. Play provided boys and girls a space where they could manipulate social rules and assume, at least temporarily, the identities of free people. Finally, play made the transition from "enslaved" to "free" possible for enslaved authors, first in their consciousness of status and even later in the way they represented themselves.

Death was another site of exploration of freedom, as articulated by Gwendolyn Brooks's poetry. Perusal of any of Brooks's collected volumes, including *The World of Gwendolyn Brooks* (1971) and *Blacks* (1987), reveals the breadth of her materials over the long span of her career. Brooks writes about women she could have known in Chicago, Illinois, including mothers, domestic laborers, sisters, friends. Her poems, however, also reveal elements of tragic black masculine experiences—men who die in war, in the streets of Chicago, and even in alleys. It is hardly unusual for an artist to effect a cross-gendered poetic self, even among Brooks's predecessors and contemporaries. Langston Hughes' "Mother to Son," for example, assumes a black maternal voice. Yet it is significant that Brooks writes herself into multiple traditions—female, African American, and modernist poetry—using multiple poetic styles (including the sonnet, balled, elegy, and free verse) and by telling male stories. Adaptations of both formal tradition and gendered personae are characteristics of Brooks's revisionist poetic style, including the use of traditional forms—the sonnet and the ballad—to attend to death.

By invoking the sonnet, Brooks gestures toward the long tradition of the sonnet, dating to the Petrarchan tradition of the 1300s (when Francesco Petrarch wrote 317 romantic sonnets in Tuscany to his idealized lover [Strand and Boland, *Making of Poetry*, 56]). Instead of invoking the attention of an outside lover, Brooks instead uses the form to ask the reader to reflect on an experience represented inside the work.

Published as the last poem in Brooks's 1945 volume *A Street in Bronzeville*, the poem "Gay Chaps at the Bar" might suggest just another stop in a black Chicago neighborhood. Its location at the end of the book could superficially be perceived as closure for the volume as a whole: the workday ends in the bar; the weekend can be spent in the bar. The bar is more than just a physical space; it is associated with notions of leisure and relaxation, a construct that opposes a place of labor. "Gay Chaps at the Bar" could easily reflect these concepts of masculine pleasure, but the epigraph of the first sonnet, a quote from Lieutenant William Couch, immediately subverts these associations: "and guys I knew in the States, young officers return from the front crying and trembling. Gay chaps at the bar in Los Angeles, Chicago, New York" (768). Brooks's speaker suggests that the "guys" returning from World War II are the ones in the bar, trying to forget what they have seen and experienced. She suggests that they are the ones in the bar who never went to war and who drink, oblivious to what their peers have gone through. The sequence is for those who need to know about a World War II experience for black soldiers and a tribute to those who already know it well, like Brooks's brother Staff Sergeant Raymond Brooks (for whom this poem is subtitled a "souvenir" [Nelson 768]). These sonnets serve all of these purposes. As the original volume in which they were published takes a reader through "a street in Bronzeville," this sequence takes the reader inside a bar and behind a "gay" post-war façade.

In "Hysterical Ties: Gwendolyn Brooks and the Rise of a 'High' Neo-modernism," James Edward Smethurst cites Brooks's "high" neomodernist style in her second volume of poetry, *Annie Allen* (1949) as "a deliberate attempt by an African-American narratorial consciousness to create an 'international' modernist documentation of the African-American subject," developed out of concerns of the "'high' cold war" (164). This style is characterized by Brooks's assumption of an "authenticating" voice that can relate the conditions of African American "folk" and the ability to penetrate and critique mass-culture. Brooks is inside this culture, Smethurst argues, and assumes a "'double consciousness' of assertion and alienation" (167). These effects are also present in the "Gay Chaps" sequence, where Brooks assumes a voice that is neither masculine nor explicitly feminine. These sonnets voice a perspective that is aware of the multiple experiences of war but is also aware of the experiences of being black in America. Brooks reminds the readers that burying practices are not the most important matters in the context of the poem—the country is at war, and men are dead.

Epilogue

Despite the alteration of the rhyme scheme, and at least the way it figures in the use of a high art form itself, the final point is that regardless of subject, the sonnet still narrates the theme of dead black bodies.

Brooks demonstrates formal mastery of the sonnet while shifting traditional content, disturbing expected rhyme schemes, among other changes. Smethurst argues that Brooks "mocks" the literariness of middle-class African American soldiers speaking; I would add that she also mocks the idea that training white soldiers to act without recognizing humanity is a farce. Brooks expands the subjectivity a sonnet can represent and revises the ways black subjects can be represented in poetry.

In addition to the fourteenth-century Petrarchan sonnet tradition Brooks also inherits the twentieth-century African American sonnet traditions produced by Langston Hughes, Claude McKay, and Countee Cullen. Although McKay, who published sonnets the earliest of the three men, stayed very close to established sonnet forms (often utilizing the Eliazbethan pattern, which consists of three quatrains and a couplet), he revised the subjectivity that sonnets had produced (e.g., "The Harlem Dancer" and "The Lynching," *Nelson, Anthology of Modern American Poetry*, 315–316). McKay's reveal the alternate self of a Harlem dancer, who represents something other than the body that people see. In "If We Must Die," one of his most famous sonnets, McKay challenges his people to die nobly by fighting like men.

The emotions McKay's sonnets portray include the anger, bitterness, hatred, and sorrow of being black in America. Cullen's "Yet Do I Marvel" also incorporates irony as he reflects on why God would have created a black poet. Hughes' oeuvre also includes these elements of irony and tragedy, along with a sarcastic humor that helps him mediate black American experiences. As both a literary predecessor and personal mentor, Hughes influences Brooks to combine themes and styles of the Harlem Renaissance with those of Modernist poetry.

In addition to skillful manipulation of the sonnet form, Hughes, and then Brooks, also use the ballad to represent black experiences. This form has a very different style and history than the sonnet; while the former has a European courtly association, the ballad was established as a medium of the "folk." The Irish balladeer, Strand and Boland write, was a village citizen and storyteller. The English balladeer stood outside the court reminding the people of their history through song. In America, the historically oral form became part of the poet's written vocabulary.[16] The ballad is characterized by its communal narrative and often marked by dialogue, elements to which Hughes and Brooks adhere as they tell folk stories.

Hughes' "Ballad of the Landlord," published eighteen years before Brooks's "Ballad of Rudolph Reed," is narrated by a Negro tenant whose complaint to a landlord about a leaky roof lands him in jail. The fixed abcb rhyme scheme and careful attention to meter mark the deliberateness with which Hughes employs this form. The straightforward dialogue about a black tenant who is jailed when a landlord refuses to do his job and fix his leaky roof makes it easy to convey a story about an ironic experience. Like Hughes, Brooks also incorporates the four-line stanzas, meter, and rhyme scheme of a traditional ballad as she returns to the theme of black men dying in "The Ballad of Rudolph Reed." Although Reed is not the narrator of his own experience, as the subject of the poem, he encounters a white housing agent who encourages him to move in, knowing, it seems, that the white homeowners would cause trouble for the family (line 21). Continuing an example set in "the white troops had their orders," Brooks uses death to show the ultimate costs of racism.

The beginning of the ballad establishes an African American subjectivity; Rudolph and his wife are described in a way that relates them to strong and brown oak trees. Their children are respectable, and they are growing into likenesses of their parents. When Rudolph speaks in the second stanza, it is in standard English, as he longs for a house where he, as a man, can protect his children from stirring plaster and falling roaches. As in "white troops had their orders," the poetic voice constructs a tension between dark bodies and "the Other"; here, the neighbors see the differences that Rudolph and his family are too excited to notice. Initially, not Rudolph neither smiles nor curses while moving in. Like Brooks's "song in a front yard," the poem is very visual and features a elegantly bannistered stairs and and the potential of a garden in the front yard. Reed still offers no unkind words when the first two rocks come through his window. As the lines mark the time passing from the first night to the second and third, Rudolph is still oaken until his daughter Mabel's gaze is finally stained by broken glass.

After transforming to angry, the description of Rudolph's rampage is still literal. He then turns into an objectified mad person, who wields a butcher knife and acts with his hands to hurt four white men. The ballad ends with Reed remaining in a permanent state of inactivity, as he is killed. Furthermore, the neighbors kick his dead body and call him "nigger," another transition in his initial definition of "man." After Reed moves into the house with his family who is physically described as dark, his temperament darkens, and he is finally marked with the ultimate racial slur. There are only two descriptors in the final stanza, the hard brown eyes of Rudoph's wife and the blood-stained gauze of young Mabel.

Continuing Smethurst's argument that Brooks's use of the ballad invokes imprisonment and repression rather than release, I argue that Brooks uses the ballad as a way to "arrest" death, to freeze a tragic moment and then tell its story.[17] Her use of the lyric voice disrupts the distinction between the empirical and poetic selves; the speaker could be an eyewitness to Rudolph Reed's demise who is close enough to even hear the words he utters or an omniscient reporter of a politicized narrative.[18] Brooks's use of the sonnet and the ballad also set the stage for her transition to representing similar themes in free verse poetry, including "The Boy Died in My Alley" (1971), in which she implicates herself and a literal or figurative family in the death of an unnamed boy. Symbolically, she manipulates a number of traditions and then finally eludes a set form to tell a universal story of death.

As nineteenth-century women writers use fictional and nonfictional narrative forms to make their audiences aware of their experiences, Brooks moves her readership through the timeline from the poetics of the Harlem Renaissance to Black Arts Movement feminist aesthetics and covers a range of topics in between.[19] Her use of traditional forms in writing about death demonstrates that any form can be used to reflect African American experiences. Brooks adapts structure and manipulates content in her poetry to write about death. While not the only subject she represents, Brooks' poetry, and that of her predecessors in African American literary traditions, would not be what it was without the violation and variation of various standard forms as she incorporates and utilizes poetic traditions to liberate her subjects from their circumstances.

Coda: From Jacobs to Giovanni—Poetics of Liberation

Nikki Giovanni, who has written for decades around issues of black liberation, published a range of poetry in the 1960s and 1970s and continues to publish today. Her work emerged, however, in a context of black women who were writing and acting within movements to counteract racism in the United States. Described by Virginia Fowler as one of the "angry young poets of the 1960s," Giovanni found her voice after helping to reinstate the chapter of the Student Nonviolent Coordinating Committee (SNCC) at Fisk University, where she began her undergraduate career. In 1967, she published her first poetry collection (*Black Feeling*). In the following three years, Giovanni published two additional volumes: *Black Talk* (1968) and *Black Judgment* (1970). Collectively, these texts propelled her into the role as a representative of issues that black people, and specifically black women, were facing in society: "[They] secured her reputation as one of the most accessible of the young writers whose poems encouraged black solidarity and revolution, and she soon became the most prominent women writer of the Black Arts Movement," writes Lisa Clayton Robinson (840).

When Stokely Carmichael, head of SNCC, issued a call for "Black Power" in his 1966 speech "What We Want," he seemed to refer to power for black communities as a whole: "'Where Negroes lack a majority, black power means proper representation and sharing of control" (Carmichael, *Let Nobody Turn Us Around*, 445). The primary goal of the movement—for black Americans to take control of their communities and change the way they were treated in society—was challenged by previous statements, including one by Carmichael himself, that all blacks should not be included in its attainment. Only two years earlier, Carmichael had made the statement that "'the only position of women in SNCC is prone'" (qtd. in Wallace, 7).

In these contradictory statements, one suggesting uniting a community in order for it to take its rightful place in society, the other asserting that the only job women were suited for in this revolution was in the bedroom, Carmichael illustrated a major barrier to women's involvement in the Black Power Movement. How could women who were ready and willing to help black people progress and effect change when some of their most vocal critics were members of their own race? It was possible, but it made the journey toward liberation bittersweet. Instead of entering an environment of collective advancement, these women had to prove they deserved to help lead the fight for liberation.

Elaine Brown, who played an invaluable role in the development of the Black Panther Party, was one of the leaders within this male dominated movement. Angela Davis worked to free the Soledad Brothers from a California prison and was indicted in allegations of armed kidnapping. Black women poets associated with the Black Arts Movement, including Nikki Giovanni and Sonia Sanchez, were also revolutionary and activist women.

Epilogue

Their arenas may have ranged from intimate audiences to large masses. Their tools of liberation may have been pens instead of weapons, but like Brown and Davis, they wrote about and acted for the same causes of which Brown and Davis spoke—freedom for all black people. Within both the political atmosphere of the Black Power Movement and the literary environment of its artistic counterpart, the Black Arts Movement, women had the difficult task of defining themselves against negative stereotypes and proving they were qualified to participate in the struggle for black representation in America.

Like Hurston and others, Giovanni expresses the urgency of responding to the position of black males in society. In "Poem (No Name No.2)," published in 1968, for example, Giovanni uses the repetition and permutation of six simple words to express the urgency of a black male response to racism and discrimination. Giovanni calls for bitterness from her male counterparts because this strong expression of emotion evokes response: "brothers" must get angry enough at their oppression that it moves them to respond. Giovanni's speaker has no patience for those who refuse to get involved in a common struggle for recognition. Additionally, it is not enough to seek this disdain or eventual rejection of actions against them, but they must do so immediately (*Selected Poems*).

Besides issuing calls for participation in the Black Power Movement, Giovanni uses poetry to redefine the roles that women were supposed to play in the revolution. In "Seduction," she narrates an intimate encounter with a revolutionary black man in which the woman takes control. Undermining prescribed rules of inferiority and re-imagining interactions in the spaces that women often inhabited in movement politics, Giovanni's female persona makes herself visible, directing the physical interaction with her partner and refusing to yield to the demands of the male persona echoed in Black Power rhetoric. The woman's removal of her partner's dashiki takes him out of his role of revolutionary leader. In this encounter, he is under command. The reversal of action here is another form of civil discourse. The speaker's gentle manner as she engages her partner's body demonstrates that there was still a need and a place for love in the midst of revolutionary action.

Sandi Russell writes, "Black women [in the Black Power Movement] were to understand and console their men" (87). Giovanni's poetry represents the response of women to the command that they be submissive. Giovanni uses direct interactions in poetry to write specifically about revolutionary politics as well as to comment on the condition of women, as in "Woman Poem," where she wishes she knew what freedom felt like (55). She praises the "beautiful" black men with afros while establishing her own career as she redefines black women within a movement that might have kept them out of the forefront.

As Houston A. Baker, Jr., and others note, the Black Arts Movement used performative, musical, authentic, and affective sounds of a black voice committed to struggle [to] serve as persuasive and effective weapons in the campaign to liberate a black nation" (Norton Anthology, 1797). The movement allowed women writers to call for their own liberation as well. Nikki Giovanni was able to write about the condition of black women and also urge African Americans to seize control of their positions in society. Giovanni created an alternative role for herself through art and used literature to express concerns that women experienced on a daily basis.

Harriet Jacobs redefined what it meant to be a Black woman writer in the 1860s, as Giovanni redefined the term "revolutionary" in the 1960s and 1970s. Her poetry articulates concerns of gender and activism in the Black Power Movement but also pays special attention to the conditions of black women. This new definition is broad enough to accommodate those who express their commitment to creating a more progressive society through writing and through creating a sense of community, as she asks in her 1975 volume *The Women and the Men*, if anyone wants to play in the new world she has a desire to create. Giovanni is revolutionary because she uses her writing to express her concerns within the "land of liberty." She is revolutionary because she believed, as she told Hobson and Smith (3) that "all black artists must be responsive to their community" (3). She truly used words as her tools of liberation.

Situating black women writers within their times and showing how their writing served as cultural criticism and critique, we can place such writers as Ntozake Shange, Gloria Naylor, Alice Walker, and Toni Morrison within their traditions and upon the themes of black women's identity. From Harriet Jacobs to Zora Neale Hurston to Nikki Giovanni, and including all the women who wrote beside and with them, women in male-dominated artistic periods, women have used tools of address, cross-gendering, staging, and other rhetorical tools to make themselves heard.

In *From #BlackLivesMatter to Black Liberation* (2015), Keeanga-Yamahtta Taylor connects African Americans' struggles for freedom after the Civil War ended in 1865 through World War II the #BlackLivesMatter

Epilogue

Movement that was formalized with the hashtag by Black women Patrisse Cullors, Opal Tometi, and Alicia Garza to bring attention to what Taylor calls the "expansive nature of Black oppression" (166). Quoting Garza, Taylor cites the women's focus through their movement against police brutality on state violence. Garza stated, "It is an acknowledgment Black poverty and genocide is state violence. It is an acknowledgment that 1 million Black people are locked in cages in this country—one half of all people in prisons or jails—is an act of state violence. It is an acknowledgment that Black women continue to bear the burden of a relentless assault on our children and our families and that assault is an act of state violence."[20] Continuing with Garza's definitions to include Black queer and trans folks, undocumented immigrants, Black girls, and "Black folks living with disabilities and different abilities" in the focus on state violence, Taylor argues, "the declaration of 'state violence' legitimizes the corollary demand for 'state action'" (167). The work of these organizers starts, Taylor argues, "from the basic recognition that the oppression of African Americans is multidimensional and must be fought on different fronts" (167). Thus, the fights for Black liberation, as documented through each of these periods discussed in this book, address each author's individual context(s) of enslavement, racial and gender discrimination, and segregation. Taylor argues:

> It should go without saying that Black women have always played an integral role in the various iterations of the Black freedom struggle. Whether it was Ida B. Wells, who risked her life to expose the widespread use of lynching in the South, or the mothers of the wrongfully accused Scottsboro Boys, who toured the world to build the campaign to free their sons, Black women have been central to every significant campaign for Black rights and freedom [165].

Beginning with black women's literary activism in the nineteenth century, documenting their interventions into campaigns to have their own freedom realized and recognized is indeed the claim of this book. This project is ongoing, as there are numbers of women who could be mentioned and whose work has yet to be realized. However, as Cooper argues, "looking back" is a first step.

Chapter Notes

Preface

1. http://www.npr.org/sections/codeswitch/2016/07/07/485078670/two-days-two-deaths-the-police-shootings-of-alton-sterling-and-philando-castile.

Introduction

1. Harris Perry, *Sister Citizen*, 20.
2. *Ibid.*, 8.
3. *Ibid.*, 21.
4. Martinez, *On Making Sense*, 159.
5. *Ibid.*
6. Reid-Pharr, *Once You Go Black*, 17.
7. I employ Evelyn Brooks Higginbotham's definition of the "politics of racial respectability" in *Righteous Discontent*.
8. Jacobs, *Incidents in the Life of a Slave Girl*, 207.
9. Sanmartin, *Black Women as Custodians of History*, 33.
10. Sanmartin, 39.
11. *Ibid.*, 47.
12. Fleischner, *Mastering Slavery*, 7, 55.
13. Invoking martial law, General John C. Frémont declared free the slaves of disloyal owners in Missouri; President Lincoln asked that he modify his order so as not to exceed congressional laws respecting emancipation (Berlin).
14. In April of 1862, at Lincoln's request, Congress pledged financial aid to any state that undertook gradual emancipation with compensation to owners. In May, General David Hunter declared free all slaves in South Carolina, Georgia, and Florida. This edict was nullified by Lincoln, who instead urged border states to embrace gradual, compensated emancipation, and, eventually, colonization outside of the United States. In September of 1862, Lincoln issued a Preliminary Emancipation Proclamation freeing all slaves in those states or portions of states still in rebellion as of January 1; these efforts culminated in his Emancipation Proclamation of January 1, 1863, which legally emancipated all slaves in select Confederate states. Emancipation history is discussed in detail by Ira Berlin and Darlene Clark Hine.
15. Darlene Clark Hine discusses the efforts of contraband wives in *A Shining Thread of Hope*, 129.
16. In *Unequal Freedom*, Evelyn Nakano Glenn argues that "in the United States, race and gender have been simultaneously organizing principles and products of citizenship and labor" (236). She reads the ways that unequal racial and gender relations have required expanded conceptualizations of citizenship. I argue in this vein that many black women extend their practices beyond the rules and regulations of local and national governments which exclude them; freedom is not only granted, but also assumed.
17. Grasso, *The Artistry of Anger*, 10.
18. Morrison, *Playing in the Dark*, 5.
19. In a more comprehensive literal explication of the terms, "liberation" might be considered a physical act that is enacted by an outside party, while "freedom" is more ambiguous and can also be metaphorical or psychological; there is more leeway in the latter term for self-perception and self-enablement. One can (but may not necessarily) consider oneself "free" without being liberated by another person or by legal acts from someone or something.
20. Anderson, *Educating Blacks in the South*, 30.
21. Frances Smith Foster, introduction, *A Brighter Day Coming* (xii–xix).
22. *Iola Leroy*, 9.
23. Harper, 15.

Notes—Chapter One

24. Challenges of publication were great for many of these writers: Jacobs, for example, had several failed publication efforts including a signed contract with Thayer and Eldridge (who also published an edition of Walt Whitman's *Leaves of Grass*), who went bankrupt. Jean Fagan Yellin discusses Jacobs' publication history in *Harriet Jacobs: A Life*. Keckley experienced a different type of publication difficulties, as the book's release was opposed by Mary Todd Lincoln's son (Women in History, Elizabeth Keckley biography, Lakewood Public Library, http://www.lkwdpl.org/wihohio/keck-eli.htm).

25. Hamilton, Jay, and Madison in *The Federalist Papers*.

26. In *Liberation Historiography*, John Ernest states the need to discuss how African Americans came to understand their historical status in the nineteenth century via multiple dialogues. Because there is no singular record of African American history, he argues, readers must consider a mix of discourses that composed African American historical writing (i.e., examine the "fragments" of African American experiences) in order to understand the production of historical literature.

27. In many influential histories of the emancipation and Reconstruction periods, including seminal texts by W.E.B. Du Bois and Eric Foner, there is a conspicuous absence of attention to black women. In the rhetoric of Emancipation itself, black women are under national surveillance but read primarily in relation to black male bodies. Additionally, Reconstruction is often written about in historical analyses but seldom discussed for its implications in literature. Histories published by Nell Painter and Darlene Clark Hine have filled in such absences in black women's history, and this study extends their investigations into the discipline of literature.

28. Hine, *Shining Thread*, 149.

29. My version of "freedom narratives" lies in between the narratives of enslavement and "liberatory narratives," as defined by Angelyn Mitchell in *Freedom to Remember*. These narratives often end with freedom, but the terms on which freedom is achieved, I argue, are as significant as the efforts and experiences leading toward it.

30. Forten's family was of the black middle class in Philadelphia.

31. Harper, *Iola Leroy*, 234.

32. *Ibid.*, 271.

33. Texts that address the duties of mothers toward cultivating the patriotism of their sons in the early American literature include *Patriotism and the Female Sex* by Rosemary Keller (Brooklyn: Carlson Publishing, 1994) and *Letters of John and Abigail Adams: 1762 to 1826* (New York: Westvaco, 2001). Linda K. Kerber coined the term "republican motherhood" in *Women of the Republic: Intellect and Ideology in Revolutionary America* (Chapel Hill: University of North Carolina Press, 2007).

34. This argument aligns with Hazel Carby's attention to early black women's writing as the source of black feminist thought and politics in *Reconstructing Womanhood* and with John Ernest's descriptions of the reformative power of African American writing in *Resistance and Reformation*.

35. Cooper, 27.

36. In *National Manhood*, Dana Nelson considers national discourse as a means of promulgating white masculinity during a period of anxiety. Her earlier book, *The Word in Black and White*, offers literature as a means for women to "stake out a clear position of subjectivity for [themselves]" (133) and reformulate the "social, political, and economic axes along which power is distributed and identities are constructed" (133).

37. Foster, *Written by Herself*, 186.

38. Cooper, 31.

39. *Ibid.*, 281.

Chapter One

1. Hurston, 14.
2. *Ibid.*, 15.
3. *Ibid.*, 14.
4. Ibid., 16.
5. *Ibid.*, 19.
6. *Ibid.*
7. *Ibid.*
8. *Ibid.*
9. *Ibid.*, 19.
10. *Ibid.*, 32.
11. *Ibid.*, 192.
12. By Howard University president Mordecai Johnson at her funeral.
13. Spillers, "Mama's Baby," 70.
14. *Ibid.*, 71.
15. See Deborah Gray White, *Arn't I a Woman*, Chapter 4.

Notes—Chapter Two

16. In Mitchell, *Righteous Propagation*, 2.
17. The Jacobs' school is discussed in "Jacobs School." *The Freedmen's Record*, March 1865. Nambi E. Kelley, Steppenwolf Theatre site on Harriet Jacobs, http://blog.steppenwolf.org/2008/03/06/harriets-legacy/#more-270.
18. Deborah Gray White both addresses the history of the organization and gives examples of specific meetings.
19. Gray White, 22.
20. Mitchell, 108.
21. *Ibid.*, 112.
22. *Ibid.*, 113.
23. Such restricted behaviors included sex outside of wedlock or open sexual attentions (Mitchell 115). Mitchell states: "conduct manuals linked character to collective salvation as they attempted to achieve far more than uplift and respectability for African Americans. The genre enabled authors to articulate concepts that the race shared a destiny, that individuals could impact collective welfare by their purposefulness—or carelessness" (109).
24. Mitchell, 113.
25. The introduction to Forten's *Journals* states that she and Grimke were extremely close; Forten even served as her guardian while her father served the consul of Santo Domingo. Both Angelina and her father Archibald lived with Charlotte Forten in her home before she died (Stevenson, 54).
26. This sister movement to the Black Power Movement of the 1960s and 1970s signaled a return to black authority and consciousness—progress on their own terms rather than those of an outside society.
27. Mitchell, 8.
28. Spillers argues, "The relative silence on the record on this point constitutes a portion of the disquieting lacunae that feminist investigation seeks to fill" (72). Previous investigations of black women's literature did much of the work of "filling" the gaps that allow contemporary critics to examine content more closely.
29. Graham, intro, 3.
30. *Ibid.*, 2.

Chapter Two

1. Hartman, *Scenes of Subjection*, 124.
2. In *Hand-Writing: Legibility and the White Body in Running a Thousand Miles for Freedom*, Lindon Barrett describes the ways that the African American body is a "vexed artifact" (315) for both free and enslaved African Americans. Barrett states, " In order to authenticate themselves as African Americans, these narrators must highlight the primary terms by which African American identity is construed—the body and the life of the body" (315).
3. *Ibid.*
4. Forten, *Journals*, p. 17.
5. Stevenson, pp. 17–19.
6. *Ibid.*, pp. 22–24
7. Stevenson in Forten introduction, 3.
8. Forten, 30.
9. Stevenson in Forten, 27–28.
10. *Ibid.*, 37.
11. *Ibid.*, 376.
12. Stevenson in Forten, 37.
13. *Ibid.*, 30.
14. Forten, 67.
15. *Ibid.* General (Rufus) Saxton was in charge of the enlistment and organization of Negroes into the Union Army and later served as Assistant Commissioner of the Freedman's Bureau. http://www.ftmac.org/Barlow-Saxton.htm.
16. Forten, 67.
17. *Ibid.*
18. *Ibid.*
19. *Ibid.*, 68.
20. *Ibid.*
21. *Ibid.*, 71.
22. *Ibid.*, 68.
23. *Ibid.*, 69.
24. *Ibid.*, 69.
25. *Ibid.*, 70.
26. *Ibid.*
27. *Ibid.*, 71.
28. Stevenson in Forten, 19. Child's rhetoric of freedom is discussed in greater detail in Chapter 3.
29. http://mac110.assumption.edu/aas/Manuscripts/masstova.html.
30. Forten, 71.
31. *Ibid.*
32. *Ibid.*
33. *Ibid.*
34. *Ibid.*, 72.
35. *Ibid.*
36. *Ibid.*, 73.
37. *Ibid.*, 74.
38. *Ibid.*
39. *Ibid.*

Notes—Chapter Two

40. *Ibid.*
41. *Ibid.*
42. *Ibid.*
43. The influence of class differences on what was deemed "respectable" behavior would be a point of contention through the end of the nineteenth and into the twentieth century. Women were criticized for personal and domestic hygiene, children's behaviors, and other aspects of domestic life when it could be argued that those with greater resources and better jobs could meet these standards more readily. The challenges of cultural "improvement" and respectability are discussed in Stephanie J. Shaw's *What a Woman Ought to Be and Do*, Evelyn Higginbotham's *Righteous Discontent*, and Deborah Gray White's *Too Heavy a Load*. In *Righteous Propagation*, Michele Mitchell adds, "The concept of racial destiny stressed collectivity, yet it enabled African American women and men to judge—often harshly—what they perceived as weaknesses, failings, and pathologies on the part of other black people" (15).
44. Frederick Douglass makes the connection between recognition of civil rights and celebration of holidays in his 1845 *Narrative of the Life of Frederick Douglass*, when he notes that slaves are given just a short moment to observe Christmas before being sent back to work. He also makes the famous inquiry "What to a slave is the fourth of July?" in a separate speech as he notes that they have no reason to celebrate liberties that they have not received through drunkenness and merriment as their masters do.
45. Forten, 74.
46. *Ibid.*, 75.
47. *Ibid.*, 79.
48. *Ibid.*
49. *Ibid.*
50. *Ibid.*, 83.
51. *Ibid.*, 82.
52. *Ibid.*
53. *Ibid.*, 71.
54. Craft, 3.
55. Sterling, 7.
56. Craft, 9–10. Charles Heglar also discusses the significant role that marriage plays in slave narratives in *Rethinking the Slave Narrative*. He emphasizes the wealth of information that can be provided about family life by examining narratives besides those written by Douglass and Jacobs. In this case, the negotiations of when to marry under the institution of slavery speak volumes about the Crafts trying to maintain their own humanity when most decisions were not under their control.
57. Craft, 10.
58. *Ibid.*, 15.
59. *Ibid.*
60. *Ibid.*, 12.
61. DeRamus, 44.
62. Craft 15.
63. *Ibid.*, 16.
64. *Ibid.*, 17.
65. *Ibid.*
66. *Ibid.*
67. He adds parenthetically that it is "not only unlawful for slaves to be taught to read, but in some of the States there are heavy penalties attached, such as fines and imprisonment, which will be vigorously enforced upon anyone who is humane enough to violate the so-called law" (17). This is another example of the way the narrative uses personal experience to offer commentary on social ills.
68. Craft, 19.
69. *Ibid.*
70. *Ibid.*
71. *Ibid.*
72. *Ibid.*, 15.
73. *Ibid.*
74. Lindon Barrett states that the supplanting of a black body with a focus on a white body in *Running a Thousand Miles* is a revision of writing, as the white body attains privilege, but in these cases that Craft cites the African American body ultimately returns.
75. Craft, 20.
76. *Ibid.*, 19.
77. *Ibid.*, 15.
78. *Ibid.*
79. *Ibid.*, 16.
80. Craft, 17.
81. *Ibid.*, 3.
82. *Ibid.*, 4.
83. *Ibid.*, 5
84. *Ibid.*, 7.
85. *Ibid.*, 8.
86. *Ibid.*, 21.
87. *Ibid.*, 22.
88. *Ibid.*
89. *Ibid.*, 23.
90. As referred to by Dorothy Sterling, *Black Foremothers*, p. 14.
91. Craft, 23.
92. *Ibid.*, 24.

Notes—Chapter Three

93. *Ibid.*
94. *Ibid.*, 25.
95. *Ibid.*
96. *Ibid.*
97. *Ibid.*, 26.
98. *Ibid.*, 28.
99. *Ibid.*, 29
100. *Ibid.*, 36.
101. *Ibid.*, 36.
102. Sterling, 19.
103. Craft, 41.
104. *Ibid.*, 42.
105. qtd. in Sterling, 23.
106. *Ibid.*
107. *Ibid.*, 24.
108. *Ibid.*, 25.
109. Craft 65–66.
110. See Blackett in Craft, 73, for additional descriptions of Ellen's idealized femininity.
111. Sterling, 26.
112. *Ibid.*
113. *Ibid.*, 27–28.
114. Craft, 42.
115. Blackett in Craft, 70–71.
116. Blackett, 71.
117. *Ibid.*, 72.
118. Craft, 87.
119. *Ibid.*
120. The concept of "rememory" comes from Toni Morrison's *Beloved*.
121. Craft, 87.
122. *Ibid.*
123. *Ibid.*
124. *Ibid.*, 88.
125. *Ibid.*
126. *Ibid.*, 89.
127. *Ibid.*
128. *Ibid.*, 89–90. Blackett writes that William secured money despite some opposition from Wendell Phillips and others who questioned the "risk" of the endeavor.
129. Blackett in Craft, 90.
130. Blackett, 90.
131. Blackett adds that "their experience was not unique," as by 1871, 1500–1600 murders were committed in Georgia in opposition to black visibility and success after emancipation (90),
132. Blackett, 91.
133. qtd. by Blackett, 92.
134. Blackett, 93.
135. *Ibid.*
136. Blackett adds: "Freedmen's Bureau officials estimated, rather conservatively, that roughly two hundred black men and women had started schools for the freedmen in at least seventy counties between 1866 and 1870" (93).
137. *Ibid.*, 94.
138. *Ibid.*
139. Blackett, 95.
140. Craft, 95.
141. See Blackett in Craft, 97, for a more comprehensive account of the suit. Blackett writes that the commissioner demanded $150 each for each witness willing to testify for the Crafts.
142. Blackett in Craft, 100, from Bryan County Deed and Record Book.
143. Craft, 100.
144. Blackett in Craft, 99.
145. Hartman, 120.
146. *Ibid.*

Chapter Three

1. Such is the tone of Becky Rutberg's biography *Mary Lincoln's Dressmaker*.
2. Jennifer Fleischner, *Mrs. Lincoln and Mrs. Keckly*, 120.
3. Keckley, *Behind the Scenes*, 3.
4. *Ibid.*, 4.
5. *Ibid.*
6. *Ibid.*
7. *Ibid.*, 5.
8. *Ibid.*
9. In his introduction to *Behind the Scenes*, Andrews asserts that Jacobs and Keckley grew up under similar circumstances as house servants and pursued similar missions to "portray their evolution from sexual exploitation in slavery to triumphant single motherhood in freedom"; however, Jacobs emphasizes her position as mother and Keckley as "female entrepreneur" (Andrews, xviii–xix).
10. Andrews notes the likelihood of Keckley's familiarity with Jacobs, given her presence in Keckley's hometown for three years and the parallels between their lives (xvii).
11. Keckley, 7.
12. *Ibid.*
13. *Ibid.*, 6.
14. *Ibid.*, 8.
15. *Ibid.*, 9.
16. *Ibid.*, 10.
17. *Ibid.*, 14.
18. *Ibid.*, 15,

Notes—Chapter Three

19. *Ibid.*
20. *Ibid.*, 17.
21. *Ibid.*, 20.
22. *Ibid.*
23. *Ibid.*, 21.
24. Douglass describes the mobility that calking ships allows him in *Narrative of the Life of Frederick Douglass*. Although he must bring his master "six to seven dollars per week," he has an amount of economic power: "I sought my own employment, made my own contracts, and collected the money which I earned. My pathway became much more smooth than before; my condition was now much more comfortable" (135).
25. Introduction, *Behind the Scenes*, p. xvii.
26. Keckley, 7.
27. *Ibid.*
28. *Ibid.*, 8.
29. *Ibid.*, 7.
30. *Ibid.*, 14.
31. *Ibid.*, 15.
32. *Ibid.*, 16.
33. *Ibid.*, 17.
34. *Ibid.*, 20.
35. *Ibid.*
36. *Ibid.*
37. Keckley is determined to purchase herself and her son on the terms established by her master rather than running away (21).
38. Santamarina, 139.
39. *Ibid.*, 140
40. *Ibid.*
41. *Ibid.*, 132.
42. Keckley, 20.
43. *Ibid.*
44. *Ibid.*, 21.
45. *Ibid.*
46. *Ibid.*
47. *Ibid.*
48. *Ibid.*, 21.
49. *Ibid.*, 22.
50. Fleischner, *Mrs. Lincoln and Mrs. Keckley*, 120.
51. Keckley includes the letters from Hobbs, who she knows as her father, 9.
52. Fleischner, *Mrs. Lincoln and Mrs. Keckly*, 124.
53. *Ibid.*
54. *Ibid.*, 126.
55. Keckley, 127.
56. *Ibid.*, 23.
57. Keckley includes quotes from one patron, Mr. Le Bourgeois, who raised money among her friends in her debt to Keckley, 23–24.
58. Fleischner, *Mrs. Lincoln and Mrs. Keckley*, 136.
59. Keckley, 26.
60. Santamarina, 140.
61. *Ibid.*, 141.
62. *Ibid.*, 145.
63. *Ibid.*, 147.
64. Keckley, 24.
65. *Ibid.*, 28.
66. Santamarina, 144.
67. *Ibid.*, 145.
68. Keckley, 33.
69. *Ibid.*, 70–71.
70. *Ibid.*, 51.
71. *Ibid.*, p. 52.
72. Keckley gives as an example a woman who claims to have "been here eight months, and Missus Lingom an't even give me one shife (shift, or dress).... My old missus us't gib me two shifes eber year" (63). This is representative of the way that many blacks carry the customs of the South into their expectations of freedom.
73. Keckley, 78–79.
74. On page 83, Keckley describes being the only person besides the wife of the Secretary of State summoned to Mrs. Lincoln's presence.
75. Keckley, 90.
76. A historically black university that her son attended briefly, destroyed by fire on the night of President Lincoln's assassination. Keckly, 90.
77. *Ibid.*, 90.
78. *Ibid.*, 99.
79. *Ibid.*, 104.
80. *Ibid.*, 114.
81. *Ibid.*, 107.
82. Even Mary Todd Lincoln thanks Keckley for her association with these "very noble men," 155.
83. *Ibid.*, 4.
84. Santamarina, 156, 158.
85. An original copy of the book is held in Alfred Whital Stern Collection of Lincolniana in the Rare Book Collection of the Library of Congress.
86. qtd. in Fleischner, 316.
87. *Ibid.*, 318.
88. Keckley, 51.
89. *Ibid.*, 118.

Notes—Chapter Four

Chapter Four

1. Boyd, *Discarded Legacy*, 120.
2. Description of Harper's tour in Foster, 19.
3. Foster, 5.
4. Foster writes that no information is known about her parents except that they were not slaves. She also cites speculation that Harper's father was white (6).
5. Foster, 7.
6. *Ibid.*
7. *Ibid.*
8. *Ibid*, 9–10. Foster adds that Harper was the first female teacher at Union but only stayed a short while due to the school's financial struggles. She left in 1852 for Little York, where she was distressed by her inability to motivate her students.
9. *Ibid.*, 11.
10. The speech was entitled "The Education and the Elevation of the Colored Race." Descriptions on Foster, 11.
11. Boyd, 12.
12. *Ibid.*
13. *Ibid.*, 11.
14. Boyd uses her poetry to create the missing context for her life. She designs her discussion to "illuminate the beliefs and practices reflected in the literature and life of Frances Harper" (27).
15. Story reprinted in Foster, 114.
16. Harper, 271.
17. *Ibid.*, 276.
18. Carby, 6–7.
19. Harper, *Minnie's Sacrifice*, 72.
20. "Offers," 114.
21. *Minnie's Sacrifice*, 67.
22. *Ibid.*
23. *Ibid.*
24. *Ibid.*, 78.
25. *Minnie's Sacrifice*, 90.
26. *Ibid.*, 92.
27. *Ibid.*, 234.
28. My analysis is very much in line with that of Hazel Carby, who sees Iola Leroy as a "vehicle for debate about the nature of black leadership and as a means for representing the relation of black intellectuals to the folk after the failure of Reconstruction" (63). Carby reads the text against analyses of Victorian entrapment, as a disruption, per se, of conventional expectations of womanhood.
29. *Minnie's Sacrifice*, 262.
30. Harper, *Iola Leroy*, 263.
31. In *Reconstructing Womanhood*, Hazel Carby argues that the desire to be represented in "'the literature of the country'" and to be "'of lasting service for the race'" are fused to form a didactic novel (71).
32. *Iola*, 236.
33. Again, I use Douglass as an example of fictionalizing subjectivity.
34. In *Resistance and Reformation*, John Ernest argues that "each individual stands as a particular configuration of various cultural influences, including not only those influences one would claim, but also those that threaten one's most fundamental sense of identity" (206–207).
35. Claudia Tate discusses ways in which early black fiction instructs on hard work and intelligence; she describes Iola Leroy, for example, as "race literature" which promotes the rise of black literary production. *Domestic Allegories*, 85.
36. See Dickson Bruce, Jr.'s *Origins of African American Literature*, 261–262, for more information on Watkins' newspaper publications.
37. Anderson, *Imagined Communities*, 6.
38. *Ibid.*, 12.
39. *Ibid.*. 36.
40. *Ibid.*, 46.
41. *Ibid.*, 98.
42. *Ibid.*, 143.
43. Foucault, 193.
44. *Ibid.*
45. *Ibid.*
46. see Dickson Bruce, Jr.'s *Origins of African American Literature*, 261–262, for more information on Watkins' newspaper publications. McHenry, *Forgotten Readers*, 137.
47. Penelope Bullock states that the African American periodical press was most active between 1854 and 1863 in *The Afro-American Periodical Press*, 12.
48. See Bruce, 286, and Chapter 2 of Robert Levine's *Martin Delany, Frederick Douglass and the Politics of Representative Identity*.
49. Bullock, 61.
50. Hazel Carby introduction, *Iola Leroy*, xvii.
51. Harper, *Trial and Triumph*, 282.
52. Details of Congress of Representative Women in Carby, 3–5.
53. Mitchell, 108–109.
54. *Ibid.*, 113.

Chapter Five

1. Cooper, *Voice from the South*, 27.
2. Michele Mitchell's *Righteous Propagation* discusses reforms that came from and during Reconstruction. Her book examines critical moments when African Americans contended that the race shared interests as "sociopolitical body"; Mitchell's is an analysis of identity formation and mobilization. She writes: "Organizing freedom was arduous work that entailed individual initiative as well as collective endeavor, but for all of its challenges Reconstruction presented novel opportunities for black mobilization" (7).
3. Du Bois, "Freedman's Bureau," 354.
4. *Ibid*.
5. *Ibid*.
6. *Ibid*.
7. *Ibid*., 355.
8. *Ibid*.
9. *Ibid*.
10. *Ibid*.
11. *Ibid*.
12. *Ibid*., 357.
13. *Ibid*., 357.
14. *Ibid*., 358.
15. *Ibid*., 359.
16. *Ibid*., 360.
17. *Ibid*.
18. *Ibid*., 363.
19. Laney's curricula have been discussed in several theses and dissertations, including *"Tell them We're Rising": Black Intellectuals and Lucy Craft Laney in Post Civil War, Augusta, Georgia* by Mary Magdalene Marshall (1998), *Lucy Craft Laney: The Mother of the Children of the People: Educator, Reformer, Social Activist* by Gloria T. Williams-Way (1998) and *"The Burden of the Educated Colored Woman": Lucy Laney and Haines Institute, 1886-1933* by Britt Edward Cottingham (1995).
20. Washington, l.
21. qtd. in Washington, li.
22. Laney lived from 1854 to 1933. McCluskey, "'We Specialize in the Wholly Impossible,'" 403.
23. McCluskey, 403.
24. *Ibid*., 404.
25. *Ibid*.
26. *Ibid*.
27. *Ibid*., 407.
28. *Ibid*. The school was named in honor of Francine F. Haines, president of the woman's department of the Presbyterian Church, who gave Laney funds after the church rejected her first appeal. They later became a sponsor.
29. Quintard Taylor, Introduction, Lucy Craft Laney, "The Burden of the Educated Colored Woman," *An Online Guide to African American History*.
30. McCluskey, 80.
31. *Ibid*.
32. *Ibid*., 81.
33. *Ibid*., footnote 38: Lucy Craft Laney, "General Mortality among Negroes," in the *Atlanta University Publications*, ed. W.E.B. Du Bois (1903; rpt. New York: Arno Press, 1968), 18–20.
34. McCluskey, 82.
35. *Ibid*.
36. *Ibid*., 76.
37. *Ibid*.
38. *Ibid*., 78.
39. *Ibid*.
40. *Ibid*., 76.
41. *Ibid*.
42. *Ibid*., 80. Footnote 29: W.E.B. Du Bois, Editorial, *The Crisis* 13.6 (1917): 26.
43. Laney, "Burden of Motherhood," 2.
44. *Ibid*.
45. *Ibid*.
46. *Ibid*.
47. *Ibid*.
48. *Ibid*., 3.
49. *Ibid*., 6.
50. *Ibid*., 4.
51. *Ibid*.
52. *Ibid*.
53. McCluskey, 78
54. Du Bois, 365.
55. *Ibid*.
56. Faulkner, 43–44.
57. *Ibid*., 45
58. *Ibid*., 101. Faulkner's description of black women's aid is that on Sojourner Truth, who served as an employment agent of the Freedmen's Bureau. Truth criticized the government's lack of compensation through land grants for the freedmen and lobbied the government for that and schools. Truth promoted land ownership in Kansas and other parts of the west to Southern blacks even after attempts at promoting land redistribution had failed in such places as Port Royal. Nell Irvin Painter also discusses the exodus to Kansas in *Standing at Armageddon*, 2.
59. Ironies evident in their resistance are that Faulkner also discusses a growing class of

African American teachers, trained in normal schools, who received less pay than white women and therefore made education more "affordable" (47). She states that societies justified withdrawing aid by claiming to advocate "self-reliance" for freedpeople but cites AFUC reports showing that freedpeople sustained 458 schools by themselves and 867 in part by 1868, paying $360,000 in tuition between July 1867 and July 1868. Thus, freedmen were already predominantly self-reliant despite appearances that the societies were doing all of the work.

60. Faulkner, 59–60.
61. *Ibid.*, 68.
62. Child, 128.
63. *Ibid.*, 129–30.
64. *Ibid.*, 131.
65. *Ibid.*
66. Documented in *Augusta Chronicle* by Bill Varian.
67. *Red and Black*, 1.
68. *Ibid.*
69. Cooper, ii.
70. *Ibid.*, iii.
71. *Ibid.*
72. *Ibid.*, 9.
73. *Ibid.*, 12.
74. *Ibid.*
75. *Ibid.*, 12–13.
76. Cooper states that Feudalism in European societies fostered chivalry, "than which no institution has more sensibly magnified and elevated woman's position in society" (13).
77. Cooper, 19.
78. *Ibid.*, 21.
79. *Ibid.*, 22.
80. *Ibid.*
81. *Ibid.*, 26.
82. *Ibid.*
83. *Ibid.*, 27.
84. *Ibid.*
85. *Ibid.*, 28.
86. *Ibid.*
87. *Ibid.*
88. *Ibid.*, 29.
89. *Ibid.*
90. *Ibid.*
91. *Ibid.*.
92. *Ibid.*, i.
93. McCluskey, 83.
94. *Ibid.*, footnote 43: Anna Julia Cooper (August 1899): 296.

Epilogue

1. Harriet Jacobs, *Incidents in the Life of a Slave Girl*, 1861 (New York: Norton, 2001), 10–11.
2. *Ibid.*, 11.
3. *Ibid.*
4. Saidiya Hartman, *Scenes of Subjection: Terror, Slavery, and Self-Making in Nineteenth Century America*. (New York: Oxford University Press, 1997), 49.
5. Douglass, *Narrative*, 300.
6. Jerome L. Singer, *The Child's World of Make-Believe: Experimental Studies of Imaginative Play* (New York: Academic Press, 1973), 9.
7. Hartman, *Scenes of Subjection*, 49.
8. *Ibid.*, 8.
9. Brian Sutton-Smith, *The Ambiguity of Play* (Cambridge: Harvard University Press, 2001), 10.
10. *Ibid.*
11. *Ibid.*, 11.
12. *Ibid.*, 81.
13. Booker T. Washington, *Up from Slavery*, 1901, 3. *African-American Classics: Up from Slavery, The Souls of Black Folk and Narrative of the Life of Frederick Douglass* (New York: Dover, 2007), 3.
14. *Ibid.*, 266.
15. Inge Bretherton, ed., "Representing the Social World in Symbolic Play: Reality and Fantasy," *Symbolic Play: The Development of Social Understanding* (New York: Academic Press, 1984), 4.
16. Referenced in Strand and Boland, 74–76.
17. Smethurst, 171.
18. In "'A Splintery Box': Race and Gender in the Sonnets of Gwendolyn Brooks," Stacy Caron Hubbard discusses Brooks' use of the lyric voice to define self and explore race and gender in her sonnets (55).
19. Gary Smith argues that Brooks rejects romantic prescriptions for Black women's lives, 45.
20. Alicia Garza, "A Herstory of the #BlackLivesMatter Movement," *Feminist Wire*, October 7, 2014, http://thefeministwire.com/2014/10/blacklivesmatter-2/. Cited in Taylor, 167.

Bibliography

Alexander, Elizabeth. *The Black Interior*. St. Paul, MN: Grey Wolf Press, 2004.

Anderson, Benedict R. *Imagined Communities: Reflections on the Origin and Spread of Nationalism*. New York: Verso, 1983.

Anderson, James. *Education of Blacks in the South, 1860-1935*. Chapel Hill: University of North Carolina Press, 1988.

Andrews, William L. Introduction. *Behind the Scenes, or Thirty years a Slave and Four Years in the White House*. 1868. New York: Penguin Books, 2005.

———. "The Novelization of Voice in Early African American Narrative." *PMLA* 105.1 (January 1990): 23-34.

———. *To Tell a Free Story: The First Century of Afro-American Autobiography, 1769-1865*. Urbana: University of Illinois Press, 1986.

Baker, Houston. *Modernism and the Harlem Renaissance*. Chicago: University of Chicago Press, 1989.

———. In *Norton Anthology of African American Literature*. Eds. Henry Louis Gates and Nellie McKay. 1st. ed. New York: Norton, 1996.

Baker, Houston, Jr. "The Black Arts Era" in *Norton Anthology of African American Literature* (second ed). Henry Louis Gates, Jr., Nellie McKay, et al., eds. New York: Norton, 2003.

Bakhtin, Mikhail M. *The Dialogic Imagination: Four Essays*. Ed. Michael Holquist. Austin: University of Texas Press, 1981.

Barrett, Lindon. "Hand-Writing: Legibility and the White Body in *Running a Thousand Miles for Freedom*." *American Literature* 69.2 (June 1997).

Berlin, Ira, et al. *Free at Last: A Documentary History of Slavery, Freedom, and the Civil War*. New York: The New Press, 1992.

———. *Slaves No More: Three Essays on Emancipation and the Civil War*. Cambridge: Cambridge University Press, 1992.

Berthold, Michael. "Not 'Altogether' the 'History of Myself': Autobiographical Impersonality in Elizabeth Keckley's 'Behind the Scenes. or, Thirty Years a Slave and Four Years in the White House.'" *ATQ* 13.2 (June 1999): 105-119.

Blackett, R.J.M. Introduction. *Running a Thousand Miles for Freedom: The Escape of William and Ellen Craft from Slavery*. Baton Rouge: Louisiana State University Press, 1999.

Boland, Eavan, and Mark Strand. *The Making of a Poem: A Norton Anthology of Poetic Forms*. New York: Norton, 2000.

Boyd, Melba Joyce. *Discarded Legacy: Politics and Poetics in the Life of Frances E.W. Harper 1825-1911*. Detroit: Wayne State University Press, 1994.

Bretherton, Inge. "Representing the Social World in Symbolic Play: Reality and Fantasy." *Symbolic Play: The Development of Social Understanding*. New York: Academic Press, 1984.

———, ed. Introduction. *Symbolic Play: The Development of Social Understanding*. New York: Academic Press, 1984.

Brooks, Gwendolyn. "Gay Chaps at the Bar," "The Ballad of Rudolph Reed," "The Boy Died in My Alley." *Anthology of Modern American Poetry*. Ed. Cary Nelson. New York: Oxford University Press, 2000. 766-779.

Brown, William Wells. *Clotelle, a Tale of the Southern States*. 1864. *William Wells Brown and Clotelle: A Portrait of the Artist in the First Negro Novel*. The Shoe String Press, 1969.

———. *Clotelle, or the Colored Heroine*. 1867. Miami: Mnemosyne, 1987.

———. *Clotel, or the President's Daughter*. 1853. New York: Penguin, 2004.

———. *Narrative of William W. Brown, a Fugitive Slave*. Boston, the Anti-Slavery Office, 1847.

Bruce, Dickson D., Jr. *The Origins of African American Literature, 1680–1865*. Charlottesville: University Press of Virginia, 2001.

Bullock, Penelope L. *The Afro-American Periodical Press, 1838–1909*. Baton Rouge: Louisiana State University Press, 1981.

Calmenson, Stephanie, and Joanna Cole. *Miss Mary Mack and Other Street Rhymes*. New York: HarperCollins, 1990.

Carby, Hazel. Introduction. *Iola Leroy*. Boston: Beacon Press, 1987.

———. *Reconstructing Womanhood: the Emergence of the Afro-American Woman Novelist*. New York: Oxford University Press, 1987.

Carmichael, Stokely. "What We Want" in *Let Nobody Turn Us Around: An African American Anthology*, Manning Marable and Leith Mullings, eds. Lanham, MD. Rowman and Littlefield: 2009.

Chakkalakal, Tess. *Novel Bondage: Slavery, Marriage, and Freedom in Nineteenth-Century America*. Urbana: University of Illinois Press, 2011.

Child, Lydia Maria. *The Freedmen's Book*. Reprint of 1865 ed. New York: Arno Press, 1968 (1980).

Cooper, Anna Julia. *A Voice from the South*. 1892. New York: Oxford University Press, 1988.

Craft, William. *Running a Thousand Miles for Freedom: the Escape of William and Ellen Craft from Slavery*. Baton Rouge: Louisiana State University Press, 1999.

Douglass, Frederick. *My Bondage and My Freedom*. 1855. New York: Penguin, 2003.

———. *Narrative of the Life of Frederick Douglass*. 1845. New York: Penguin, 1982.

———. *Narrative of the Life of Frederick Douglass*. 1845. *The Classic Slave Narratives*. Ed. Henry Louis Gates, Jr. New York: Penguin, 1987, 255.

Du Bois, W. E. B. *Black Reconstruction*. New York: Atheneum, 1962.

———. "The Freedmen's Bureau." *Atlantic Monthly* 87 (1901): 354–365.

Du Cille, Ann. *The Coupling Convention: Sex, Text, and Tradition in Black Women's Fiction*. New York: Oxford University Press, 1993.

Ernest, John. *Liberation Historiography: African American Writers and the Challenge of History, 1794–1861*. Chapel Hill: University of North Carolina Press, 2004.

———. *Resistance and Reformation in Nineteenth-Century African-American Literature*. Jackson: University Press of Mississippi, 1995.

Faulkner, Carol. *Women's Radical Reconstruction: the Freedmen's Aid Movement*. Philadelphia: University of Pennsylvania Press, 2004.

Fleischner, Jennifer. *Mastering Slavery: Memory, Family, and Identity in Women's Slave Narratives*. New York: New York University Press, 1996.

———. *Mrs. Lincoln and Mrs. Keckly: The Remarkable Story of the Friendship Between a First Lady and a Former Slave*. New York: Broadway Books, 2005.

Foner, Eric. *Forever Free*. New York: Knopf, 2005.

———. *Short History of Reconstruction*. New York: Harper and Row, 1990.

Forten, Charlotte. *The Journals of Charlotte Forten Grimké* New York: Oxford University Press, 1988.

———. "Life on the Sea Islands." 1864. In *Two Black Teachers during the Civil War*. New York: Arno Press, New York Times, 1969.

Foster, Frances Smith. Introduction. *A Brighter Coming Day*. New York: Feminist Press at the City University of New York, The Graduate Center, 1990.

———. *Witnessing Slavery: The Development of Ante-bellum Slave Narratives*. Westport, CT. Greenwood Press, 1979.

———. *Written By Herself: Literary Production by African American Women, 1745–1892*. Bloomington: Indiana University Press, 1993.

Foucault, Michel. "On *The History of Sexuality*: Interview with Lucette Finas." *Power/Knowledge: Selected Interviews & Other Writings*. Ed. Colin Gordon. New York: Random House, 1980.

Gaines, Kevin. *Uplifting the Race: Black Leadership, Politics, and Culture in the Twentieth Century*. Chapel Hill: University of North Carolina Press, 1996.

Giovanni, Nikki. *The Selected Poems of Nikki Giovanni*. New York: William Morrow, 1996.

Glenn, Evelyn Nakano. *Unequal Freedom: How Race and Gender Shaped American*

Bibliography

Citizenship and Labor. Cambridge: Harvard University Press, 2002.

Graham, Maryemma. Introduction. *The Cambridge Companion to the African American Novel.* Ed. Maryemma Graham. Cambridge: Cambridge University Press, 2004

Grasso, Linda. *The Artistry of Anger: Black and White Women's Literature in America, 1820-1860.* Chapel Hill: University of North Carolina Press, 2002.

Haines Institute. *Red and Black Yearbook.* Augusta, Georgia, 1923.

Harper, Frances E.W. *Iola Leroy, Or Shadows Uplifted.* Boston: Beacon Press, 1987.

———. *Minnie's Sacrifice.* In *Minnie's Sacrifice. Sowing and Reaping. Trial and Triumph: Three Rediscovered Novels by Frances E.W. Harper.* Ed. Frances Smith Foster. Boston: Beacon Press, 1994.

———. *Poems.* 1871. *The Complete Poems of Frances Ellen Watkins Harper.* Ed. Maryemma Graham. New York: Oxford University Press, 1988.

———. *Sketches of Southern Life.* 1872.

———. *The Two Offers* and *Our Greatest Want. Anglo-American Magazine,* September and October 1859.

Hartman, Saidiya. *Scenes of Subjection: Terror, Slavery, and Self-Making in Nineteenth Century America.* New York: Oxford University Press, 1997.

Heglar, Charles. *Rethinking the Slave Narrative: Slave Marriage and the Narratives of Henry Bibb and William and Ellen Craft.* Westport, CT: Greenwood Press, 2001.

Higginbotham, Evelyn Brooks. *Righteous Discontent: The Women's Movement in the Black Baptist Church, 1880-1920.* Cambridge: Harvard University Press, 1993.

Hine, Darlene Clark, and Kathleen Thompson. *A Shining Thread of Hope: The History of Black Women in America.* New York: Broadway Books, 1998.

Hubbard, Stacy Carson. "'A Splintery Box': Race and Gender in the Sonnets of Gwendolyn Brooks." *Genre XXV* (Spring 1992): 47-64.

Hughes, Langston. "Ballad of the Landlord." *Anthology of Modern American Poetry.* Ed. Cary Nelson. New York: Oxford University Press, 2000. 522.

Hunter, Tera. *To 'Joy My Freedom': Southern Black Women's Lives and Labors After the Civil War.* Cambridge: Harvard University Press, 1997.

Hurston, Zora Neale. "John Redding Goes to Sea." http://english204-dcc.blogspot.com/2011/04/john-redding-goes-to-sea-hurston.html.

———. *Their Eyes Were Watching God.* 1937. New York: HarperCollins, 1998.

Jacobs, Harriet. *Incidents in the Life of a Slave Girl.* 1861. New York: Norton, 2001.

——— [as Linda Brent]. *Incidents in the Life of a Slave Girl: Written by Herself.* 1861. Orlando: Harcourt Brace, 1973.

Jenkins, Candice M. *Private Lives, Proper Relations: Regulating Black Intimacy.* Minneapolis: University of Minnesota Press, 2007.

Keckley, Elizabeth. *Behind the Scenes, or Thirty Years a Slave and Four Years in the White House.* 1868. New York: Penguin Books, 2005.

Laney, Lucy Craft. "Burden of the Educated Colored Woman." *Report of the Hampton Negro Conference* (1899). http://www.blackpast.org/?q=1899-lucy-craft-laney-burden-educated-colored-woman.

Lawson, Bill E., and Howard McGary. *Between Slavery and Freedom: Philosophy and American Slavery.* Bloomington: Indiana University Press, 2002.

Levine, Robert S. *Martin Delany, Frederick Douglass, and the Politics of Representative Identity.* Chapel Hill: University of North Carolina Press, 1997.

Martinez, Ernesto Javier. *On Making Sense: Queer Race Narratives of Intelligibility.* Stanford: Stanford University Press, 2013.

McBride, Dwight A. *Impossible Witnesses: Truth, Abolitionism, and Slave Testimony.* New York: New York University Press, 2001.

McCluskey, Audrey Thomas. "'We Specialize in the Wholly Impossible': Black Women School Founders and Their Mission." *Signs* 22.2 (1997): 403.

McHenry, Elizabeth. *Forgotten Readers: Recovering the Lost History of African American Literary Societies.* Durham: Duke University Press, 2002.

Mitchell, Angelyn. *Freedom to Remember.* New Brunswick: Rutgers University Press, 2002.

Mitchell, Michele. *Righteous Propagation: African Americans and the Politics of Racial Destiny After Reconstruction.* Chapel Hill: University of North Carolina Press, 2004.

Morrison, Toni. *Playing in the Dark: Whiteness and the Literary Imagination.* New York: Vintage Books, 1992

Bibliography

Mulvey, Christopher. "Freeing the Voice, Creating the Self: The Novel and Slavery." *The Cambridge Companion to the African American Novel*. Ed. Maryemma Graham. Cambridge: Cambridge UP, 2004.

Nelson, Cary. *Anthology of Modern American Poetry*. New York: Oxford University Press, 2000.

Nelson, Dana. *National Manhood: Capitalist Citizenship and the Imagined Fraternity of White Men*. Durham: Duke University Press, 1998.

———. *The Word in Black and White: Reading "Race" in American Literature, 1638–1867*. New York: Oxford University Press, 1992.

Painter, Nell. *Southern History across the Color Line*. Chapel Hill: University of North Carolina Press, 2002.

———. *Standing at Armageddon: United States: 1877–1919*. New York: W.W. Norton, 1987.

Perry, Melissa Harris. *Sister Citizen: Shame, Stereotypes, and Black Women in America*. New Haven: Yale University Press, 2011.

Peterson, Carla. "Commemorative Ceremonies and Invented Traditions: History, Memory, and Modernity in the 'New Negro' Novel of the Nadir." *Post-Bellum, Pre-Harlem: African American Literature and Culture*. Eds. Barbara McCaskill and Caroline Gebhard. New York: New York University Press, 2006.

———. *Doers of the Word. African-American Women Speakers and Writers in the North (1830–1880)*. New York: Oxford University Press, 1995.

Potter, Vilma Raskin. *Reference Guide to Afro-American Publications and Editors, 1827–1946*. Ames: Iowa State University Press, 1993.

Reid-Pharr, Robert. *Conjugal Unions: The Body, the House and the Black American*. Oxford: Oxford University Press, 1999.

———. *Once You Go Black: Choice, Desire, and the Black American Intellectual*. New York: New York University Press, 2007.

Robbins, Sarah. "Gendering the Debate over African Americans' Education in the 1880s: Frances Harper's Reconfiguration of Atticus Haygood's Philanthropic Model." *Legacy* 19.1 (2002) 81–89.

Russell, Sandi. *Render Me My Song: African-American Women Writers from Slavery to the Present*. London: Rivers-Oram Press, 1990.

Rutberg, Becky. *Mary Lincoln's Dressmaker: Elizabeth Keckley's Remarkable Rise from Slave to White House Confidante*. New York: Walker and Company, 1995.

Sanmartin, Paula. *Black Women as Custodians of History: Unsung Rebel (M)Others in African American and Afro-Cuban Women's Writing*. New York: Cambria Press, 2014.

Santamarina, Xiomara. *Belabored Professions: Narratives of African American Working Womanhood*. Chapel Hill: University of North Carolina Press, 2005.

Shaw, Stephanie. *What a Woman Ought to Be and to Do: Black Professional Women Workers During the Jim Crow era*. Chicago: University of Chicago Press, 1996.

Singer, Jerome L. *The Child's World of Make-Believe: Experimental Studies of Imaginative Play*. New York: Academic Press, 1973.

Smethurst, James Edward. *The New Red Negro: The Literary Left and African American Poetry, 1930–1946*. New York: Oxford University Press, 1999.

Smith, Barbara. "Toward a Black Feminist Criticism." In *All the Women Are White, All the Blacks Are Men, but Some of Us Are Brave*. Ed. Gloria T. Hull, Patricia Bell Scott, and Barbara Smith. Old Westbury, NY: Feminist Press, 1982.

Smith, Gary. "Gwendolyn Brooks's *A Street in Bronzeville*, The Harlem Renaissance and the Mythologies of Black Women." *MELUS* 10.3 (Autumn 1983): 33–46.

Sorisio, Carolyn. "Unmasking the Genteel Performer: Elizabeth Keckley's *Behind the Scenes* and the Politics of Public Wrath." *African American Review* 34.1 (Spring 2000): 19–38.

Spillers, Hortense J. "Mama's Baby, Papa's Maybe: An American Grammar Book." *The Black Feminist Reader*. Ed. Joy James and T. Denean Sharpley-Whiting. Malden, MA: Blackwell, 2000.

Stanford, Ann Folwell. "Dialectics of Desire: War and the Resistive Voice in Gwendolyn Brooks's 'Negro Hero' and 'Gay Chaps at the Bar.'" *African American Review* 26.2 (Summer 1992): 192–211.

Sterling, Dorothy. *Black Foremothers: Three Lives*. Old Westbury, NY: Feminist Press, 1979.

Stevenson, Brenda, ed. Introduction, *The Journals of Charlotte Forten Grimké*. New York: Oxford University Press, 1988.

Bibliography

Stewart, Maria. "Religion and the Pure Principles of Morality." *Maria W. Stewart, America's First Black Woman Political Writer: Essays and Speeches*. Ed. and introd. Marilyn Richardson. Bloomington: Indiana University Press, 1987.

Talbert, C.A. Lincoln Day Address, Northwestern University, 1931.

Tate, Claudia. *Domestic Allegories of Political Desire: The Black Heroine's Text at the Turn of the Century*. New York: Oxford University Press, 1992.

Taylor, Diana. *Archive and the Repertoire: Performing Cultural Memory in the Americas*. Durham: Duke University Press, 2003.

Taylor, Keeanga-Yamahtta. *From #BlackLivesMatter to Black Liberation*. Chicago: Haymarket Books, 2016.

Truth, Sojourner. "Arn't I a Woman?" 1851. http://www.blackpast.org/?q=1851-sojourner-truth-arnt-i-woman.

Wald, Priscilla. *Constituting Americans: Cultural Anxiety and Narrative Form*. Durham: Duke University Press, 1995.

Washington, Booker T. *Up from Slavery*. 1901. *3 African-American Classics: Up from Slavery, the Souls of Black Folk and Narrative of the Life of Frederick Douglass*. New York: Dover, 2007.

Washington, Mary Helen. *Invented Lives: Narratives of Black Women, 1860–1960*. Garden City, NY: Doubleday, 1987.

Wheatley, Phillis. *Poems of Phillis Wheatley*. 1773. Chapel Hill: University of North Carolina Press, 1989.

White, Deborah Gray. *Arn't I a Woman: Female Slaves in the Plantation South*. New York: W.W. Norton, 1985

_____. *Too Heavy a Load: Black women in Defense of Themselves, 1894–1994*. New York: W.W. Norton, 1999.

Zafar, Rafia. *We Wear the Mask: African Americans Write American Literature, 1760–1870*. New York: Columbia University Press, 1997.

Index

activism 18–19, 48, 101, 112, 124, 157–58
African Methodist Episcopal Church 12
Akron, Ohio 21
Alexandria, Virginia 31
Ambiguity of Play 144
Amendment, Fifteenth 14, 148
Amenia Conference 125
American Freedmen's Union 121, 130
American Missionary Association 121, 129–30
Anderson, Benedict: *Imagined Communities* 114
Andrews, William 69
Anglo-African Magazine 109, 113, 117
Anti-Slavery Bugle 113, 116
Atlanta, Georgia 124
Atlanta University 123–24; conferences 124–25
Atlantic Monthly 36, 120
Augusta, Georgia 18, 119–20, 123–24, 126, 133
authorship 6, 12; self-authorship 8

Baker, Houston, Jr. 25, 157
Baltimore, Maryland 107
Baptist church 42
Baton Rouge, Louisiana 1
Belabored Professions: Narratives of African American Working Womanhood 66, 75
Beloved 34
Bethune, Mary McLeod 31, 120, 123–24, 126
Black Arts Movement 33, 155–57
black female subjectivity 13
#BlackLivesMatter 2, 157
Black Power Movement 155–56; women's involvement 155–58
Black Women as Custodians of History 8
Blackett, R. 60
Blake; or, the Huts of America 20
body: economies 63; illness 57; legibility, ownership 53; reconstructing 62; remembering 59; violence 47; writing 37
Boston 58, 60
Boyd, Melba J.: *Christian Recorder* 107

Brent, Linda *see* Jacobs, Harriet Ann
Bretherton, Inge 143, 149; "Representing the Social World in Symbolic Play" 143, 149
"Bring Back Our Girls" 147
Brooks, Gwendolyn 19, 150–54; "Ballad of Rudolph Reed" 153–54; *Blacks* 150; *A Street in Bronzeville* 151; *The World of Gwendolyn Brooks* 150
Brown, Charlotte Hawkins 31, 123
Brown, Elaine 155
Brown, Hallie Quinn 118
Brown, Michael 146
Brown, William Wells 34, 38, 116
Bruce, Dickson 116
Burroughs, Nannie Helen 31, 123
Burwell, Col. A. 69, 73

Calmenson, Stephanie 146
Cambridge Companion to the African American Novel 33
Carby, Hazel 107–8; *Reconstructing Womanhood* 108
Carmichael, Stokely 155
Castile, Philando 1
Chakkalakal, Tess 6
Charlotte, North Carolina 1
Child, Lydia Maria 39, 43, 130–32; *The Freedmen's Book* 130–31
Christian Recorder 12, 38, 108
citizenship 3–6, 9, 14, 19–20, 147–48
civil discourse 20
civil rights 6, 14
Civil War 11, 31, 35, 45, 65, 68–69, 72, 85, 87, 90, 93, 94, 102, 104, 157
Clotel 34, 114
Cole, Joanna 146
The Colored Girl Beautiful 31
coming of age narratives 143
community engagement 6; community rebuilding 7; participation 14; relationships 6
conduct literature 32–33
Constitution, U.S. 147–48
contrabands 40
contraception 51

Index

Cooper, Anna Julia 2, 3, 13, 17–18, 31, 118–20, 123, 129–30, 133–40, 158
Coppin, Fannie Jackson 118
Craft, Ellen 2, 16, 30, 35–37, 46, 49- 65, 124, 134
Craft, William 16, 30, 35–36, 46, 49–62, 65
Crawford, Janie 28–29
Crawford, Leafy 29
Crawford, Nanny 28–29
Crisis Magazine 26, 126
Crummell, Dr. Alexander 136
Cullen, Countee 152
Cullors, Patrisse 158

Daughters of America 149
Daughters of Liberty 149
Davis, Angela 155
Davis, Jordan 147
Davis, Varina 68
Daytona, Florida 126
death 150–51
Delany, Martin 19, 117
democracy 14
DeRamus, Betty 51
disguise 52–53, 56; court 62; illness 57
Douglass, Frederick 20, 70, 75, 110, 131, 142, 144, 150; *The Heroic Slave* 20; *My Bondage and My Freedom* 142
Du Bois, W.E.B. 18, 120–23, 126, 129, 131
du Cille, Ann 6, 107

Early, Sarah J. 118
education 6, 7, 11, 46, 59, 62, 64, 124, 126, 129, 130–32, 139
emancipation 9, 64, 113, 115, 119, 123, 129
Emancipation Proclamation 5, 9–10, 13, 120
Emerson, Ralph Waldo 135
England 35–36
Epes Grammar School 38

family 5, 125
Farmer's Conferences 124
Ferrell, Jonathan 2, 146
fiction 105, 108, 112
Fisk University 123
Fleischner, Jennifer 9; *Mastering Slavery* 9; *Mrs. Lincoln and Mrs. Keckly* 65–66
Forest Leaves 106, 107
Forten (Grimke), Charlotte 2, 13, 15, 33, 35–49, 62–64, 65, 121, 124
Foster, Frances Smith 18, 106
Foucault, Michel 115
Frederick Douglass' Paper 113, 116
free black female subjectivity 9
Freedmen's Aid Societies 121
Freedmen's Bureau 120–22, 129
Freedmen's Primer 12

freedom narratives 5, 10
Fremont, Gen. John 9
Fugitive Slave Law 24

Gage, Frances 21
Garland family 68
Garner, Margaret 34
Garrison, William Lloyd 38, 43, 106
Garza, Alicia 158
"Gay Chaps at the Bar" 151
Gilbert, Olive 21
Giovanni, Nikki 2, 19, 154–57; *Black Feeling* 155; *Black Judgment* 155; *Black Talk* 155; *The Women and the Men* 157
girlhood 147
Graham, Maryemma 33, 107
Grasso, Linda 10
Grimke, Angelina Weld 33
Groos, Karl 143

Hackley, Emma Azalia 31
Haines Industrial and Normal Institute 119, 124, 126, 129, 133
Haitian Revolution 44
Hampton-Tuskegee Negro Conference 125, 127–28, 130
Hampton University 123
Harlem Renaissance 4, 33
Harper, Frances Ellen Watkins 12–13, 17, 105–18, 133, 147; "Colored Women of America" 117; "Duty to Dependent Races" 117; *Minnie's Sacrifice* 107–8, 133; *Sowing and Reaping* 107; *Trial and Triumph* 107, 116–17; "Two Offers" 107, 108
Harriet Ann Jacobs (as Linda Brent) 2, 7–11, 13, 19, 21–22, 25, 29, 69, 131, 141, 147, 150, 157
Hartman, Saidiya 15, 63, 142–43; *Scenes of Subjection* 142
Hickory Hill, South Carolina 60
Hillsboro, North Carolina 71, 74
Hilton Head, South Carolina 40
Hine, Darlene Clark 14
holidays, celebration 46–47
Hope, John 124
Howard University 123, 133
Howard, Oliver 122, 129
Hughes, Langston 152–53; "Ballad of the Landlord" 153
Hurston, Zora Neale 3, 19, 25–26, 33, 156–57; *John Redding Goes to Sea* 25–28

identity: collective 6; cultural 6; individual 6
Incidents in the Life of a Slave Girl 6, 7, 10
intellectualism 7, 105, 110, 112, 123
Iola Leroy 12, 17, 30, 108–11, 114, 117, 133

Index

The Jacobs School 31
Jenkins, Candice 6
Johnson, Charles 26

Keckley, Elizabeth 2, 13, 16, 10, 31, 33, 65–119, 133
Kerber, Linda: *Women of the Republic* 17
Killicks, Logan 29
kindergartens 125

labor 6, 7, 8, 14, 16, 36, 60–63, 71, 75, 80, 83, 121, 141–43; black women's 7, 14–16, 36, 65–68, 72–80, 84, 101; spaces 3
Laney, Lucy Craft 18, 30–31, 119–20, 123–30, 132, 133, 138–40
Latimer, Dr. 111
Lawson, Bill: *Between Slavery and Freedom* 13
legal implications, attachment, contracts 8–9
Leroy, Iola 17, 19, 108–12, 114, 117
liberation writing: Harriet Jacobs 141, 157; Nikki Giovanni 154–57
Liberator 38, 107, 113, 116
Life on the Sea Islands 15, 40
Lincoln (film) 65
Lincoln, Abraham 65; Emancipation Proclamation 5, 9–10, 13, 120
Lincoln, Mary Todd 16, 65, 67–68
literacy 12, 35; reading 12–13
Little York, Pennsylvania 106
Locke, Alain 25
L'Ouverture, Toussaint, 44
Lucy Craft Laney Museum 133

Macon, Georgia 35, 50, 124
Maine Anti-Slavery Society 107
marriage 5, 7–8, 15–16, 46, 50–51, 53, 71, 109, 125, 127, 129, 139
Martin, Trayvon 146
Martinez, Ernesto J. 4
Mary Lincoln's Dressmaker 66
Maryland 106
masculinity 150
maternal lineage: ambiguity 30; blood, bloodline 31
maternity 149
McCluskey, Audrey 124–26
McGary, Howard: *Between Slavery and Freedom* 13
McKay, Claud 152
Minnie (and Louis) 108–12, 116
Miss Mary Mack 145–46
Mr. Sands 24
Mitchell, Angelyn: *The Freedom to Remember* 7
Mitchell, Michele 32–33, 118

mobility 5, 36, 39, 44, 51, 61, 63, 120
Modernism and the Harlem Renaissance 25
Morehouse College 124
Morrison, Toni 2, 11, 34, 157
Moss, Otis, III 1
motherhood 12, 23–24, 119, 125–26

Narrative of the Life of Frederick Douglass 6, 72, 142
National Anti-Slavery Standard 38
National Association of Colored Women 9, 18, 32, 124–25
National Freedmen's Relief Association 121
nationalism 113
naturalization 148
Naylor, Gloria 157
New England Freedmen's Aid Society 131
New York 36
New York Anglo-African 113, 116
newspapers 105, 113–14, 116

Obama, Barack H. 1
On Making Sense 4
Opportunity magazine 26

paternity 149
Perry, Melissa Harris 3
Philadelphia, Pennsylvania 1, 35–36, 38, 57
Pierce, Edward 121
play 141–44, 146, 150
Playing in the Dark 10
pleasure 143
Poems of Miscellaneous Subjects 107
poetry 150–56; ballad 153; sonnet 150–52
Port Royal 38–39
pregnancy 71

queer race narratives 4, 158

racial progress 18, 35, 105, 108, 110, 112, 119, 136, 155
racial uplift 125, 131, 140
Raleigh, North Carolina 3
Reconstruction 9, 106, 111, 115, 120, 123–24, 129–30, 130; legislation 9, 130; narratives 107–8, 111, 114–15, 117, 120, 128–30, 138–39
Red and Black yearbook 133
Redding, John 25–28
Remond, Charles Lenox 38
respectability 6, 33, 140
Running a Thousand Miles for Freedom 16, 35, 49–50
Russell, Sandi 156
Rutberg, Becky 66

St. Paul, Minnesota 1
Salem, Massachusetts 38

175

Index

Sanchez, Sonia 155
Sanmartin, Paula 8
Santamarina, Xiomara 66, 75
Savannah, Georgia 56, 61
Saxton, Gen. Rufus 40, 45, 121
#SayHerName 2
Scott, Keith Lamont 2
Sea Islands, South Carolina 35–37, 39, 41–43, 48–49, 121
"Seduction" 156
self-liberation 6
sexuality 6
Shange, Ntozake 157
Sierra Leone 60
Singer, Jerome 143; *Child's World of Make-Believe* 143
Sister Citizen 3
Smethurst, James Edward 151, 154
Souls of Black Folk 129
Spillers, Hortense 30
sports 145
Starks, Joe (Jody) 29
state violence 158
Sterling, Alton 1
Sterling, Dorothy 50
Stevenson, Brenda 38–39
Stowe, Harriet Beecher: *Uncle Tom's Cabin* 107, 117
Student Nonviolent Coordinating Committee 155
Stylus (Howard University) 25
subjectivity 7, 9, 13, 15, 36, 105, 115–16
Sundquist, Eric: *To Wake the Nations* 117
Sutton-Smith, Brian 144; *Ambiguity of Play* 144

Taylor, Keeanga-Yamahtta 157–58
teaching texts: 130–32, 140
Terrell, Mary Church 32
Their Eyes Were Watching God 3, 25, 28

Tometi, Opal 158
Too Heavy a Load 32
travel 6, 55
Truth, Sojourner 21, 127, 130
Tuskegee, Alabama 125–26
"The Two Offers" 107, 109

Union camps 38
Union Theological Seminary 106
University of Paris-Sorbonne 3
Up from Slavery 145

A Voice from the South 119, 133–34, 139

Walker, Alice 33, 157
Wall, Cheryl 26
Washington, Booker T. 18, 120, 126, 145, 150
Washington, Margaret Murray 126
Washington, Mary Helen 123
Washington, D.C. 3, 139, 147
Watkins, the Rev. William 106
Watson, Pheoby 29
weddings 71
Weekly Anglo-African 117
Wheatley, Phillis 127, 149
White, Deborah Gray 21, 32
White, William J. 124
Whittier, John Greenleaf 38, 43
Williams, Fannie Barrier 118
Wilmington, North Carolina 56–57
witness 41, 47–48, 67, 100, 101, 114
Woman's Rights Convention 21
Women of the Harlem Renaissance 26
Women's Conference of 1893 18
"Women's Era" 9, 32, 123
Woods, Vergible "Tea Cake" 29
Woodville 61
World Congress of Representative Women 139
Wright, Richard R., Sr. 126

www.ingramcontent.com/pod-product-compliance
Lightning Source LLC
Chambersburg PA
CBHW032104300426
44116CB00007B/877